Contents

Teacher Preparation for Bilingual Student Populations

"La vida se me pasa en el viento sobre las alas de la mariposa. ¿Será tiempo?"

—Amado Peña, artist 1974

"As an invaluable resource for teacher educators, this book carefully engages the ideologies, structures, and pedagogical conditions that most impact the teaching and learning of bilingual/bicultural students in the United States. Solidly grounded upon the cultural, linguistic, and community values of bicultural populations, it is by far the most comprehensive articulation of a critical bicultural vision and praxis of teacher formation. Moreover, despite these precarious times, it is a formidable tribute to all those who have courageously kept the revolutionary promise of equal education alive for bilingual children in this country."

Antonia Darder, University of Illinois, Urbana Champaign

"No task in education is more important than the preparation of teachers. More than any other factor, outstanding teachers make a significant difference in students' learning and life chances. However, given the great diversity of students in public schools, teachers' technical competence must be matched by increased language and cultural sophistication to develop pedagogies that expand, rather than restrict, learning opportunities for students, especially those who are bilingual. This book features an admirable collection of articles written by expert bilingual teacher educators who provide transformative models of schooling that engage students' experiences to enhance their social and intellectual development. There is power and commitment in this teaching; our children deserve nothing less."

Luis C. Moll, University of Arizona

The growing number of bilingual students in public schools coupled with a critical shortage of teachers specially prepared to serve this population calls for a critical examination of policies and practices in bilingual and ESL teacher preparation. This volume focuses on understanding the structural, substantive, and contextual elements of preparation programs, and provides transformative guidelines for creating *Educar* signature programs. Designed to improve the practice of teacher preparation by promoting dialogic conversations and applications of praxis in the preparation of bilingual/ESL teacher candidates, it emphasizes that exemplary teacher preparation requires transformative teacher educators.

Simultaneously organizing the scholarship in the field and advancing new understandings, this book is a must-have resource for current and future teacher educators. Contributors include María Brisk, Sylvia Celédon-Pattichis, Lourdes Díaz-Soto, Eugene E. García, Virginia González, Guillermo Solano-Flores, María Torres-Guzmán, Carmen I. Mercado, Bertha Pérez, Mari Riojas-Cortez, Francisco Rios, Concepción M. Valadez, and Angela Valenzuela.

Belinda Bustos Flores, Professor, Interdisciplinary Learning and Teaching, University of Texas at San Antonio.

Rosa Hernández Sheets, Curriculum and Instruction, Texas Tech University.

Ellen Riojas Clark, Professor, Bicultural Bilingual Studies, University of Texas at San Antonio.

Preface

In spite of maturation in the field and a solid theoretical knowledge base, there is minimal empirical evidence regarding the nature of bilingual education teacher preparation models and their impact on teacher quality and effectiveness. Therefore, understandings on the structural and substantive elements of bilingual education teacher preparation programs as a whole; and, examination of its various components, including procedural and contextual factors is the strength of this volume. Additionally, the accelerated growth of bilingual students/learners (BLs) in public schools coupled with the critical shortage of teachers specially prepared to serve this emerging majority population creates the need for a text explicitly examining effective bilingual education teacher preparation programs.

Teacher Preparation for Bilingual Student Populations: Educar para Transformar adopts a sociocultural perspective, recognizing that exemplary preparation of *aspirantes*/candidates for BLs requires transformative teacher educators and bilingual education program leaders. The purpose of this text is to help teacher educators understand how to facilitate *aspirantes'* learning throughout the various components in bilingual teacher preparation programs. Four major guiding goals are:

1 To introduce *Educar para Transformar*, an exemplary model conceptualized within two overarching, interdependent, complementary frameworks, *transformación* and *revolución*, with three interconnecting dimensions— *iluminación, praxis,* and *concientización,* directing programmatic content. Its vision, *Dar Luz*, guides the transformative-revolutionary spirit permeating throughout.

2 To provide teacher educators with research-based information from key proponents in the field on best practices in bilingual education teacher preparation to improve the practice of teacher education.

3 To acknowledge that teacher educators can assume responsibility to create and sustain emotional and cognitive conditions in preparation coursework and field experiences that enable *aspirantes* from different ethnic, linguistic, economic, and cultural groups learn what is required of future teachers of BLs.

4 To instill in teacher educators that pedagogical effectiveness and achievement success with BLs often depends on their commitment and ability to prepare *aspirantes* with relevant experiences, knowledge, and skills.

García, E. E., & Cuellar, D. (2006). Who are these linguistically and culturally diverse students? *Teachers College Record, 108*(11), 2220–2246.

García, E. E., & Jensen, B. T. (2009). *Language development and early education of young Hispanic children in the United States.* Available from http://www.ecehispanic.org/work/lang_dev_6August2007.pdf

García, E. E., & Miller, L. S. (2008). Findings and recommendations of the National Task Force on Early Childhood Education for Hispanics. *Child Development Perspectives, 2*(2), 53–58.

Hernández, D. J., Denton, N. A., & Macartney, S. E. (2008). Children in immigrant families: Looking to America's future. *Social Policy Report: A Publication of the Society for Research in Child Development, 22*(3), 1–24.

Jensen, B. T. (2008). Immigration and language policy. In J. González (Ed.), *Encyclopedia of Bilingual Education* (pp. 372–377). Thousand Oaks, CA: Sage.

National Center for Education Statistics. (1995). *Approaching kindergarten: A look at preschoolers in the United States.* National household survey. Washington, DC: US Department of Education, Office of Educational Research and Improvement.

- Tracking limits access to academic courses and justifies learning environments that do not foster academic development and socialization or perception of self as a competent learner and language user.
- A lack of opportunities to engage in developmentally and culturally appropriate learning experiences.

The implication of this re-thinking has profound effects for the teaching/ learning enterprise related to BLs. This new pedagogy redefines the classroom as a community of learners in which speakers, readers, and writers come together to define and redefine the meaning of the academic experience. It might be described by some as pedagogy of empowerment, by others as cultural learning, or as a cultural view of providing instructional assistance/guidance. In any case, it argues for teachers to respect and integrate students' values, beliefs, histories, and experiences and recognizes the active role that BLs must play in the learning process.

Of course, a teaching and learning community that is responsive to the dynamics of social, cultural, and linguistic diversity within the broader concerns for high academic achievement requires and emerges from a particular schooling environment. While considerable work has been devoted to restructure schools and change the fundamental relationships that exist among school personnel, students, families, and community members, seldom have these efforts included attention to the unique influences of the linguistic and sociocultural dimensions of these same relationships and structures.

In summary, a knowledge base put forward in this volume recognizes that academic learning has its roots in processes both out-of-school and in school. Diversity is perceived and acted on as a resource for teaching and learning instead of a problem. A focus on what BLs bring to the schooling process generates a more asset-resource oriented approach.

This redirection or *transformación* considers a search for and documentation of particular implementations of principles of teacher development, which serve a diverse set of educational environments. This volume reaffirms that an understanding of how individuals with diverse sets of experiences, packaged individually into cultures, "make meaning," communicate and extend that meaning, particularly in the social contexts we call schools. Such a mission requires in-depth treatment of the processes associated with producing diversity, issues of socialization in and out of schools, coupled with a clear examination of how such understanding is actually transformed into pedagogy and curriculum resulting in high academic performance and overall social well-being for BLs.

References

Capps, R., Fix, M. E., Murray, J., Ost, J., Passel, J. S., & Hernández, S. H. (2005). *The new demography of America's schools: Immigration and the No Child Left Behind Act.* Accessed online link from the Urban Institute: http://www.urban.org/url.cfm?ID=311230

García, E. E., Arias, M. B., Harris Murri, N. J., & Serna, C. (2010). Developing responsive teachers: A challenge for a demographic reality. *Journal of Teacher Education, 61*(1–2), 132–142.

Teacher Development: The Critical Factor in Addressing Education Well-Being

This volume appropriately frames the significance of teacher development in an educationally relevant theoretical context. This text cogently and consistently acknowledges that linguistically and culturally diverse populations call for a deeper understanding of the interaction of BLs' language and culture and the prevailing school language and culture. This position is supported by a rich contribution of research, which suggests that the educational failure of diverse student populations is related to a culture clash between home and school. In essence, the volume's contributors suggest that without attending to the distinctiveness of the contribution of culture, educational endeavors for BLs are likely to fail.

To facilitate discussion of how considerations of cultural diversity can be integrated into the development of a pedagogy and practice that improve the educational conditions of BLs, the volume provides a depiction of the continuum of approaches suggested by the research literature, education practices, and lessons learned from contributors to the volume. The conclusions are clear: BLs who should succeed, who have no intellectual reason for not succeeding, do not succeed due to differences between home and school culture. Teachers perpetuate this dissonance when they fail to integrate the family's cultural knowledge (García, Arias, Harris Murri & Serna, 2010). The mission for educators is to identify critical differences between and within ethnic minority groups and individuals within those groups and to incorporate this information into classroom practice. Although the teacher and their development is not the only critical variable, without well prepared, responsive teachers, the educational high aspiration of schools, families, and students will not be attained. This volume helps us better understand this mission, the challenges manifested in the mission, and, a road map to navigate this new educational landscape.

Embedded is the understanding that language, culture, and their accompanying values are acquired in the home and community environment, that BLs come to school with knowledge about what language is, how it works, and ways it is used. Children learn higher-level cognitive and communicative skills as they engage in socially meaningful activities, and their development and learning is best understood as the interaction of linguistic, sociocultural, cognitive knowledge, and experiences. A more appropriate perspective on teaching and learning recognizes that learning is enhanced when it occurs in contexts that are socioculturally and linguistically meaningful for the learner. Further, BLs learn best and teachers feel most satisfied when they are allies in the learning process. Therefore, a more appropriate perspective on teacher development is one that recognizes that learning is enhanced when it occurs in meaningful contexts. Such meaningful contexts have been notoriously inaccessible to BLs. On the contrary, schooling practices and teachers often contribute to educational vulnerability. The monolithic culture transmitted by the US schools in the form of pedagogy, curricula, instruction, classroom configuration, and language dramatizes the lack of fit between BLs and the school experience. The culture of schools in the US is reflected in such practices as:

- The systematic exclusion of the histories, languages, experiences, and values of BLs from classroom curricula and activities.

Foreword

Eugene E. García

Currently, over 5 million students in the US are learning English as a second language (García & Jensen, 2009). How we define these children and the labels we ascribe to them can be confusing. I use the term bilingual learner (BL) rather than limited English proficient as a way of emphasizing their strengths, learning, and progress. In doing so, I also recognize the contribution of this volume by its editors and contributors to change the way we think about and behave towards BLs, their families, communities, and the educators that serve them. Flores, Sheets, and Clark make abundantly clear, that it no longer serves anyone to ignore the education of Latinos or to relegate it only to the teaching and learning of English.

It strikes me as quite odd that some teachers of BLs can have no formal preparation and minimal workshop training and yet obtain a state-issued credential. While they may be labeled English as a Second Language teacher, Bilingual Education teacher, English Language Development teacher, or Sheltered English Immersion teacher, they all teach BLs. Overall, too many BLs have teachers who themselves admit that they are not prepared to teach these students (García & Miller, 2008).

The academic performance patterns of BLs as a whole cannot be adequately understood without considering their social and economic characteristics in comparison with native English speakers (Jensen, 2008). While socioeconomic variation exists among BLs, they are more likely than native English-speaking children to live in poverty and have parents with limited formal education (Garcia & Cuellar, 2006). BLs are more likely to be an ethnic/racial minority (Capps et al., 2005). Each of these factors—low income, low parent education, and ethnic/racial minority status—decreases their group achievement averages across academic areas.

Thus, rather than pointing to background factors that account for BLs' low achievement, it should be understood that educational risk is attributable to a myriad of interrelated out-of-school factors, including parent education levels, family income, parent English language proficiency, mother's marital status at the time of birth, and single- versus dual-parent homes (NCES, 1995). The more risk factors children are subject to, the lower the probability that they will do well in school. Because BLs, on average, exhibit three of the five risk factors at higher rates than native English speakers, they are generally at greater risk for academic underachievement (Hernández, Denton, & Macartney, 2008).

Dedicación

To those who dared before us, who provided the shoulders for us to climb, who gave us the *alas* for the preparation of bilingual education teachers; we acknowledge the early proponents and advocates of bilingual education—Joe Bernal, Albar Peña, José Cardenas, Gloria Zamora, William. Justice, Ralph Yarborough, Arcadia López, and Tomás Rivera. Their courage and vision sustains and allows us to continue *la lucha* and see possibilities beyond. And to all who will dare to persist to change existing structures for better and equitable lives, we dedicate our work.

First published 2011
by Routledge
270 Madison Avenue, New York, NY 10016

Simultaneously published in the UK
by Routledge
2 Park Square, Milton Park, Abingdon, Oxon OX14 4RN

Routledge is an imprint of the Taylor & Francis Group, an informa business

© 2011 Taylor & Francis

The right of Belinda Bustos Flores, Rosa Hernández Sheets, and Ellen Riojas Clark to be identified as the authors of the editorial material, and of the authors for their individual chapters, has been asserted by them in accordance with sections 77 and 78 of the Copyright, Designs and Patents Act 1988.

Typeset in Minion by
HWA Text and Data Management, London
Printed and bound in the United States of America on acid-free paper by Walsworth Publishing Company, Marceline, MO

Cover art: "*Sera Tiempo*" (Amado Pena, 1974, silkscreen, 17/20), Private collection – Ellen Riojas Clark.

Library of Congress Cataloging-in-Publication Data
Teacher preparation for bilingual student populations : educar para transformar / [edited by] Belinda Bustos Flores, Rosa Hernández Sheets, Ellen Riojas Clark.
     p. cm.
  Includes index.
  1. Teachers–Training of–United States. 2. Bilingual education–United States. I. Flores, Belinda Bustos. II. Sheets, Rosa Hernández. III. Clark, Ellen Riojas.
  LB1715.T432 2011
  370.71´1–dc22

ISBN 13: 978-0-415-87739-8 (hbk)
ISBN 13: 978-0-415-87740-4 (pbk)
ISBN 13: 978-0-203-85097-8 (ebk)

SUSTAINABLE
FORESTRY
INITIATIVE

Certified Chain of Custody
Promoting Sustainable
Forest Management
www.sfiprogram.org

NSF-SFI-COC-C0004285
The SFI label applies to the text stock.

Teacher Preparation for Bilingual Student Populations

Educar para Transformar

Edited by

Belinda Bustos Flores
University of Texas at San Antonio

Rosa Hernández Sheets
Texas Tech University

Ellen Riojas Clark
University of Texas at San Antonio

Routledge
Taylor & Francis Group

NEW YORK AND LONDON

Intended Audience

This volume is specifically designed as a core text or resource for teacher educators and for graduate students in bilingual teacher education programs, especially doctoral students with a specialization in teacher education. It is intended to be used as a primary text in graduate courses on pedagogy of teacher education, research on teacher learning, bilingual education foundational courses, and English as a Second Language (ESL) endorsement coursework. Other audiences are current teacher educators in the field of bilingual, ESL and general teacher education. While our focus is primarily Spanish/English populations, we contend that content examined are applicable and can be adapted to generalist programs.

Description

This text draws from the existing research in bilingual education teacher preparation. It expands the field by examining the structural and substantive aspects of bilingual teacher preparation models, as well as responding to issues, such as *aspirante* knowledge base, bilingual/bicultural pedagogical approaches, and teacher learning. ESL methodology is included as an aspect of bilingual education teacher preparation.

Organization

This volume uses a balance of empirical research and conceptual pieces to address components of exemplary bilingual education teacher preparation programs. The preparation of teacher candidates, the majority whom are English-speaking monolinguals seeking ESL endorsement through university course work, is addressed. The book is organized in five sections: *Transformación, Iluminación, Praxis, Concientización,* and *Revolución.* Each section is discussed below.

Part I: Transformación

In Part 1, Chapter 1 establishes the rationale for the volume and introduces the vision for the *Educar* model. Chapter 2, *Educar para Transformar,* discusses the conceptual framework, characteristics, and components of the transformative model.

Part II: Iluminación

Issues pertinent to *aspirantes'* development are addressed in this section. Chapter 3 examines identity development as a metamorphic recursive process. Chapter 4 explores candidate ideology reflected in motives, efficacy, epistemology, and cultural teaching beliefs and Chapter 5 focuses on *aspirantes'* bilingualism. Chapter 6 analyzes the role of diversity courses in the preparation of candidates and teacher educators. This section concludes with Chapter 7, which metaphorically uses chrysalis to describe a process for nurturing personal and professional growth.

Part III: Praxis

In Part III, we move beyond personal development towards specific, recommended curricular knowledge bases, pedagogical approaches, and program experiences. The foundational premise in this section is that *aspirantes* must acquire transformative ideological positions and specific knowledge and skill to promote and encourage BLs' linguistic, sociocultural, academic, and cognitive growth. Chapter 8 presents the philosophical and theoretical underpinnings for play as a cultural and developmental approach for young BLs. Biliteracy preparation and development is examined in Chapter 9. *Aspirantes'* knowledge of language and culture as conduits for teaching mathematics and science are discussed in Chapter 10. The importance of *aspirantes'* demonstrating assessment knowledge and skills is presented in Chapter 11. The preparation of ESL candidates is examined in Chapter 12, while Chapter 13 proposes ways to prepare *aspirantes* to work with gifted BLs. To counter the current reality that the majority of teachers are not prepared to work with BLs, Chapter 14 uses a case study to illustrate that all candidates must assume this responsibility.

Part IV: Concientización

In this section, contributors examine policies and practices influencing the schooling of BLs. Chapter 15 reveals the difficultly in creating sound policy and calls for the development of *aspirantes'* political identity. In Chapter 16, the authors discuss indigenous Latin@ immigrant families and elucidates how deficit thinking becomes part of discourse. Two cases of community-based and inquiry-oriented approaches for preparing *aspirantes* to become *concientizadas* are documented in Chapter 17. The power of apprenticeship for affirming candidate consciousness and social justice beliefs, while linking theory and praxis is the focus of Chapter 18.

Part V: Revolución

Educar asks that we take necessary risks to systematically challenge and transform institutional conditions. We consider transformative program change as a form of *revolución*; and, as such, cannot be separate from or unrelated to the practice of bilingual teacher preparation. A call for transformative action is the heart of Chapter 19. The afterword inspires and illuminates all teacher educators to *Educar para Tranformar*.

Conclusion

All chapters advance the dialogue to transform the practice of bilingual teacher preparation and suggest topics for research. *Educar para transformar* presents a conceptual premise to begin and sustain a meaningful discourse on transformative models of teacher preparation. Specifically, we offer our vision—*Dar Luz* to guide the knowledge and skill base focusing on "teaching about teaching" to address teacher learning.

We ask that you consider joining in the movement to transform schooling opportunities of BLs using the *Educar* model. *El pueblo unido jamás será vencido.*

Acknowledgments

Damos muchísimas gracias to all who joined and helped us in the development of *Educar*, especially our contributors who actively participated in the realization of our vision—*Dar Luz*. We thank the Academy for Teacher Excellence (ATE) at the University of Texas at San Antonio, which embodies, supports, and actualizes our mission. We are most grateful to Margaret Graham, manuscript editor at Texas Tech University, for her expertise and willingness to proof multiple drafts within tight deadlines. Special appreciation goes to Naomi Silverman, Routledge, Acquisition Editor, who recognized the value of this volume to the field and provided continual support and guidance throughout this project. To Amado Peña, *amigo*, who gave us permission to use his artwork for the cover; we honor his artistic creativity, which reflects our vision. We thank our colleagues, scattered throughout the country, who participated in the blind-review process.

We give special thanks to Mario Enrique Flores for his careful review of Spanish text. We are grateful to Sungwon Chung, Texas Tech University, for *Educar's* webpage and graphic design as well as Eduardo Valenzuela and Lucretia Fraga, University of Texas at San Antonio, for helping with book design, publication materials, and links on ATE website. We also wish to express gratitude for our past, present, and future teachers. And for our families *damos gracias, agradecimos su aliento y les damos nuestro cariño para siempre.*

A mi querido esposo, Mario y *mi linda hija*, Janelle, who share my vision of making education equitable and accessible *para nuestros niños. Y para mi familia Bustos y mi mamá Julia, gracias por su amor*—Belinda

Muchísimo amor a mis niños y nietos—you embody the hope of the future. To Joseph, my beloved, you give space and place in heart and mind. I am indebted to you for always—Rosa

Adelante to my daughters and granddaughters who will always strive for a better world *y gracias* to Hector for his support and constant supply of *café*— Ellen

Part I

Transformación

Let us breathe through the cracks of our open hearts.
And may our collective breath be the vision
of a transformative dream of education
that speaks the language of heart and mind
and the truth of wholeness, harmony,
social justice, and liberation.

Laura Rendón. (2010). *Sentipendante pedagogy: Educating for wholeness, social justice, and liberation*. Sterling, VA: Stylus Publishing, LLC, p. 151.

1 *Dar Luz*

Visionary Teaching about Teaching

*Belinda Bustos Flores, Ellen Riojas Clark,
and Rosa Hernández Sheets*

Our vision for the *Educar* model, *Dar luz* illuminates transformative ways of thinking, knowing, and being in exemplary bilingual education teacher programs. *Dar luz*—as a transformational framework—provides constructs representing who we are as bicultural bilingual beings and promotes our desire to prepare bilingual education teacher *aspirantes*/candidates, who are *bien educados*. In this text, the term *aspirante* refers to bilingual education teacher candidates, unless otherwise specified. *Transformación* and *revolución* are the impetus driving the conceptualization of teacher preparation through the dimensions of *iluminación*, praxis, and *concientización*.

Foremost, for *transformación* to occur, it is important to recognize that issues of power are central in distinguishing schooling from *educación*. While the purpose of schooling is socialization and control, *educación* results in learning and empowerment within multiple arenas including school, home, and community. "It is evident that school serves the purpose of the society for which they have been constructed and that social and political forces shape the practice and purpose of schooling" (Hollins, 2008, p. 17).

In proclaiming freedom from hegemonic discourses that approach schooling from monolithic lenses, in this text we use Latin@s to refer to pan-ethnic groups who share similar languages, cultures, and genotypes. However, beyond genetic makeup, it is important to recognize that Latin@s are a heterogeneous group, whose languages, literacies, rituals, and practices vary based on diverse sociocultural contexts. While Latin@s represent the emerging majority ethnic group in the US, our connections extend beyond boundaries and borders. Latin@s' multilinguality and multiculturality as intuitive cultural knowledge provides conduits to cognitive shifts and helps us critically analyze appropriate cultural behaviors in different contexts (Clark & Flores, 2007). Thus, in this text, this knowledge is brought to the forefront.

In resistance to hegemonic discourse giving English monolingualism and monoculturalism prominence, we counter by assuming a sociocultural transformative position. Erroneously labeling bilingual learners (BLs) acquiring English as a second language as English language learners (ELLs) fails to recognize that:

1   monolingual English speakers are learning and developing their English proficiency as English learners, and as such are the true ELLs, and

2   bilinguals who speak another language possess linguistic, lexical, grammatical, and cultural knowledge and are simultaneously acquiring dual languages.

Consequently, we demand BLs be labeled accurately by programs and institutions. We recognize that within their speech communities, BLs are simultaneously constructing and developing their native language, while acquiring English. They possess both languages along a continuum of proficiencies (Hornberger, 2003). Moreover, there is an acknowledgement that bicultural practices, values, and norms are also being learned and shared in varying sociocultural contexts. We also maintain that multilingualism and multiculturalism are recognized as the norm throughout the world, not the exception.

The purpose of this chapter is to organize the overall content of the volume and to elucidate our vision—*dar luz*—to guide the practice of teaching about teaching with optimal potential for the preparation of transformative, knowledgeable, skilled, and empowered *aspirantes* for BLs. We begin with the current demographic trends, followed by the text's organizational components.

Demographic Trends

We assume the country was not shocked when Latin@s were proclaimed the largest and the fastest growing ethnic minority group in the US. In fact, demographers concluded that numbers were probably underreported, since undocumented immigrants, with estimates as high as 11.5 to 12 million, were not included in official counts (PEW, 2006). While the current growth is stimulated by immigration; the future projected distribution will be expressed through increased birth rates (Verdugo, 2006). Nearly two-thirds of Latin@s are US born and one fourth of US newborns are Latin@s (PEW, 2009). To illustrate, between the years of 1990–2005, two-thirds of newborns in Georgia were Latin@ and in Arkansas the percentage of new babies rose from 14.3% to 23.7% due to Latin@ births (National Task Force on Early Education for Hispanics, 2007). Undoubtedly, this projected demographic shift tests political, health, and economic structures; and, there is no question this shift requires changes to educational institutions.

The Latin@ populace was estimated at 42.7 million, 15% of the total population (US Census Bureau, 2005). This figure did not include Puerto Rico's 3.9 million residents. Demographers project that within 40 years, one in four individuals living in the US will be Latin@ (US Census Bureau, 2005). Presently, the US ranks as the fourth largest Latin@ population in the world, trailing behind Mexico, Spain, and Colombia. The Latino Diaspora establishes Latin@ as the minority-majority in 19 states; however, almost half (49%) call California and Texas home, and approximately, 74% live in five states—California, Texas, New York, Florida, and Illinois. Though, between 1990–2004, states with largest Latin@ growth rates were North Carolina, 575%, Arkansas, 508%, Georgia, 449%, Tennessee, 410%, and Nevada, 328% (Verdugo, 2006).

In the US, the Mexican ethnic group is not only the largest (66%), but it is also the least formally schooled; while, Cubans, the smallest (4%), are the most skilled and schooled. Mexicans, especially undocumented workers with low-levels of formal schooling, visibly sift into the bottom of the labor market, contributing to the stereotype of Latin@s as an impoverished, uneducated group of menial workers (Portes, 2004). However, as a pan-ethnic group, Latin@s have the least formal schooling (National Center for Educational Statistics, 2007); only 77% of all Latin@s, as compared to all other groups, complete high school (PEW, 2009). Latinas are even less likely to pursue post-secondary education (González, Stoner, & Jovel, 2003). As a group, Latin@s, age 16–25 value education; educational attainment is dependent on various factors including generational status (native versus foreign-born), income, familial obligations, and language proficiency (PEW, 2009). Several reasons were identified for low schooling outcomes, 44% of the Latin@ students reported being taught by teachers unprepared to work with them (PEW, 2009). While there are commonalities among Latin@s such as familialism, there are generational, linguistic, and acculturation differences.

Currently, Latin@ children (under age 18) are the fastest growing and the second largest student population, after White students; and, Latin@ children account for more than half (58%) of all immigrant youth in the US (Kohler & Lazarín, 2007). Trends indicate that 19% speak a language other than English at home; and, 62% in this group speak Spanish (US Census, 2005). Student public school population patterns for the past 32 years (1972–2004) show significant changes in the ethnic backgrounds and linguistic heritage of students. Numbers show that linguistically diverse, ethnic minority children are increasing, while the monolingual White student enrollment is decreasing. Between 1979 and 2004, the number of children "who spoke a language other than English at home and who spoke English with difficulty increased by 114%" with Spanish "being most frequently spoken at home by both those who spoke a language other than English at home and by those who spoke English with difficulty" (Condition of Education, 2006, p. 1). In 2004, 37% of 5–9 year-olds and 24% of 10–17 year-olds spoke Spanish at home and 67% of school-age children came from homes where Spanish was spoken (Condition of Education, 2006). Latin@s, ages 16 to 25, language proficiency ranges with the majority being (41%) being bilingual, 36% English dominant, and 23% Spanish dominant (PEW, 2009).

Proportionately, more Latin@s live in poverty than any other racial and ethnic group. In 2004, the national poverty rate was 12.7% and 8.6% for White; however, for Latin@s it was substantially higher, 21.9% (National Poverty Center, 2005). Nearly one-fourth of Latin@s live in poverty with 53% living in households with less than $50,000 mean income (PEW, 2009). Most Latin@s earn less, suffer recurring unemployment, and work in unskilled occupations (Valenzuela, 2001).

Given the lack of educational access and attainment for Latin@s, we should not be astounded that nationally the teaching population is predominately White, 83.5% (NCES, 2008), yet nearly 47% of the student population is classified as ethnic minorities with Latin@s accounting for 20% of the total US student population. Other trends show a critical shortage of bilingual education teachers (see Chapter 2) and data showing that BLs do not have access to teachers with knowledge and skill to support BLs' schooling needs (NCES, 2000).

An overview of these demographic trends demonstrates the urgency for exemplary bilingual education preparation programs focusing on the exponentially growing Latin@ group. We maintain that a generic, universal, multilinguistic group approach invalidates the specificity, contextual, and situational factors present in a sociocultural learning-teaching process. Demographic trends clearly demonstrate the need for preparing teachers *bien educadas* for Latin@ bilingual student populations.

Organizational Components

Teacher Preparation for Bilingual Student Populations: Educar para Transformar adopts a sociocultural transformative perspective, recognizing that exemplary preparation for BLs requires transformative programs with a measurable vision and an explicit conceptual framework with well-defined dimensions (see Chapter 2).

Since the purpose of this text is to transform the practice of teacher preparation, the major goals guiding this text are grounded in our *sabiduría*:

1   *Donde no hay voluntad, no hay fuerza: Transformación* occurs when there is recognition that change is necessary. We begin this journey with our vision *Dar luz*, establish *Educar* as a preparation model, *iluminar* through the examination of issues pertinent to *aspirantes'* development, examine *praxis* as we move towards specific pedagogical approaches, promote *concientización* as we examine policies and practices to transform schooling, and continue a *revolución* as we advocate for equity in BLs' schooling.
2   *Busca tu mejores bienes, que adentro de ti los tienes*: We suggest that to advance teacher educators' knowledge of research-based best practices and assist in the *transformación* of the teacher preparation program requires acknowledgement that cultural and linguistic knowledge and power are central.
3   *Querer es poder:* Teacher educators must be prepared to have the courage and desire to design, sustain, and evaluate social and cognitive conditions in preparation programs for *aspirantes* from different ethnic, linguistic, economic, and cultural groups.
4   *El pueblo que pierde su historia, pierde su destino:* Teacher educators must be inspired and encouraged to use our epistemological knowledge and enact social justice advocacy in developing exemplary bilingual education teacher preparation programs that result in pedagogical effectiveness and achievement success for BLs.

Based on our ideology, it is with intentionality that we chose to pair established scholars with emerging scholars, for we recognize that we must *apoyarlos* as we build on the shoulders of others. This collective scholarship documents a balance of empirical research and conceptual pieces to address the various components of the *Educar* model, an exemplary bilingual education teacher preparation program.

We believe that programs guided with the vision—*Dar luz*—of the *Educar* model has optimal potential to prepare *aspirantes* with relevant bilingual/bicultural pedagogical knowledge and consciousness to assist them to interpret and respond to schooling events with social, political, and ideological purpose and clarity. We choose to *educar aspirantes* to become *iluminados, concientizados,* engage in praxis *y tener el poder para educar.* These *aspirantes* will have the capacity to become culturally efficacious teachers characterized as having cultural competency, positive teaching efficacy, dynamic epistemological knowledge, and bilingual/ bicultural transformative pedagogical skills. As culturally efficacious teachers, they will understand how to contextualize and facilitate instruction in diverse, situational settings. The actualization of these skills, attitudes, and behaviors in practice assure BLs success. ¡*Sí se puede!*

References

Clark, E. R., & Flores, B. B. (2005). Creating a just society: Multicultural teacher education and the changing classroom. *Teacher Education and Practice, 18*(3), 315–332.

Clark, E. R., & Flores, B. B. (2007). Cultural literacy: Negotiating language, culture, and thought. *Voices in the Middle, 15*(2), 6–12.

Condition of Education. (2006). *Participation in education, elementary/secondary education: Language minority school-age children.* Retrieved from http://nces.ed.gov/programs/coe/2006/section1/indicator07.asp

González, K. P., Stoner, C., & Jovel, J. E. (2003). Examining the social capital in access to college for Latinas: Toward a college opportunity framework. *Journal of Hispanic Higher Education, 2*(1), 146–170.

Hollins, E. R. (2008). *Culture in school learning: Revealing the deep meaning of culture,* (2nd ed.). New York: Routledge.

Hornberger, N. H. (Ed.) (2003). *The continua of biliteracy: An ecological framework for educational policy, research, and practice in multilingual settings.* Clevedon, UK: Multilingual Matters.

Kohler, A. D., & Lazarín, M. (2007). *Hispanic education in the United States: Statistical brief No. 8.* Washington, DC: National Council of La Raza.

Martínez, M. D. (2003). Missing in action: Reconstructing hope and possibility among Latino students placed at risk. *Journal of Latinos and Education 2*(1), 13–21.

National Center for Education Statistics. (2000). *Teacher preparation and professional development, NCES 2001-088* by B. Parsad, L. Lewis, & E. Farris. Washington, DC. Retrieved from http://nces.ed.gov/surveys/frss/publications/2001088/index.asp

National Center for Education Statistics. (2007). Status and trends in the Education of racial and ethnic minorities. Retrieved from http://nces.ed.gov/pubsearch/pubsinfo.asp?pubid=2007039.

National Center for Education Statistics. (2008). Schools and Staffing Survey (SASS), Public School Teacher, BIE School Teacher, and Private School Teacher Data Files, 2007–08. Table 2. Percentage distribution of school teachers, by race/ethnicity, school type, and selected school characteristics: 2007–2008. Retrieved from http://nces.ed.gov/pubs2009/2009324/tables/sass0708_2009324_t12n_02.asp.

National Poverty Center. (2005). *Poverty facts.* Retrieved from http://www.npc.umich.edu/poverty/#4

National Task Force on Early Education for Hispanics. (2007). Working papers. www.ecehispanic.org

Pew Hispanic Center. (2006). *Fact sheet, April 5, 2006: Recently arrived migrants and the congressional debate on immigration.* Retrieved from http://pewhispanic.org/files/factsheets/15.pdf

Pew Hispanic Center. (2009, December 11). *Between two worlds: How young Latinos come of age in America.* Washington, DC.

Portes, A. (2004). *The new Latin nation: Immigration and the Hispanic population in the United States.* CMD Working Paper #04–02. Center for Migration and Development, Working Papers Series, Princeton University.

US Census Bureau. (2005). *American community survey*. Retrieved from http://www. census.gov/acs/www.index.html

Valenzuela, A. (2001). *The remarkable rise of the Hispanic population in the United States and its implications for hemispheric relations*. Retrieved from http://www.nuevamayoria. com/english/analysis/valenzuela/ivalenzuela230301.htm

Verdugo, R. (2006). *A report on the status of Hispanics in education: Overcoming a history of neglect*. Washington, DC: National Educational Association.

2 *Educar Para Transformar*

A Bilingual Education Teacher Preparation Model

Rosa Hernández Sheets, Belinda Bustos Flores,
and Ellen Riojas Clark

The *Latinization of America,* a term used by Henry Cisneros (1989) over twenty years ago, is no longer prophetic in nature. Descriptive demographic snapshots show the Latin@ Diaspora spreading quickly and completely across the entire country (see Chapter 1). This dramatic exponential growth pattern of this emerging majority calls for immediate changes in educational policy and practice. Data profiling the historical and continual neglect of Latin@ children clearly shows that this group is shamefully underserved. Many Bilingual Learners (BLs) attend low-quality, under-performing, hyper-segregated schools, staffed with high numbers of non-credentialed teachers. Actually, they are the most segregated ethnic minority student population in the nation (Sheets, 2007). Schooling institutions have moved slowly and methodically, often perpetuating substandard public school conditions placing this group at the lowest achievement level of any ethnic group in the US (Kohler & Lazarín, 2007). These depressing conditions generate low achievement and the resulting outcomes follow children into adulthood. According to the Pew Hispanic Center (2010) Latin@s display the lowest high school and college completion rates. This undeniable data is disproportionate and disturbing.

The unprecedented growth of Latin@s, coupled with federal requirements, acute bilingual education teacher shortages, and lack of qualified English as a Second Language (ESL) teachers further compounds the issue. Scholarship, both conceptual and empirical, reveal the need to study, evaluate, and transform the ways we prepare bilingual teacher education *aspirantes*/candidates and monolingual candidates for BLs, as well as graduate students entering the professoriate as teacher educators and researchers; or, as future curriculum specialists, administrators, and policy makers.

Cochran-Smith and Zeichner (2005) organize the field of teacher education as follows: teacher characteristics, demographic profiles, indicators of quality, effects of non-education coursework and educational foundations, methods courses and field experiences, pedagogical approaches in preparation programs, preparation for diverse populations and students with ability differences, accountability, and program preparation models. Even though BLs comprise the largest ethnic minority school population, a category for bilingual teacher education is conspicuously missing.

This chapter focuses on preparation program models. We briefly examine characteristics of signature models and introduce *Educar para Transformar*

(*Educar*), as an exemplary model for the preparation of bilingual education *aspirantes*. We conclude with implications for transforming practice and discussion on research directions.

Background

US Secretary of Education Duncan claims the need for "revolutionary change" in colleges of education; he states, "we should be studying and copying the practices of effective teacher preparation programs, and encouraging the lowest-performers to shape up or shut down" (Associated Press, 2009, p. 1). Darling-Hammond (2006) maintains that traditional programs are characterized by "fragmentation, weak content, poor pedagogy, disconnect from schools, and inconsistent oversight of teachers-in-training" (p. 6). According to Cochran-Smith and Zeichner (2005) "empirical evidence relevant to practices and policies in preservice education" (p. 3) reveal serious issues, including significant variation in the structure of programs and obvious disconnect between mission and practice. They conclude that the research examining the effectiveness of preparation models is limited, contradictory, and conflicting.

Generalists' Programs

While formal preparation programs began in the 1930s, research surfaced in the mid-1960s. Cochran-Smith and Fries (2005) reported that the first publication addressing teacher preparation was in 1964. According to Zeichner and Conklin (2005), most of the empirical evidence on preparation models focuses on structural elements, such as program length and comparisons between 4th- and 5th-year designs. Other research analyzes conceptual frameworks (Feiman-Nemser, 1990); discusses specific elements such as cohorts and partnerships (Arends & Winitzky, 1996); or describes self-studies on particular courses (Borko, Liston, & Whitcomb, 2007; Wilson, Floden, & Ferrini-Mundy, 2001). Most scholars concede that information on the substantive aspects and effects of teacher preparation on student learning outcomes is sorely missing—"There is no research that directly assesses what teachers learn in their pedagogical preparation and then evaluates the relationship of that pedagogical knowledge to student learning or teacher behavior" (Wilson et al., 2001, p. 46). Conversely, studies report that generalists are ill equipped and not prepared to meet the needs of diverse learners (Garcia & Miller, 2008; Hollins & Torres-Guzman, 2005) or bilingual learners (Garcia, Arias, Harris Murri, & Serna, 2010).

Alternative Certification Programs (ACPs)

Nationally 47 states, plus the District of Columbia, offer some type of ACPs (NCEI, 2010). While Darling-Hammond (2000) alleges that ACPs reduce standards, these programs view themselves as the "wave of the future," especially with the development of complete on-line distance delivery options (etools4Education, 2007). A problem with the ACP proliferation is whether qualified instructors and relevant models prepare competent teachers for BLs, especially since these easily established convenient programs address bilingual teacher education shortages (Baines, McDowell, & Foulk, 2001). ACP's explosive growth is associated with high demand disciplines such as mathematics, science; particular grade levels including early childhood and middle school; and, specialized areas such as bilingual, ESL, and special education (Clewell & Forcier, 2001). For example, in Texas, 45% of the bilingual teachers prepared in 2005–2006 were trained by ACPs; 29% by traditional university-based programs; and, 26% were certified through appeals and testing procedures (SBEC, 2010). Although research is either missing or inconclusive in terms of ACPs in Texas, they produce the majority of certified bilingual teachers.

Bilingual Teacher Shortage

Satisfying the national need for bilingual teachers is not likely to happen soon. This disparity in teacher qualification profoundly affects BLs. The concern for qualified bilingual education teachers has been an on-going debate (Burnett, 1979; Macías, 1989). Over 20 years ago, researchers at the Tomas Rivera Center realized that bilingual teacher preparation was one of the most pressing issues. Scholars advocated for their recruitment, preparation, and retention (Macías, 1989). They predicted that BLs were growing at a faster rate than institutional ability to prepare specialized teachers for this population (Díaz-Rico & Smith, 1994; Maroney, 1998).

Today, a crisis mode prevails, especially when one considers the increasing enrollment of BLs and the decreasing rates of bilingual education teachers. Capacity to produce the needed numbers is exacerbated by federal mandates for highly qualified teachers, retirements, high attrition, and the overwhelming numbers of monolingual English-speaking teachers entering the field (Hollins & Torres-Guzman, 2005). Inequitable schooling conditions experienced by BLs in public schools limits their opportunity for higher education and potentially eliminates the recruitment of large numbers from this pool of native Spanish speakers. Also relevant is growing additions of full day kindergarten and universal preschool programs with high BL enrollment in public schools. These young BLs will demand large numbers of specially prepared early childhood bilingual teachers (see Chapter 8).

Bilingual Education Teacher Preparation

Although the need for bilingual education teacher preparation existed prior to the Bilingual Education Act (1968), institutions of higher learning were excluded from initial funding. Instead, funds went directly to school districts to train teachers (Canales & Ruiz-Escalante, 1993; Stewner-Manzanares, 1988). In 1975, under Public Law 93-330, universities and colleges became eligible to apply for bilingual teacher training funds (Canales & Ruiz-Escalante, 1993).

Almost four decades later, empirical research examining the nature and efficacy of bilingual preparation program models remains thin; however, there is a rich body of conceptual and anecdotal scholarship describing frameworks, standards, and goals (Sheets & Salazar, 2008). To illustrate, Tinajero and Spencer (2002) describe components of their university model. Most of the early conceptual scholarship focused on teacher competencies, which evolved into nationally adopted standards guiding current competency-based models (Blanco, 1977; Canales & Ruiz-Escalante, 1993). Presently, the majority of the research in bilingual education addresses areas other than programmatic models, such as: Spanish language assessment (Sutterby, Ayala, & Murillo, 2005) candidate beliefs (Artiles, Berreto, Pena & McClafferty, 1998), recruitment and retention (Diaz-Rico & Smith, 1994), diversity concerns (Sheets & Chew, 2002), and self-studies on specific courses (Arias & Poynor, 2001). There is also scholarship related to specific candidate populations, such as para-educators and *normalistas* (Carrier & Cohen, 2003; Clark & Flores, 2001; Flores, 2001; Flores & Clark, 2004). Thus, in spite of maturation of the field and a solid theoretical knowledge base, there is minimal empirical evidence on program type and its impact on *aspirante* effectiveness.

Two studies examined bilingual teacher preparation models in Texas and California. Flores and Clark (2002) studied Project *Alianza* implemented in five public universities in Texas and California. *Alianza's* goals were to remove institutional barriers and create pathways for three distinct groups of Latin@ candidates: college-age undergraduates, non-traditional paraprofessionals, and US resident *normalistas*. To determine candidate need, *Alianza* assessed levels of bilingual proficiency, beliefs, and pedagogical and content knowledge. They found that *Alianza* provided institutional, programmatic, personal, and curricular support. Support included financial aid, advising, mentoring, flexible course schedules, temporary waivers of entry exams, recognition of foreign credentials, and heterogeneous cohort groupings. To accommodate the different candidate needs, *Alianza* adapted curricular content and pedagogical approaches taking into consideration language proficiency, literacy skills, and personal development aspects such as ethnic identity, biculturalism, and efficacy. School principal evaluations showed that *Alianza* completers were viewed as effective teachers of BLs.

A qualitative study by Sheets and Salazar (2008) examined seven teacher preparation models in Texas public (5) and private (2) university programs, one of which was identified as exemplary. The findings showed that programs: had similar vision statements, followed state bilingual teaching competencies, adapted to meet specific candidate populations, provided extensive field experiences, offered test preparation, had strong Spanish foundations, and aligned course content in multiple sections. Shared challenges included: dependence on grants for funding and survival, recruitment of qualified instructors, dealing with Spanish language loss affecting candidate bilingualism, difficulty maintaining continuity for courses taken out of the bilingual program, need to strengthen collegial practices among faculty, issues with constant changes in state policies, awareness of anti-immigration movements associated with bilingual education, and lack of a strong diversity component throughout.

Exemplary Program Characteristics

Shulman (2005) uses the term "signature" to describe exemplary teacher preparation programs. According to Shulman, signature pedagogies have three dimensions: a surface structure, what teaching looks like; a deep structure, assumptions about teaching/learning; and an implicit structure, beliefs about what should be valued. Hollins' (2008) framework, specifically addresses preparation for culturally diverse students. She includes three major elements: focused inquiry—approaches for acquiring essential knowledge for practice; directed observation—specifically designed protocol to document and analyze classroom practices and relationships; and guided practice—ways to facilitate learning for particular students.

We found two empirical studies that examined programs with signature characteristics. Darling-Hammond (2006) studied seven generalist teacher preparation programs. She found six common strengths: coherent clear vision grounded in student learning understandings; strong core curriculum taught within a sociocultural context; extensive connected clinical experiences closely interwoven with coursework; reflective inquiry approach which included case methods and teacher research; school–university partnerships and experiences in professional communities; and, assessment-based professional standards addressing evaluation of teaching performance.

Leighton, Hightower, and Wrigley's (1995) study identified 12 exemplary bilingual education preparation programs across the country. Their selection framework included five broad areas: research-based second language pedagogy promoting high standards of skill and knowledge in content areas; value orientation for language-culture preservation and family/community involvement while promoting English language acquisition; extended field experiences monitored for theory to practice connections; effective recruitment strategies for preparation and professional development to increase numbers and quality of teachers; and a context supporting a climate for life-time professional growth, leadership, advocacy, reflection, and accountability.

Actualizing the *Educar para Transformar* Model

There are considerable differences among the vision and conceptual framework characterizing traditional models, signature programs, and the *Educar para Transformar* (*Educar*) model. The systematic, substantive, and conscientious curricular reform in *Educar's* design and implementation focuses on transforming program faculty, as well as *aspirantes'* ideological positions, knowledge, and skills. Once commitment, leadership, and consensus to dismantle an existing program to an *Educar* model is at hand, we suggest faculty consider the following: develop a procedural protocol to organize and guide the process for learning to change and changing to learn about teaching about teaching; conduct a critical analysis of existing contextual institutional strengths and limitations; and, evaluate existing curricular content and acknowledge that transformation requires making substantive shifts, adjustments, and modifications to program.

Additionally, if design and implementation issues, applicable to individual institutional situations, are considered, these factors will be less able to constrain, obstruct, or thwart the collaborative process of transformation. As faculty engage in transformation, at times, change may appear contradictory or impossible. The change process might generate argumentative positions, which may require reconciliation. Changes to the existing structures may create issues of ownership, identity, time, persistence, conflict, values, power, and perspectives. Actualizing transformative change takes dedication, compassion, and expertise. ¡*Pero con ganas, claro que se puede!*

Educar para Transformar *Model*

The *Educar* model is conceptualized within two overarching, interdependent, complementary frameworks, *transformación* and *revolución*, with three interconnecting dimensions—*iluminación*, praxis, and *concientización*, directing programmatic content. Its vision, *Dar Luz*, guides the transformative-revolutionary spirit permeating throughout. *Educar* asks that we take necessary risks to systematically challenge and transform institutional conditions. We consider transformative program change as a form of *revolución*; and, as such, cannot be separate from or unrelated to the practice of bilingual teacher preparation. The vision, *Dar Luz* clarifies the purpose, describes the mission, and justifies a desired transformed future (see Chapter 1). It conveys goals, objectives, values, and responsibilities of a transformed, empowered, skilled faculty who prepare culturally competent *aspirantes* with a deep sense of responsibility to nurture and educate our children (see Chapter 1).

Educar's focus on deep understandings of sociocultural learning theory and transformative bicultural/bilingual pedagogical skills is enhanced by explicit curriculum examining issues such as identity, efficacy, epistemological belief systems, advocacy, teacher responsibility, and commitment to sustained service in bilingual communities.

Aspirantes embraced and supported by continual movements of *transformación* and *revolución* flourish throughout. Upon completion, they emerge with knowledge, tools, skills, socio-political positions, responsibility, and agency. *Aspirantes* prepared in an *Educar* model are distinguishable from others in the field—their transformed identity stands out. They teach for freedom. Prepared to lead, they advocate and join the struggle to bring about change in self, BLs, schools, and community (see Chapter 19). Description and discussion of *Educar's* three dimensions follow.

Educar's Dimensions

We maintain that curriculum in a preparation program has the power to illuminate *aspirantes'* development, shape praxis, and generate consciousness. *Educar's* dimensions and attendant subsections are neither hierarchal nor discrete; rather they intersect, combine, and unite in practice. The first dimension, *iluminación*, centers on the awakening and development of *aspirantes'* personal and professional identities and beliefs. Its goal is to strengthen bilingualism, critical reflective thinking, and cultural competency. Praxis, the second dimension, focuses on the learning process with emphasis on teacher as mediating learning. The curricular content in this dimension includes sociocultural learning theory, pedagogical knowledge, and evaluation/assessment. *Concientización* requires faculty to critically scrutinize institutional issues, which will be encountered by *aspirantes* in the field; and, provide them multiple opportunities to examine the socio-political, economic, familial, and legal influences of schooling, as well as acknowledge the developmental nature of learning to teach. While there are more topics to consider in this dimension we include three: sociopolitical issues, policy matters, and apprenticeships. Discussion on the dimensions follow and are elaborated further in other chapters in this text. See Figure 2.1: *Educar para Transformar*

Iluminación

Educar's program design contains specific and sustained curricular content and field experiences for *aspirantes* to experience a personal evolution that questions existing beliefs, enhances ethnic identity, initiates teacher identity, and promotes efficacy (see Chapter 3 and 7). This dimension also focuses on the development of knowledge and skill in bilingualism (see Chapter 5) critical reflexive thinking, and cultural competency (see Chapter 4 and 6). A goal is to support *aspirantes* as they gain knowledge and develop skills to help them nurture BLs' development. These developmental attributes guide successful learning-teaching practices and intensify their commitment to advocate for social justice.

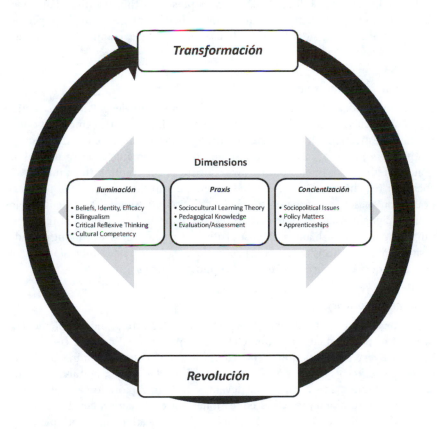

Figure 2.1 Educar para Transformar. Dar Luz—Illuminates Transformative Ways of Thinking, Knowing, and Being

Beliefs, Identity, Efficacy

Ideology, when viewed as a belief system, is integrated into a philosophy that guides educational principles, shapes learning--teaching behaviors, affects identity construction, and influences efficacy development. Since the *aspirantes'* ideology is socially and politically constructed, it is highly influenced by their socialization in the dominating culture. These ingrained, automatic belief systems steer thinking, judgment, and receptiveness to knowledge; therefore, *Educar* maintains that *aspirantes* discover, acknowledge, and often deconstruct previously held beliefs (see Chapter 3, 4, 6 and 7).

Bilingualism

Most agree that language is one of the most powerful cultural tools humans possess; thus, the construct of bilingualism in a preparation program must be viewed as more than academic dual language proficiency. The acquisition of academic dual language expertise gives *aspirantes* ability to learn and teach in both languages, and as such should not be discounted; however, an *Educar* program, fully recognizes, cultivates, and extends the extraordinary force contained within the attitudes, knowledge, skills, and experiences present within two lived languages. *Aspirantes* must experience and understand that languages embody a people's identity, traditions, history, values, rituals, voice, culture, cognition, knowledge, and worldviews (see Chapter 5).

Critical Reflexive Thinking

Similar to the acquisition of other essential skills and knowledge, the construction of an *Educar* curriculum includes critical reflexive thinking as a specific component. In the investigation of the social, political, cultural, and economic aspects of schooling, *aspirantes* learn to apply standards and elements of critical thinking (Paul & Elder, 2006) and become aware of the traits framing their intellectual character (Ritchhard, 2004). Repeated experiences in the analysis, synthesis, and evaluation of schooling issues coupled with critical thinking knowledge helps them become consciously attentive to the strengths and limitations in their own thinking patterns and habits and those of others. Critical reflexive thinking provides insights into their decision-making process and leads to greater understandings of how their decisions affect BLs' access to opportunity to learn.

Cultural Competency

In *Educar,* the term cultural competency has dual, intersecting, and complementary overtones—personal cultural competency and professional cultural competency in the delivery of instruction. Personal cultural competence requires *aspirantes* to recognize, respect, and cherish their identities, languages, cultures, families, and communities. This competence develops through exploration and analysis of the social, cultural, political, and educational power dynamics faced within self, families, neighborhoods, prior schooling, higher education, and work place (see Chapter 3). *Educar* also recognizes that positive social and academic outcomes for BLs depend on *aspirantes'* capacity to conceptualize the role of culture and language in schooling and to apply it to the learning-teaching process (see Chapter 5 and 6). They must be given multiple opportunities throughout their coursework to develop and demonstrate cultural competency using BLs' out-of-school-learning and problem-solving skills acquired through participation in and use of linguistic traditions, cultural practices, ethnic rituals, and community resources. Culturally relevant, extended field experiences provide practice for instructional accommodations as well as strengthen their observational skills, which helps them respond and interpret the cultural nuances BLs disclose (see Chapter 6 and 7).

Praxis

Freire (1986) defines praxis as "reflection and action upon the world in order to transform it" (p. 36). Whereas *Iluminación* uses reflection to center on various aspects of *aspirantes'* self-development, Praxis moves toward conscious actions and skilled pedagogical behaviors in classrooms. Since we view learning–teaching as a symbiotic, inseparable process, *Educar's* coursework, in this dimension, upholds central ideas that must be reinforced throughout, through faculty modeling, such as —teachers are responsible for student learning; a teacher's role is to facilitate and mediate learning, and teachers purposefully advance BLs' self-development and strive to build positive interpersonal relationships with children and their families. This dimension has three interrelated components: sociocultural learning theory, bilingual/bicultural pedagogy, and evaluation/assessment.

Sociocultural Learning Theory

Sociocultural theory is at the heart of the theoretical framework for the *Educar* model. Highly influenced by the work of Vygotsky (1962, 1978), this learning theory maintains that a learner's social interaction within a cultural, historical context affects cognitive growth. Sociocultural theorists acknowledge critical connections among the social, language, and cultural dimensions of learning (Kozulin, 2002, 2003; Lave & Wenger, 1991; Moll, Amanti, Neff, & González, 2001). This differs from viewing cognitive development as an isolated, individualistic cognitive process. *Educar's* vision is to improve *aspirantes'* potential to mediate instruction and co-construct new knowledge; enhance their ability to design and evaluate optimal learning conditions in classrooms; and, develop skill to contextualize instruction in particular situations under specific conditions. Therefore, sociocultural learning theory is a major component in the human development required course; and its tenets must be incorporated and applied throughout all other coursework and extended field experiences.

Pedagogical Knowledge

In *Educar*, the bilingual/bicultural transformative pedagogical foundation is consciously, deliberately, and systematically screened through BLs' and *aspirantes'* cultural, linguistic, and experiential repertoires. An outcome is to instill transformative pedagogical knowledge and skill in areas of curriculum evaluation and design; interdisciplinary approaches to knowledge, and technology literacies (see Chapters 8–14).

Educar promotes an interdisciplinary approach to curriculum. This encourages integration and connections among disciplines. The examination of issues through interdisciplinary lens requires *aspirantes* to be open-minded and provides meaningful experiences in perspective-taking, problem-solving, inquiry, critical thinking, ambiguity, and integration of conflicting ideas or concepts (Lattuca, Voight, & Fath, 2004). This approach aligns with sociocultural transformative perspectives since it requires *aspirantes* to activate prior learning and acknowledge the situational and cultural context in which learning occurs.

There can be no doubt that *aspirantes* must be prepared with necessary skills to use technology as a conduit for learning. To achieve high levels of twenty-first century knowledge, in an *Educar* program, technology is integrated throughout the preparation program. We acknowledge that knowledge of technology literacies encourages exploration, opens doors to BLs' economic future, provides access to inexhaustible knowledge resources, and creates meaningful ways to examine, question, express, and reflect on cultural, social, and political realities.

To ensure that *aspirantes* can conditionalize the declarative and procedural knowledge contained in praxis, program design allows for extended, guided, cultural exposure in practice, including ethnographic community studies (see Chapter 9). *Educar* strongly recommends "framing experiences" (Hollins, personal conversation) throughout the program to help *aspirantes* explore and apply community resources to learning events. *Aspirantes* must develop sharp observational skills to document, interpret, and respond to what they see and experience. All field experiences are linked explicitly to learning theory, framed by bilingual/bicultural transformative pedagogy, and connected with course content, goals, and objectives.

Evaluation/Assessment

This component includes honest and rigorous program evaluation since teacher educators are responsible for the acquisition and development of *aspirantes'* attitude, knowledge, and skill, which in turn translates to their effectiveness in classrooms. Likewise, through program activities and experiences, *aspirantes* learn strategies to self-evaluate, as well as ability to assess learners' progress, since they are responsible for BLs academic and social achievement (see Chapter 13).

Concientización

This dimension extends the circle of knowledge, commitment, and responsibility. We begin with self (*Iluminación*), move to spaces in the classroom (Praxis) and finally our journey takes us into places where societal issues affect the community (*Concientización*). Experiences in coursework addressing this dimension includes *aspirantes'* participation in reflexive processes of reconsidering, reframing, questioning, and challenging sociopolitical contextual elements, existing policies, and community resources influencing the schooling of BLs. Deliberate efforts are made to inspire and motivate *aspirantes* to become *concientizados* to concerns affecting the schooling of BLs.

Socio-political Issues

Aspirantes have course experiences that specifically scrutinize socio-political issues and explore community resources impacting schooling and impinging on practice. As teachers, they will realize that many factors are within their influence; therefore, they must be prepared to assume social responsibility and understand ways to utilize community resources in rich, authentic ways. Likewise, they will become conscious that school and societal culture perpetuates problematic systemic conditions, such as lack of accessibility to equitable schooling opportunities, unequal power representation and distribution in school and community; and, weak or nonexistent familial support structures. While some of these issues may be out of *aspirantes'* immediate control, opportunity to critically analyze these factors can help them understand how these factors affect practice (see Chapter 15).

Policies Matters

Since schools are impacted by educational policies and legal mandates from the federal, state, district, and school level, *aspirantes* can identify these directives in practice and observe how they affect BLs, teachers, schools, and community. Educational policies include items such as teacher certification requirements, school budgets, length of school year, daily schedules, assessment programs, salaries, textbook adoptions, and curriculum standards. While legislative policies differ from state to state, Chapter 15 provides an example from Texas. *Aspirantes* realize that teaching is a political act; and, at times, they might need to assume social and political responsibility to the community beyond the classroom.

Apprenticeships

Aspirantes who participate in an apprenticeship are more likely to receive the services needed to develop cultural competency and carry out ethical practices. Research shows that *aspirantes* need support, especially during their first three years (Ingersoll & Kralik, 2004). Mentoring and coaching from more "expert others"'is viewed as an integral part of the *Educar* model. Programs that assign mentors to novices scaffold their learning classroom experiences, support learning to teach, promote participation in learning communities of practice, minimize isolation, and encourage novices to identify with and advocate for BLs (see Chapter 18). Induction has potential to improve student achievement (Villar & Strong, 2007).

Guided by its vision, *Dar Luz,* and framed by a collective, courageous wisdom of *transformación and revolución, Educar's* three dimensions—*iluminación*, praxis and *concientización* began during preparation, remains active throughout their teacher-life. *Educar's* culturally competent novices in various stages of learning to teach, continue their journey toward excellence through continual commitment and development.

Transforming Teacher Preparation

We have cited research clearly showing that for the most part, BLs do not have fair access to schooling opportunities readily available to native English speakers. In some states, adequate language polices appear to be in place; however, a myriad of educational, political, and economic reasons impede equitable implementation (see Chapter 15). Granted, while factors affecting optimal schooling conditions for BLs are complex; one way to improve their schooling is through exemplary teacher preparation and professional development for under-qualified teachers. However, even in the arena of teacher preparation, there are several stumbling blocks, which at times seem out of control.

First, neoliberalism in education—the social process making education marketable, competitive, and capital producing—is alive and well in schooling, including teacher preparation (Hursh, 2005; Rikowski, 2006). This movement is quite visible in the preparation of bilingual teachers. University-based programs are being replaced by competitive ACPs who push out teachers cheaply and quickly. Although ideally, these entities are monitored and accredited, what actually happens in practice is debatable.

Under-qualified, monolingual teachers, often last-minute-hires, generally work in hard-to-staff schools located in high-poverty urban areas with large emerging majority student populations, many being BLs. This is particularly troubling since research shows that they share the following characteristics: twice as many have GPAs below 2.75; more have BAs from less competitive schools; are three times as likely to have failed a portion of the teaching exam at least once; and, more are uncertified, inexperienced, and "out of field;" and 71% of Bilingual/ESL secondary teachers are uncertified (Cochran-Smith & Zeichner, 2005; Zumwalt & Craig, 2005).

Another problem resides with teacher educators. Who are they? Who is being prepared as future teacher educators? The majority of full-time faculty in colleges of education across the US are White monolinguals (Ladson-Billings, 2005). While many existing professors in the various disciplines—mathematics, science, social studies, literacy, and technology—do not have basic knowledge in bilingual foundations and ESL methodology, it appears that neither will the new cadre of teacher educators. Professors' ideological perspectives and authority enjoyed in graduate schools of education, has a consequential effect on the effectiveness of preparation programs, including who receives exposure to bilingual education and ESL pedagogy. In many institutions, *aspirantes* take a significant portion of their methods courses outside the bilingual department and doctoral students, many who will become future teacher educators, can graduate without course work in bilingual education. Many professors do not incorporate bilingual/ESL pedagogy in their methods courses and some may not see the need for advanced courses in bilingual/ESL in doctoral degree plans. Compounding the problem is that many professors and doctoral students lack knowledge of culture and teaching experience with BLs (Sheets, 2003).

Unfortunately, it takes more than good intentions. Minimally, we need well-prepared bilingual and ESL teachers. Exemplary programs, traditional and alternative, need to prepare large numbers of culturally, linguistically competent bilingual education teachers. Solutions must come from the field. University teacher education programs have potential to serve as vehicles to construct powerful coalitions with community leaders. Together we can:

- Make positive impacts in educational reform efforts affecting policy at the local, district, state, and national level.
- Use critical voices to transform schooling opportunities for BLs through the development of transformative preparation programs, presentations, and publications delineating program strengths and challenges.

Future Research Directions

Though there is solid theoretical and empirical evidence that bilingual education is effective for BLs (Rolstad, Mahoney, & Glass, 2005), there is minimal empirical evidence of the impact of specific bilingual teacher preparation program type on teacher quality, teaching effectiveness, and BLs' achievement outcomes. Clearly, research is needed on preparation models. Many practitioners in the field from tier-two institutions experience heavy teaching loads along with a myriad of time-consuming responsibilities characteristic of their positions. These working conditions often make it difficult for them to sustain a line of inquiry needed to generate scholarship. Collaborative efforts might support their scholarship. Some areas to consider:

- *Educar*: Examination of the process involved in its design, development, and implementation including assessment of its dimensions. Findings from this work can refine the model and provide institutions with information on ways to make procedural and substantive program changes.
- Alternative Certification Programs: Although research is missing, conflicting, or inconclusive, in terms of the merits of ACPs, they are producing large numbers of certified bilingual education teachers. They also draw extensively from a non-traditional population—more males, more mature people, and second-career individuals. Empirical research is needed to examine ACP's contribution to the preparation of bilingual education teachers.
- Self-studies: Research examining strengths and challenges of specific models.

References

Arends, R., & Winitzky, N. (1996). Program structures and learning to teach. In F. B. Murray (Ed.), *The teacher educator's handbook: Building a knowledge base for the preparation of teachers* (pp. 526–556). San Francisco: Jossey-Bass.

Arias, B., & Poynor, L. (2001). A good start: A progressive, transactional approach to diversity in pre-service teacher education. *Bilingual Research Journal, 25*(4), 417–434.

Artiles, A. J., Berreto, R. M., Pena, L., & McClafferty, K. (1998). Pathways to teacher learning in multicultural contexts: A longitudinal case study of two novice bilingual teachers in urban schools. *Remedial and Special Education, 19*(2), 70–90.

Associated Press. (2009). Retrieved from: http://www.usatoday.com/news/education/2009-10-22-obama-teachers_N.htm

Baines, L., McDowell, J., & Foulk, D. (2001). One step forward, three steps backward: Alternative certification programs in Texas, Georgia, and Florida. *Educational Horizons, 80*(1), 32–37.

Blanco, G. (1977). Competencies needed by bilingual education. *Educational Leadership, 35,* 123–127.

Borko, H., Liston, D., & Whitcomb, J. (2007). Genres of empirical research in teacher education. *Journal of Teacher Education, 58*(1), 3–11.

Burnett, R. W. (1979). *National estimates of bilingual education teachers.* Retrieved from   http://eric.ed.gov/ERICWebPortal/Home.portal?_nfpb=true&_pagELLabEL L=RecordDetails&ERICExtSearch_SearchValue_0=ED176557&ERICExtSearch_ SearchType_0=eric_accno&objectId=0900000b800fe4b1

Canales, J., & Ruiz-Escalante, J. A. (1993). A pedagogical framework for bilingual education teacher preparation programs. In *Proceedings of the Third National Research Symposium on Limited English Proficient Student Issues: Focus on Middle and High School Issues.* Vol 1. Washington, DC: US Department of Education, Office of Bilingual Education and Minority Language Affairs. Retrieved from Bilingual Education Act, the. (1968). Public Law 90-247. http://www.ncela.gwu.edu/pubs/symposia/third/ canales.htm

Carrier, K. A., & Cohen, J. A. (2003). Personal and professional success in a bilingual teacher training program. *NABE Journal of Research and Practice,* 1(1), 50–69.

Cisneros, H. (1989). *Doing more for more: Hispanic issues for Texas and the nation.* Austin, TX: Hogg Foundation for Mental Health.

Clark, E. R., & Flores, B. B. (2001). Is Spanish proficiency simply enough? An examination of *normalistas'* attitudes towards Spanish, bilingualism, and bilingual teacher pedagogy. *MexTesol Journal, 25*(3), 13–27.

Clewell, B., & Forcier, L. (2001). Increasing the number of mathematics and science teachers: A review of teacher recruitment programs. *Teaching and Change, 8*(4), 331–361.

Cochran-Smith, M., & Fries, K. (2005). Researching teacher education in changing times: Politics and paradigms (pp. 69–109). In M. Cochran-Smith & K. M. Zeichner (Eds.), *Studying teacher education: The report of the AERA panel on research and teacher education.* Mahwah, NJ: Erlbaum/AERA.

Cochran-Smith, M., & Zeichner, K. M. (Eds.). (2005). *Studying teacher education: The report of the AERA panel on research and teacher education.* Mahwah, NJ: Erlbaum/AERA.

Darling-Hammond, L. (2000). *Studies of excellence in teacher education.* New York: National Commission on Teaching and America's Future.

Darling-Hammond, L. (2006). *Powerful teacher education: Lessons from exemplary programs.* San Francisco: Jossey-Bass.

Diaz-Rico, L. T., & Smith, J. (1994). Recruiting and retaining bilingual teachers: A cooperative school community-university model. *The Journal of Educational Issues of Language Minority Students, 14,* 255–268.

Etools4Education (2007). *Alternative certification.* Retrieved from http://www.online-distance-learning-education.com/article_info.php/articles_id/37

Feiman-Nemser, S. (1990). *Conceptual orientations in teacher education.* Retrieved from http://ncrtl.msu.edu/http/ipapers/html/pdf/ip902.pdf

Flores, B. B. (2001). Thinking out of the box: One university's experience with foreign-trained teachers. *Educational Policy Analysis Archives, 9*(18). Retrieved from http://epaa. asu.edu/epaa/v9n18.html

Flores, B. B., & Clark, E. R. (2002). *El desarrollo del proyecto Alianza: Lessons learned and policy implications.* CBER, Arizona State University.

Flores, B. B., & Clark, E. R. (2004). A critical examination of *normalistas'* self-conceptualization and teacher efficacy. *Hispanic Journal of Behavioral Sciences, 26*(2), 230–257.

Freire, P. (1986). *Pedagogy of the oppressed.* New York: Continuum.

García, E. E., & Miller, L. S. (2008). Findings and recommendations of the National Task Force on Early Childhood Education for Hispanics. *Child Development Perspectives,* **2(2), 53–58.**

García, E. E., Arias, M. B., Harris Murri, N. J., & Serna, C. (2010). Developing responsive teachers: A challenge for a demographic reality. *Journal of Teacher Education, 61(1–2),* 132–142.

Hollins, E. (2008, March). *A teacher preparation framework: Improving diverse student learning outcomes.* Paper presented at the Annual American Educational Research Association (AERA), New York.

Hollins, E., & Torres-Guzman, M. E. (2005). Research on preparing teachers for diverse populations. In M. Cochran-Smith & K. Zeichner (Eds.), *Studying teacher education: The report of the AERA panel on research and teacher education* (pp. 477–548). Mahwah, NJ: Erlbaum/AERA.

Hursh, D. (2005) Neo-liberalism, markets and accountability: Transforming education and undermining democracy in the United States and England. *Policy Futures in Education, 3*(1), 3–15. Retrieved from http://www.wwwords.co.uk/pdf/viewpdf.asp?j=pfie&vol=3&issue=1&year=2005&article=2_Hursh_PFIE_3_1_web&id=195.93.21.7

Ingersoll, R. M., & Kralik, J. M. (2004). *The impact of mentoring on teacher retention: What the research says.* Education Commission of the States, Research Review. Retrieved from http://www.ecs.org/clearinghouse/50/36/5036.htm.

Kohler, A. D., & Lazarín, M. (2007). *Hispanic education in the United States: Statistical brief No. 8.* Washington, DC: National Council of La Raza.

Kozulin, A. (2002). Sociocultural theory and the mediated learning experience. *School Psychology International, 23*(1), 7–35.

Kozulin, A. (2003). *Psychological tools: A sociocultural approach to education.* Cambridge, MA: Harvard University Press.

Ladson-Billings, G. (2005). Is the team all right? Diversity and teacher education. *Journal of Teacher Education, 56,* 229–234.

Lattuca, L. R., Voigt, L. J., & Fath, K. Q. (2004). Does interdisciplinarity promote learning? Theoretical support and researchable questions. *The Review of Higher Education, 28*(1), 23–48.

Lave, J., & Wenger, E. (1991). *Situated learning: Legitimate peripheral participation.* Cambridge, MA: University of Cambridge Press.

Leighton, M. S., Hightower, A. M., & Wrigley, P. G. (1995). *Model strategies in bilingual education: Professional development.* Report by the US Department of Education, Contract #LC920960.

Macias, R. F. (1989). *The national need for bilingual teachers* (ERIC Publication No. 334153). Claremont, CA: Thomas Rivera Center.

Maroney, O. H. (1998). Who is teaching the children? More trained bilingual teachers are needed for excellent education. *The Intercultural Development Research Association Newsletter, 25*(1), 6–8.

Moll, L., Amanti, C., Neff, D., & González, N. (2001). Funds of knowledge for teaching: Using a qualitative approach to connect homes and classrooms. *Theory Into Practice 31*(2), 132–141.

National Center for Educational Information (NCEI). (2010). *Alternative routes to teacher certification: An overview.* Retrieved from http://www.ncei.com/Alt-Teacher-Cert.htm

Paul, R., & Elder, L. (2006). *Critical thinking: Tools for taking charge of your learning and your life* (2nd ed). Upper Saddle River, NJ: Prentice Hall.

Pew Hispanic Center (2010). *Statistical portrait of Hispanics, 2008*. Retrieved from http://pewhispanic.org/factsheets/factsheet.php?FactsheetID=58

Rikowski, G. (2006, October 30). *Caught in the storm of capital: Teacher professionalism, managerialism, and neoliberalism in schools* (EDU 3004). A paper prepared for Education, Culture & Society Students. Retrieved from http://www.flowideas.co.uk/?page=articles&sub=Caught%20in%20the%20Storm%20of%20Capital

Ritchhart, R. (2004). *Intellectual character: What it is, why it matters, and how to get it.* San Francisco: Jossey-Bass.

Rolstad, K., Mahoney, K., & Glass, G. (2005). The big picture: A meta-analysis of program effectiveness research on English language learners. *Educational Policy, 19*(4), 572–594.

Sheets, R. H. (2003). Competency vs. good intentions: Diversity ideologies and teacher competency. *International Journal of Qualitative Studies in Education, 16*(1), 111–120.

Sheets, R. H. (2007, February). *Risking the nation: Are schools ready for the Latino majority.* Paper presented at the 2007 National Association of Bilingual Education, San Jose, CA.

Sheets, R. H., & Chew, L. (2002). Absent from the research, present in our classrooms: Preparing culturally responsive Chinese American teachers. *Journal of Teacher Education, 53*(2), 123–137.

Sheets, R. H., & Salazar, D. (2008, March). *Texas bilingual teacher preparation models: Strengths and limitations.* Paper presented at the Annual American Educational Research Association (AERA). New York.

Shulman, L. S. (2005). Signature pedagogies in the disciplines. *Daedalus, 134*, 3, 52–59.

State Board for Educator Certification (SBEC). (2010). *Educator certification.* Retrieved from http://www.sbec.state.tx.us/SBECOnline/default.asp

Stewner-Manzanares, G. (1988). *The bilingual education act: Twenty years later.* National Clearing House for Bilingual Education, No. 6. Retrieved from http://www.ncela.gwu.edu/pubs/classics/focus/06bea.htm

Sutterby, J. A., Ayala, J., & Murillo, S. (2005). *El sendero torcido al español* [The twisted path to Spanish]: The development of bilingual teachers' Spanish-language proficiency. *Bilingual Research Journal, 29*(2), 435–452.

Tinajero, J. V., & Spencer, D. A. (2002). Models of bilingual teacher preparation: What worked at the University of Texas at El Paso. In L. Minaya-Rowe (Ed.), *Teacher training and effective pedagogy in the context of student diversity* (pp. 241–268). Greenwich, CT: IAP.

Villar, A., & Strong, M. (2007). Is mentoring worth the money? A benefit-cost analysis and five-year rate of return of a comprehensive mentoring program for beginning teachers. *ERS Spectrum, 25*(3), 1–17.

Vygotsky, L. (1962). *Thought and language.* Cambridge, MA: MIT Press.

Vygotsky, L. (1978). *Mind in society: The development of higher mental processes.* In M. Cole, V. John-Steiner, S. Scribner, & E. Souberman (Eds. & Trans.), Cambridge, MA: Harvard University Press.

Wilson, S. M., Floden, R. E., & Ferrini-Mundy, J. (2001). *Teacher preparation research: Current knowledge, gaps, and recommendations.* A research report prepared for the US Department of Education (Document R-01-3). Retrieved from http://depts.washington.edu/ctpmail/PDFs/TeacherPrep-WFFM-02-2001.pdf

Zeichner, K. M., & Conklin, H. G. (2005). Teacher education programs (pp. 645–735). In M. Cochran-Smith & K. M. Zeichner (Eds.), *Studying teacher education: The report of the AERA panel on research and teacher education.* Mahwah, NJ: Erlbaum/AERA.

Zumwalt, K., & Craig, E. (2005). Teachers' characteristics: Research on the indicators of quality. In M. Cochran-Smith & K. M. Zeichner (Eds.), *Studying teacher education: The report of the AERA panel on research and teacher preparation* (pp. 157–260). Mahwah, NJ: AERA/Erlbaum.

Part II

Iluminación

Dar Luz —
Para preparar aspirantes bien educados,
necesitamos transformar lo que somos,
pensamos, sabemos, y hacemos. ¡Adelante!
Flores, Sheets, & Clark, 2011.

3 Identity

A Central Facet of Culturally Efficacious Bilingual Education Teachers

Ellen Riojas Clark, Linda Guardia Jackson,
and Linda Prieto

The majority of teachers in culturally and linguistically diverse (CLD) classrooms are not representative of the shift in US demographics (see Chapter 1). This demographic gap between the students' and teachers' cultural and linguistic experiences can have negative effects on the academic successes of ethnic minority students (Peña, 1997), including Bilingual Learners (BLs). Dilemmas in meeting the educational needs of BLs include the lack of Latin@ teachers as role models (Flores & Clark, 2005). According to Valencia (2002), the low percentage of Latin@ teachers compared to Latin@ school-age students must be addressed for several reasons: (a) the presence of Latin@s in professional positions provides role models for this school-age population; (b) teachers with similar cultural [and linguistic] backgrounds engage students more effectively; and (c) diversity in the teaching force offers the possibility for culturally responsive teaching. Hence, it is important to recruit, prepare, and retain Latin@ teachers (Flores & Clark, 2005; Prieto, 2009).

As important as these points are, the challenge of effective schooling for BLs is not simply an issue of the quantity of Latin@ teachers but about the quality of teachers' identities, pedagogies, philosophies, and sensibilities. The call from researchers, policymakers, and educational leaders for a more diverse group of teachers is based on the hope that their educational approaches will benefit the BLs they teach. However, that may not always be the case since pedagogies reflect identities and worldviews constructed through interactions in a particular socio-historical context.

Critical education scholars argue that schools are inclined to reproduce cultural systems and positions of power related to race, ethnicity, class, gender, and language. Apple (2004) and Freire (2000) contend that educators are involved in a political act whether they are conscious of it or not. Thus, education is not a neutral process. Specifically, bilingual education and ESL programs cannot proceed without serious attention to social and historical issues connected to identity formation.

Literature

Various identity theories stem from the areas of sociology, psychology, or cultural studies. Erikson (1950) popularized the construct of identity based on eight stages. We move away from his perspective of sequential stages passed through, never revisited, and that happen within particular age ranges. We view identity making as a heuristic developmental process dependent on sociocultural interactions and historical moments. This sociocultural approach leads to the understanding of identity as multiple, fluid, and always in the process of formation.

Ethnic Identities

An individual's ethnic and cultural identities reflect the socialization processes experienced in homes and communities. Scholars have examined the interaction among ethnic identity, social class, and power (Alba, 2005; Castillo-Speed, 1995; Waters, 1999). Other research documents the complex process of boundary crossing for ethnic and racial groups and the challenges of cultural identity in diverse school settings (Anzaldúa, 1987; García, 1997; Pettman, 1996; Hondagneu-Sotelo, 1994). The construction of students' racial and ethnic identities, gender roles, socioeconomic status, and the mismatch of cultural and linguistic student–teacher relationships are prevalent in our classrooms, schools, and communities (Flores & Clark, 2004; Guardia Jackson, 2009; Prieto, 2009; Romo, 1999). Recent studies examine the importance of developing bilingual education teacher candidates' cultural and ethnic identities and consciousness (Clark & Flores, 2010) to inform their decisions to teach and improve their teaching practices with BLs (Guardia Jackson, 2009; Prieto, 2009). Flores and Clark (2004) call for teachers to comprehend that student identities are tempered by the sociocultural, historical, and political context. In this chapter, we propose a conceptual framework for the development of ethnic and teacher identity that will lead to the preparation of culturally efficacious teachers, who, as described by Flores, Clark, Claeys and Villarreal (2007), have strong identities, practice bilingual/bicultural pedagogy, and display positive teaching efficacy beliefs.

Ethnic and Teacher Identity Conceptual Framework

We draw upon Holland et al.'s (1998) understanding of multiple identities as socially constructed through power relations embedded within particular social practices. Holland et al. state, "Persons are now recognized to have perspectives on their cultural worlds that are likely to differ by gender and other markers of social positions" (p. 31). The fundamental shift in the views of the relationship between culture and identity pushes researchers "to ask a broader range of questions about experience and subjectivity and the role of cultural resources in the constitution of this experience" (p. 31). This calls for a framework to "describe how specific, often socially powerful, cultural discourses and practices both position people and provide them with the resources to respond to the problematic situations in which they find themselves" (p. 32).

Holland and Lachicotte (2005) explain that people "creatively direct the sets of collective meanings to their selves, and through this orchestration come to be able to organize and narrate themselves in practice in the name of an identity, and thus achieve a modest form of agency" (p. 32). Agency, a necessary condition for choice, is the power of a person for action (Holland, et al., 1998; Urrieta, 2009). For teachers, the possibility of agency within the bounded structures of society and self can result in decisions to bring or circumvent cultural resources and to reject or promote a deficit perspective as they navigate and negotiate the public school system. The idea of agency is a crucial aspect of identity production, as we are not carbon copies of our cultural system (Holland et al., 1998; Urrieta, 2009). Our perspective considers both agency and identity rejecting the notion of the reproduction of static cultural norms (Holland, et al., 1998; Holland & Lachicotte, 2005; Urrieta, 2009). This leads us to the dismissal of the simplistic notion that identity production is a rubber stamp of the social internalized by the self. The construction of identity must take into consideration cultural parameters (Holland et al., 1998). What you *want* to be or become must be weighed against what you are *allowed* to be or become.

Norton (2000) defines identity as "how a person understands his or her relationship to the world, how that relationship is constructed across time and space, and how the person understands possibilities for the future" (p. 5). This identity production is necessarily co-constructed, happening both in social practice that transforms the individual, as well as discourse in multiple realities. Holland et al. (1998) explain, "Identity is a concept that figuratively combines the intimate or personal world with the collective space of cultural forms and social relations" (p. 5). An aspect of this co-construction inevitably involves power and positionality, which are inextricably linked to the forming of identities. Every individual participates in this positioning in some way. Therefore, identity production can be conceptualized as constantly answering and orchestrating multiple voices, which are often in conflict (Holland & Lachicotte, 2005; Holland et al., 1998; Holquist, 1990; Moraes, 1996).

Bridging Ethnic Identity to Teacher Identity

Ethnic minority educators' cultural experiences can enhance their teacher identity by bridging their ethnic and teacher identities. Experiences within a sociocultural and political context are central to how ethnic minority teachers engage with students, parents, and colleagues (Galindo, 1996; Guardia Jackson, 2009; Prieto, 2009). Prieto (2009) maintains that Latin@ *aspirantes* learn to become teachers in the home. At an early age they contribute to the household by caring for others as bicultural brokers, translators, surrogate parents, financial contributors, and by tutoring relatives, family, friends, and neighbors.

Researchers argue that *aspirantes* need opportunities to learn about their ethnic heritage to enhance their development of consciousness and transform their teaching (Clark & Flores, 2001, 2010; Prieto, 2009). The critical components of this understanding are essential for teacher identity. Through these explorations, teachers become aware of the ways language, culture, and ethnicity mediate the social construction of student identity. These explorations lead teachers to begin understanding the implications of their ideologies on their students' outcomes (Ogbu & Matute-Bianchi, 1986). Franzak (2002) clarifies these notions:

> We live in a world of negotiated identity, one where we continually construct and revise our vision of us. Those of us who create "teacher" as part of our identity must negotiate the particular implications of our professional identity in relation to students, peers, the general public, our intimates, and ourselves.
>
> (p. 258)

Teachers' identity is mediated through the social interactions with students, parents, and colleagues (Zembylas, 2003). Using Bakhtin's (1981) notion of dialogicality, Zembylas suggests that a teacher's identity is determined by others' affirmation and recognition. Rather than expecting recognition from others, Clark and Flores (2010) recommended that *aspirantes* engaged in critical reflections to affirm their teacher identity. For example, some *aspirantes* reveal that commitment to the community is the primary motive for pursuing the teaching profession (see Chapter 4). Likewise, Prieto (2009) found that aspiring Latin@ teachers "recalled their individual experiences as bilingual children and children of immigration and identified such experiences as contributing to their desire to teach Latina/o students in Spanish/English bilingual [education] classrooms" (p. 325). It is not unusual for *aspirantes* to be questioned as to their motives for choosing teaching as a profession or dedicating their teaching profession within certain communities (see Chapter 4). Clark and Flores (2010) recommend that teacher educators engage *aspirantes* in critical analysis to understand views of race, ethnicity, socioeconomics, and power. They further encourage role-playing situations to develop voice to respond to these challenges.

Metamorphic Transformation Model

We examine Clark's (1996) metamorphic transformative model to elucidate the shaping of teacher identities. Consistent with Clark and Flores (2010), the teacher is at the center of their development and learning within this teacher transformation model. Guardia Jackson (2009) and Prieto (2009) perceive teacher transformation as a process that involves reflection and dialogue wherein the examination of cumulative life experiences provides *apoyo* [support] and impact instructional philosophies and practices for teachers serving BL communities. Conversely, teachers prepared to be culturally responsive do incorporate these ideals into their teacher identity. After a year-long self-assessment of their teacher identity, Vavrus (2002) observe that candidates accommodated democratic principles as part of their teaching practices thereby countering hegemonic discourse and assuming an advocacy role.

Clark and Flores (2010) suggest that through critical reflection and action, teacher candidates can begin developing a strong sense of ethnic and cultural consciousness, self-conceptualization, cultural teaching efficacy, and constructivist epistemological beliefs. Through this metamorphic process, a transformative teacher identity can result. Clark and Flores persuasively argue that self-determined, empowered, and actualized teachers have the tools to confront hegemonic discourse.

Metamorphosis: A Model of Change and Transformation

The idea of metamorphosis captures both biological physical changes and psychological processes of transformation. As *aspirantes* undergo metamorphosis, they either become transformative agents or remain stagnant. To become an efficacious teacher requires critical reflection of identity, beliefs, and attitude within the social, cultural, ethnic, linguistic, and economic context. Clark and Flores (2010) espouse that through a process of struggle, denial, acceptance, revitalization and validation of self, teachers can develop a salient ethnic and cultural identity.

In *Metamorphosis: A Model of Identity Transformation* (1996), Clark described four stages based on the metamorphosis of a butterfly:

1   Dormancy: characterized as a lack of self-awareness as an ethnic being and having limited contact with other cultural group members.
2   Exploration: characterized as a process in which an individual begins to reflect and explore identity and self within the sociocultural context.
3   Crystallization: characterized as process of acquiring clarity for defining and articulating self-identity.
4   Flight: characterized as a transformative process in which individuals experience a paradigm shift developing new ways of believing, seeing, and thinking.

In reconsidering the original Clark (1996) model, Clark and Flores (2010) determined that the process is not linear, but rather a recursive process. They further stipulate that this process leads *aspirantes* to acceptance, empowerment, revitalization, and self-realization. Dependent on the individual's identity formation, consciousness, and experiences, further identity development occurs at differing rates throughout a candidate's course of study or throughout the teaching career. Those who undergo metamorphosis usually also experience a change in *habitus* or behavior. For teachers, their process of metamorphosis or identity development depends on their situation, historical moment, and environment.

The Trajectory of Identity Formation of a Mexican American Bilingual Educator

For the purposes of this chapter, Guardia Jackson's (2009) case study of an exemplary Mexican American bilingual educator is viewed through a metamorphic transformational lens. The participant, Luz, a first-grade teacher with 28 years of classroom experience in the same district, was interviewed and observed over a four-year span. The findings revealed a dialectic and dialogic process between personal experiences, schooling, imposition of policies, daily-lived classroom experiences, and the challenges of teaching BLs.

Luz, second of five children born to Mexican immigrant parents, entered public school as a monolingual Spanish speaker. She was one of the few among her high school friends who went to college. Luz taught kindergarten through third grade in the same school district throughout her career. In addition to several certifications, she earned a Master's degree in Curriculum and Instruction with an emphasis on bilingual education and has been recognized in Texas and nationally for her exemplary bilingual education teaching.

Unexplored Identity: Who am I?

In dormancy, long-held beliefs and worldviews will remain static if unchallenged due to lack of awareness or limited ethnic contact with others. Assisting a teacher to explore her identity begins with Who am I? (Connelly & Clandinin, 1999; Clark & Flores, 2001, 2010). An egocentric perspective usually is the basis for an individual's identity. Group ethnic identity remains unexplored when the individual is not in contact with the perspectives of other group members; so then patterns within their sociocultural experiences are not perceptible. Luz grew up in a largely Latino community having only limited contact with other ethnic groups. Her family and community did not encourage her to develop ethnic consciousness.

> In my hometown, people were not as outspoken about their culture and language. They wanted to be like Americans.
>
> (Interview, August 8, 2008)

Similar to Luz's experience, Clark and Flores (2001) document that often *aspirantes* have not developed ethnic consciousness. The *aspirantes*' interpretation of events, which are accepted as the norm, stem from a lack of political or ideological clarity (Bartolomé & Balderrama, 2001).

It was not until Luz left for college that she had experiences that enabled her to explore her cultural identity. Understanding that we are works-in-progress with multiple identities, exploratory questions during dormancy include: "Who am I in my story of teaching? Who am I in my administrator's stories? Who am I in my parents' stories?" (Connelly & Clandinin, 1999, p. 3). Only then can we come to understandings about what is self, selfhood, and identity. We agree with Holland et al. (1998):

> People tell others who they are, but even more important, they tell themselves and then try to act as though they are who they say they are. These self-understandings, especially those with strong emotional resonance for the teller, are what we refer to as identities.
>
> (p. 3)

Clark and Flores (2010) maintain that identity exploration is a critical aspect in candidate and teacher development; this process assists in understanding their professional roles. Since there is a significant relationship between self-concept and cultural diversity awareness, Brown (2004) proposes that self-concept development is required to challenge candidates' resistance toward differences. To expand *aspirantes*' thinking and beliefs, a continuous self-exploration of "Who am I?" is necessary to nurture identity development.

Exploration: Cultural Identity as a Way of Seeing and Understanding

Exploration as a process extends beyond understanding self and others' identities; there is an intentional introspection to broaden personal perspectives for articulating cultural identity (Clark & Flores, 2010). Certain events or experiences may trigger exploration where differing views emerge as in the case of Luz. At the university, Luz was faced with the assimilated thinking of her family and community colliding with her awakening *conciencia* (consciousness):

> When I learned and studied and read what Chicanismo was to some people and what it meant to others, I was really proud that there had been some working on empowering themselves. I liked the fact that some people had stood up for their rights and for their jobs and for different things and for their education. I remember when we started reading a lot about Raza Unida in the cultural courses at the university. It just opened up my mind. That's what made me realize that I was so proud to be part of the Mexicano, Chicano, you know, that trend. I was so glad to be part of the culture.
>
> (Interview, August 8, 2008)

As individuals explore the exogenous factors, such as historical, political, cultural, and economic, within their sociocultural contexts, identity is heightened and views are changed. As in the case of Luz, she begins to examine colonization, marginalization, assimilation, and accommodation. As she focused on the historical and political conditions, Luz begins to affirm her ethnic identity.

Her university experiences forged her awareness about the intersectionality of race/ethnicity, language, class, and gender. The feedback loop of interactions and knowledge production led her to become aware of issues and understand different perspectives:

> So I learned a lot. Well, what really helped me understand those, I guess, misconceptions and the misunderstandings about minorities made me realize later on that those were the things that were being said about Mexicanos, and about the children, and about Blacks. You know what I mean. I guess I was more open-minded knowing that certain things are not true. I was more open-minded.
>
> (Interview, August 8, 2008)

As Luz continues to explore these exogenous factors, her perspective changes and her identity is further forged. It is easy to see why this process occurs at dissimilar rates for different individuals; we explore identity through our world view, perspectives, beliefs, and thinking. The goal is for the teacher candidate to cognitively and psychologically situate their identity within the sociocultural context, while expanding their perspectives and beliefs. As a dialogic process, there is a deliberate course of action for exploring self and understanding others' views. Ríos, Trent, and Castañeda (2003) promote perspective taking as a means to cultivate candidates' empathy and advocacy for social justice. Clark and Flores (2010) affirm that when teachers appreciate and comprehend differing perspectives, they are more likely to become culturally efficacious and promote student success.

Internal Change: Working Towards Becoming Culturally Efficacious

Internal change occurs as the individual evaluates and redefines how one has come to be within the sociocultural context. As Luz illustrates:

> In college, I realized that I didn't know of things about my culture that I felt I should have been taught in high school, and I was disappointed because having come from an all Mexicano community, I was real disappointed that my Mexicano teachers—there were not too many, but the ones that were there—were not—what is it?—they did not give us the information that I feel I should have had then. You know? The majority were Anglo teachers, so I understood that, but there were also ... there must have been, like, at every grade level—seventh grade, eighth grade, there were Mexicanos there, but I'm disappointed that they were not the Mexicanos to be promoting their culture and their language. You know? So I was real disappointed in that when I learned that in college. I wish I had gotten into it earlier.
>
> (Interview, August 8, 2008)

As a result of a dialogical process, Luz's cognitive understanding evolves and encompasses new knowledge and acceptance of another dimension of her cultural identity. Luz's experiences throughout the university years shaped her professional identity. These pre-career, daily lived experiences uniquely situated her to reflect on current events as well as on past events. She commented on one particular school:

> One of the other things is that I really felt empowered at Martinez, and I think that was the most important. And I was really learning. And my self-esteem was really good.
>
> (Interview, November 4, 2008)

Luz's acceptance of self helps define who she is as an ethnic being. As Natalicio and Hereford (1969) remind us:

> [T]rue self-acceptance often comes with great difficulty or not at all ... (It is) a process which involves self-awareness, self understanding, and self realization ... (it includes) those facets of the personality which cannot be understood but which, nevertheless, must be accepted and adjusted to an empirical or a trial and error basis.
>
> (p. 37)

Clark and Flores (2010) poignantly indicate that having a strong self-concept coupled with strong identity assists *aspirantes* to respond to the enigmatic question of Who am I? However, we must go beyond understanding self, as Flores and Clark (2004) observe that in the case of *normalistas* having a national identity did not ensure positive teaching efficacy beliefs about BLs. Hence, *aspirantes* should also critically consider responding to the prompt: What can I do? Clark and Flores contend that the response to the question is revealed in the teacher's efficacy beliefs. Teachers with positive cultural teaching efficacy believe that they can engage in culturally responsive pedagogies and can affect student achievement. Clark and Flores further indicate assisting *aspirantes* to develop a strong ethnic identity and positive culturally teaching efficacy provokes them to become cultural efficacious.

Paradigm Shift: Self-determination and Empowerment

As internal change or self-realization occurs, the candidate continues through the transformative process. Once acceptance of self and identity are firmly underway, the teacher becomes self-determined. As we see in Luz, through her increased astuteness of her ethnic and cultural identities, she feels empowered. For example, while Luz struggles to provide educational equity for BLs throughout her teaching career, her professional trajectory reflects sharing ideas, speaking up, and taking action.

During a 13-year span at this particular school, from 1983 to 1996, her circle of action moved from inside her classroom to her school community, district, state, and, ultimately, the nation. She sat on a state textbook committee and attended workshops about Montessori-based practices and additive bilingual education. Luz reflects:

> I think what kept me going is that—and it's not to say that I'm the only person that the children would get anything from—it's just that I've always believed innovation should be for children who can't afford to go to private schools. I feel that I can offer them that. I've always believed that it should be in the public schools.
>
> (Interview, November 8, 2008)

We note that these experiences further affirm Luz's resolve of her identity. Revitalization of identity occurs when she realizes that it can more easily be reproduced in others. The heuristic identity development of this exemplary Mexican American bilingual education teacher provides valuable lessons for all involved in the field, while her trajectory demonstrates the possibilities of becoming culturally efficacious. For Luz, her philosophy and practices had to make sense for teaching BLs. She actively worked toward transforming school and district bilingual education programs as additive models. Although exiting bilingual education students in the first or second grade was the accepted practice for the time, Luz pushed for late exit, wherein BLs would learn English and continue in Spanish through the remainder of the elementary years:

> But they were exiting children early, and so when we brought it up, these people were upset that we were coming in and saying, "Wait a minute, this is not what should be done. You don't take someone's culture and language and just say, 'Forget it after third grade.'" And so we were looking at maintaining their language and their culture.
>
> (Interview, November 4, 2008)

We see Luz's heightened sociopolitical consciousness as she continues developing toward cultural competency. Her actions demonstrate the internal change and paradigm shift emerging as Luz recognized that teachers must not only act as cultural brokers, but they must also believe that what they do in the classroom will have a positive impact on students' achievement. It is also evident that Luz's epistemological stance about learning characterizes knowledge as being dynamic, culturally determined, and socially constructed. As an empowered teacher, Luz advocates for students because she sees them as capable learners and she uses her voice to ensure equity for her BLs.

Summary

The shaping of personal and professional identity is linked to cultural, schooling, and teaching experiences. The social, political, historical, and cultural context of family, school, and community provide the context for these experiences (Clark & Flores, 2010; Guardia Jackson, 2009; Quiocho & Ríos, 2000). As this work demonstrates, ethnic minority teachers with a strong identity bring a certain cultural knowledge to their experiences as educators of BLs. Their cultural resources play a powerful part in the shaping of their identity. Prieto (2009) verifies that Latin@ candidates draw on their cultural resources and lived experiences as gendered, racialized, and classed individuals to inform their perspectives on becoming bilingual education teachers. Even from their early schooling experiences, the identity of an *aspirante* is constructed and re-constructed. Guardia Jackson (2009) found that the teacher is an agent helping to create and maintain a cultural system negotiating between the way they were raised and what they now see as most beneficial for students. How teachers see themselves as professionals is influenced by how they view themselves as individuals and as members of an ethnic/cultural group. The dialogic process, by whatever method, can serve several purposes in guiding classroom practices by: a) assisting in the continuous development of a philosophy of bilingual education; b) augmenting teachers' understanding of bilingualism and multiculturalism; c) lessening the sense of isolation that some novice bilingual education teachers experience; d) providing mentoring to assure the retention of bilingual education teachers in the classroom; and e) preparing candidates to serve BLs.

The work of Guardia Jackson (2009) and Prieto (2009) illustrate an examination of personal and professional life experiences by bilingual education teachers and candidates. Exploration of life experiences can be utilized to document and understand how implicit and explicit cultural values impact and guide actions in the classroom. This perspective considers that teachers are not just reproducing themselves and their culture. Rather, they appropriate, produce and improvise allowing for the possibility of identity transformation.

The culturally efficacious teacher uses students' cultural knowledge to construct school knowledge. In essence, providing candidates with a sense of ethnic identity enhances self-concept and actualizes cultural teaching efficacy leading to empowerment, enhanced understanding of others, and enriches communication and social relationships with students. Essentially, transformed teachers will have deeper senses of how they have been constructed, how others' identities have been constructed, and how they can support their students whose identity is also being constructed. They own the power to make a change in the lives and learning of their students. As a result of this metamorphosis, a stronger socially constructed teacher identity emerges which in turn impacts students. Through engaged pedagogy, educators and students

> develop their power to perceive critically the way they exist in the world with which and in which they find themselves; they come to see the world not as a static reality, but as a reality in process, in transformation.
>
> (Freire, 2000, p. 71)

It is by this process of reflection and action that assumptions and beliefs that have been co-constructed socially and historically can be examined; it is also by this process, Freire argues, that educators can make explicit the beliefs, values, and principles that guide their actions. It is in this manner that identities can be transformed and a teacher becomes culturally efficacious.

Transforming Teacher Preparation

Understanding ethnic identity is a critical aspect in teacher development; this process assists teachers in their identity formation, defining their teaching role, and their transformation toward becoming culturally efficacious. Therefore, preparation programs must consider:

- Providing candidates with the tools for identity exploration.
- Challenging *aspirantes'* thinking and beliefs through the self-exploration of "Who am I?" as a beginning point to nurture identity development.
- Expanding *aspirantes'* multiple identities to augment their perspectives about others.
- Exploring identities and perspectives through critical discourse as a conduit for reflection and change should be embedded in a teacher preparation course.
- Engaging teacher candidates in self-reflections through threaded discussions with peers along with professors' critical feedback.
- Using life histories to understand self, context, and decision-making.
- Providing specific coursework and experiences such as diversity pedagogy theory, powerful, meaningful field experiences, rich social cultural experiences, and presence of cultural activities.
- Focusing explicitly on the candidate personal identity development.

Research Directions

There is a need for empirical scholarship in the following areas:

- Exploring the relationship between ethnic identity and teacher identity.
- Investigating the relationship between identity and efficacy.
- Examining the effect of identity transformation on student achievement.
- Refining Clark's (1996) Metamorphosis Model.
- Analyzing the outcome of implementing the Metamorphosis Model on teacher candidate/*aspirante* identity formation.

References

Alba, R. (2005). Bright vs. blurred boundaries: Second-generation assimilation and exclusion in France, Germany, and the United States. *Ethnic and Racial Studies, 28*(1), 20–49.

Anzaldúa, G. (1987). *Borderlands/La frontera: The new mestiza.* San Francisco: Spinsters/ Aunt Lute.

Apple, M. (2004). *Ideology and curriculum.* (3rd ed.). New York: Routledge.

Bakhtin, M. M. (1981). *The dialogic imagination.* M. Holquist, Ed., C. Emerson & M. Holquist. Trans. Austin, TX: University of Texas Press.

Bartolomé, L. I., & Balderrama, M. V. (2001). The need for educators with political and ideological clarity: Providing our children with "The Best." In M. L. Reyes & J. J. Halcón (Eds.), *The best for our children: Critical perspectives on literacy for Latino students* (pp. 48–64). New York: Teachers College Press.

Brown, E. L. (2004). The relationship of self-concept to changes in cultural diversity awareness: Implications for urban teacher educators. *The Urban Review, 36*(2), 119–145.

Castillo-Speed, L. (Ed.). (1995). *Women's voices from the borderlands.* New York: Simon & Schuster.

Clark, E. R. (1996). *Metamorphosis.* Unpublished document.

Clark, E. R., & Flores, B. B. (2001). Who am I? The social construction of ethnic identity and self-perceptions of bilingual preservice teachers. *The Urban Review, 33*(2), 69–86.

Clark, E. R., & Flores, B. B. (2010). The metamorphosis of teacher identity: An intersection of ethnic consciousness, self-conceptualization, and belief systems. In P. Jenlink (Ed.), *Teacher identity and the struggle for recognition.* New York: Routledge.

Connelly, F. M., & Clandinin, D. J. (1999). Shaping a professional identity: Stories of educational practice. New York: Teachers College Press.

Erickson, E. (1950). *Childhood in society.* New York: W. W. Norton & Company, Inc.

Flores, B. B., & Clark, E. R. (2004). *Normalistas*: A critical examination of *normalistas'* self-conceptualization and teacher efficacy. *Hispanic Journal of Behavioral Sciences, 26*(2), 230–257.

Flores, B. B., & Clark, E. R. (2005). The centurion: Standards and high-stakes testing as gatekeepers for bilingual teacher candidates in the new century. In A. Valenzuela (Ed.), *Leaving children behind: How "Texas-style" accountability fails Latino youth* (pp. 225–248). Albany, NY: SUNY.

Flores, B. B., Clark, E. R., Claeys, L., & Villarreal, A. (2007, Fall). Academy for teacher excellence: Recruiting, preparing, and retaining Latino teachers through learning communities. *Teacher Education Quarterly, 34*(4), 53–69.

Franzak, J. K. (2002). Developing a teacher identity: The impact of critical friends' practice on the student teacher. *English Education, 34*(4), 258–280.

Freire, P. (2000). *Pedagogy of the oppressed* (M. B. Ramos, Trans. 30th Anniversary ed.). New York: Continuum.

Galindo, R. (1996). Reframing the past in the present: Chicana teacher role identity as a bridging identity. *Education and Urban Society, 29*(1), 85–102.

García, E. E. (1997). The education of Hispanics in early childhood: Of roots and wings. *Young Children, 52*(3), 5–14.

Guardia Jackson, L. (2009). *Becoming an activist Chicana teacher: A story of identity making of a Mexican American bilingual educator.* Unpublished dissertation, University of Texas at Austin.

Holland, D., & Lachicotte, W. (2005). Vygotsky, Mead, and the new sociocultural studies of identity. In H. Daniels, M. Cole, & J. Wertsch (Eds.), *Vygotsky* (pp. 101–135). Cambridge, MA: Cambridge University Press.

Holland, D., Lachicotte, W., Skinner, D., & Cain, C. (1998). *Identity and agency in cultural worlds.* Cambridge, MA: Harvard University Press.

Holquist, M. (1990). *Dialogism: Bakhtin and his world.* New York: Routledge.

Hondagneu-Sotelo, P. (1994). *Gender transitions: Mexican experiences of immigration.* Berkeley, CA: University of California Press.

Moraes, M. (1996). *Bilingual education: A dialogue with the Bakhtin circle.* New York: SUNY.

Natalicio, L. F., & Hereford, C. F. (Eds.). (1969). *The teacher as a person* (2nd ed.). Dubuque, IA: William C. Brown.

Norton, B. (2000). *Identity and language learning: Gender, ethnicity and educational change.* New York: Longman.

Ogbu, J. U., & Matute-Bianchi, M. E. (1986). Understanding sociocultural factors: Knowledge, identity, and school adjustment. *Beyond language: Social and cultural factors in schooling language minority students.* Los Angeles: Evaluation, Dissemination, and Assessment Center, California State University.

Peña, R. A. (1997). Cultural differences and the construction of meaning: Implications for the leadership and organizational context of schools. *Education Policy Analysis Archives, 5*(10). Retrieved from http://olam.ed.asu.edu/epaa/v5n10.html.

Pettman, J. (1996). Border crossings/shifting identities: Minorities, gender and the state international perspective. In M. Shapiro & H. Alker (Eds.), *Challenging boundaries* (pp. 261–283). Minneapolis, MN: University of Minnesota Press.

Prieto, L. (2009). *Conciencia con compromiso: Maestra perspectives on teaching in bilingual education classrooms.* Unpublished dissertation, University of Texas at Austin.

Quiocho, A., & Ríos, F. (2000). The power of their presence: Minority group teachers and schooling. *Review of Educational Research, 70*(4), 485–528.

Ríos, F., Trent, A., & Castañeda, L. V. (2003). Social perspective-taking: Advancing empathy and advocating justice. *Equity & Excellence, 36*(1), 5–15.

Romo, H. (1999). *Reaching out: Best practices for educating Mexican-origin children and youth.* ERIC. Charleston, WVA: Clearinghouse on Rural Education and Small Schools. (ERIC Document Reproduction Service No. ED 432432).

Urrieta, L., Jr. (2009). *Working from within: Chicana and Chicano activist educators in whitestream schools.* Tucson, AZ: The University of Arizona Press.

Valencia, R. (Ed.). (2002). *Chicano school failure and success: Past, present, and future* (2nd ed.). New York: Routledge.

Vavrus, M. (2002). Connecting teacher identity formation to culturally responsive teaching. Paper presented at The Annual Meeting of the National Association of Multicultural Education, Washington, DC/Arlington, VA, Oct 30–November 3, 2002.

Waters, R. (1999). Teachers as researchers: Making sense of teaching and learning. *Language Arts, 77*(1), 44–46.

Zembylas, M. (2003). Emotions and teacher identity: A poststructural perspective. *Teachers and Teaching, 9*(3), 213–239.

4 Bilingual Education Candidate Ideology

Descubriendo sus Motivos y Creencias

Belinda Bustos Flores, Lucila D. Ek,
and Patricia Sánchez

For nearly 20 years, scholars have reported the impact of ideology on teacher preparation (Armaline & Hoover, 1989). However, not all researchers use ideology to examine candidates' belief systems. Studies on teachers and candidates examine isolated concepts such as: attitudes (Cho & DeCastro-Ambrosetti, 2005/2006; García-Nevarez, Stafford & Arias, 2005), dispositions (Borko, Liston & Whitcomb, 2007; Villegas, 2007), beliefs (Flores, 2001; Karabenick, & Clemens-Noda, 2004), and values as individual phenomena rather than as intersecting and mutually influencing notions. We view ideology as socially and politically constructed, intersecting and mutually influencing attitudes, dispositions, beliefs, values, and worldviews.

Teacher ideology shapes behavior and classroom practices as well as student achievement expectations. Taylor and Wasicsko (2000) state, "there is a significant body of research indicating that teachers' attitudes, values, and beliefs about students, about teaching, and about themselves, strongly influence the impact they will have on student learning and development" (p. 2). Wilkerson (2006) argues: "dispositions are, in the long run, more important than knowledge and skills" (p. 2). Teachers have particular beliefs about "the role of teachers and schools, the nature of knowledge, the process of teaching and learning, and about students and families" (Villegas, 2007, p. 373)—all with potential to influence pedagogy and classroom climate. Examining *aspirantes'* epistemological beliefs about learning is vital in understanding their approaches to teaching (Flores, 2001). We agree that ideology is critical to teacher development, along with curricular knowledge and pedagogical skills because *aspirantes* are not "blank slates who simply need to learn the latest in teaching" (Bartolomé & Trueba, 2000, p. 281).

Theoretical Framework

In this mixed-methods study, we use a sociocultural lens to examine bilingual education teacher *aspirantes'* ideologies by investigating four intertwined constructs: (1) motives for pursuing bilingual teacher education; (2) efficacy beliefs, relating to self-confidence and self-perceived competence; (3) epistemological beliefs or implicit theories on the nature of knowledge; and (4) projected cultural teaching beliefs.

Teacher Candidates' Ideology

Because of the dearth of research on the ideologies of this population, we begin with research about teachers and candidates in general, followed by research conducted with Latin@ bilingual teachers and candidates. Villegas (2007) surmises, "Because teacher candidates' beliefs are powerful filters that not only make new phenomena understandable but also organize new ideas, teacher educators cannot ignore their students' entering and developing beliefs" (p. 373).

Reyes and Garza (2005) found that the two groups of Latin@ teachers from Mexico and the US—shared a common set of beliefs, even though they did not intend to measure teacher ideology. Border teachers: "placed significant import on affirming students' cultural identities, on bilingualism and multiculturalism, on providing opportunities for students' voice, on allowing some choice on learning activities, and on recognizing their social needs" (Reyes & Garza, 2005, p. 158). Sánchez and Ek (2008) found that Latin@ candidates' immigrant identities and backgrounds influence their political perspectives and pedagogical philosophies; a large majority also vehemently rejected deficit views of Mexican immigrants. However, even with their political and ideological clarity intact, these candidates were not fully informed on how certain laws protect the rights of immigrant children (Sánchez & Ek, 2008). Thus, ideologies also need to be accompanied by certain skill sets and useful information.

Motives for Teaching

Decisions to teach are developmental and change over time. They are based on various motives: (a) love for working with children, (b) passion for a specific content area, (c) desire to give back to the community, (d) commitment to make a difference in the lives of children, and/or (e) degree of job security and benefits (Sinclair et al., 2006; National Comprehensive Center for Teacher Quality and Public Agenda, 2007). According to Sinclair et al., teacher motives differ depending on age, gender, minority status, academic achievement, and prior career; and, may predict teacher commitment. Flores (2001) reported that cultural, literacy, and schooling experiences influenced motives for pursuing bilingual education teacher preparation. Sandoval-Lucero (2006) observed that bilingual paraprofessionals with a strong commitment to the community aspired to become bilingual teachers.

Candidate Efficacy

Efficacy is an individual's belief about ability and confidence towards a specific task (Bandura, 1993). Individuals with positive self-efficacy demonstrate competence, persistence, and perseverance (Pajares, 1997). When learners experience academic success, their competence affirms self-efficacy. In the case of teachers, teaching efficacy is observable when they create learning environments that promote knowledge acquisition (Bandura, 1993). Cultural values also mediate candidates' efficacy beliefs (Lin, Gorrell, & Taylor, 2002).

Teacher self-efficacy is comprised of two factors, general and personal (Ashton & Webb, 1986; Tschannen-Moran & Hoy, 2001). General teaching efficacy is the belief that internal or external factors influence competency. Personal teaching efficacy is the confidence that your teaching makes a difference in students' lives. Research also demonstrates the impact of teaching efficacy on creativity (Tschannen-Moran & Hoy, 2001) and urban student achievement (Goddard, Hoy, & Hoy, 2000; Swars, 2005).

Flores and Clark (2004) explored the teaching efficacy of Latin@ *normalista* candidates. They observed that these candidates reported confidence that their teaching would impact students' achievement; however, they believed that their efforts would be affected by external factors beyond their control. Subsequently, Flores, Desjean-Perrotta, and Steinmetz (2004) compared the teaching efficacy of bilingual, early childhood, reading, and special education candidates. Bilingual candidates' general teaching efficacy means were significantly higher, compared to their peers. Classroom observations confirmed these differences. They surmised that preparation, specifically addressing bilingual learners (BLs) contributed to *aspirantes'* beliefs about their teaching ability.

Candidate Epistemological Beliefs

Brownlee, Purdie and Boulton-Lewis (2001) defined candidates' epistemological beliefs as "views on what knowledge is, how it can be gained, its degree of certainty, and the limits and criteria for determining knowledge" (p. 286). Schommer-Aikins (2004) revealed that prior experiences mediate epistemological beliefs. *Aspirantes'* epistemological beliefs are often naïve because their beliefs about learning may reflect prior schooling experiences. Their naïveté is reflected in beliefs about the process of acquiring knowledge, students' role in the acquisition of knowledge, degree of concept complexity, absoluteness of knowledge, and perspectives toward inherent knowledge (Flores, 2001).

Examining bilingual teachers' epistemological beliefs, Flores (2001) used Schommer-Aikin's (2004) framework. Factor analysis resulted in four knowledge perspective dimensions: (a) certainty/absoluteness (dualistic vs. relative); (b) control (incremental vs. inherent); (c) structure (simplicity vs. complexity); and (d) interaction (interplay vs. disconnect). Flores (2001) considered the interaction of the knowledge acquisition belief dimension as the interactive processes of culture, language, and thought.

In sum, *aspirantes* must not only be prepared to provide effective instruction in two languages; they must be perspicacious of the sociopolitical contexts of BLs and the political nature of becoming a bilingual teacher. This includes comprehending the shifting contexts of immigration, family and community resources; the dynamism of culture; and, legislative changes adversely affecting bilingual programs (see Chapter 15). For these reasons, *aspirantes* should understand how their ideologies are influenced and constructed.

Methodology

The study explores motives for teaching and exploring their efficacy, epistemology, and projected cultural efficacy teaching beliefs. We also examine *aspirantes'* backgrounds and context to better understand their ideologies.

Context

South Texas

Our study was located in a city with 1.3 million residents with predominantly Latin@ population (61%) and 13% foreign-born (US Census 2006–2008). Not surprisingly, 44% of the population speaks Spanish (US Census 2006–2008). "Living in a transnational city ... 'blurs the boundaries' (Alba, 2005) between recent immigrants who have many connections with Mexico and second- and third-generation Mexican Americans who may have never been to Mexico" (Romo, 2008, p. 78).

University

The university is a Hispanic-serving institution. *Aspirantes* pursuing bilingual education certification obtain a degree in Interdisciplinary Studies, taking courses from Interdisciplinary Learning and Teaching and Bicultural Bilingual Studies departments. Twenty-seven of 30 hours are taught in Spanish. Prior to student teaching, *aspirantes* enroll as a cohort in four blocked field-based courses two days per week; the other three days in groups of two to ten, they complete 85 hours of field experience at local elementary schools. The Academy for Teacher Excellence's (ATE) Teacher Academy Learning Community (TALC) provides *aspirantes* academic, personal, and professional support commencing in the freshman year and continuing through the first three novice years (Flores, Clark, Claeys, & Villarreal, 2007).

Participants

The study includes 82 Latin@ *aspirantes*. For the purpose of the quantitative analysis, data for Latin@s (n = 25) were extracted from a larger sample. The participants are overwhelmingly female (n =79), seeking certification in PK-fourth grade. While they are all bilingual (Spanish/English), they exhibit varying levels of oral and written bilingualism. Participants come from different backgrounds: long-term *Tejanas*, border town second-generation Mexican Americans, *Fronterizas* who grew up on both sides of the Texas-Mexico border, Mexican nationals, South American immigrants, *Puertorriqueñas,* and self-identified *Chicanas*. Ages include: 49 between the ages of 21 and 28; 22 between 29 and 38; 11 are 42 or older with three over 52. Forty-two candidates are second-generation immigrants, having either one or two foreign-born parents. Twenty-nine are foreign born, with the majority from Mexico, while 11 are third-generation and beyond. The largest group was raised in San Antonio (25). The second category had 20 participants; 14 were raised either in the Texas Río Grande Valley, a well-known zone along the US–Mexico border with a unique history and bilingual community, or in a different Texas city; the remaining six grew up in another state or a combination of places. The third group had 17 participants who grew up in Mexico.

Design

We employed a sequential mixed-methods study (Creswell, 2009). The study occurred in two phases with the first phase examining the *Academic Self-Identity: Self-Observation Yearly* (*ASI SOY*) data for Latin@ *aspirantes* (*n* = 25). During the second phase, we analyzed in-class assignments of 82 *aspirantes* across three semesters. These assignments delved into the candidates' immigrant-ethnic backgrounds, upbringing, and the ways in which they became bilingual.

Quantitative Data Collection

During phase one, we gathered archival *ASI SOY* data completed during their freshman year for 25 *aspirantes*. *ASI SOY* is a multidimensional, validated instrument measuring the individual's educational experiences, motives for teaching, ethnic identity, acculturation issues, efficacy, and epistemology (Flores et al., 2010). The *ASI SOY* test-retest reliability is strong (r^2 = .995, p < .001, n = 217) and Cronbach reliability is high (α = .82, n = 654) [Flores et al.]. With the current sample, a similar high Cronbach reliability was determined (α = .96, n = 25).

Qualitative Data Collection Process

During phase two, over three academic semesters, we collected various data, including *aspirantes'* language history maps written and illustrated in Spanish, adapted from Olsen and Jaramillo (1999); essays written in Spanish on language and literacy learning trajectories *(trayectorias);* short ethnographies of local community funds of knowledge (González, Moll, & Amanti, 2005); field notes and/or audio- or video-recordings of in-class discussions; and short surveys on immigration beliefs. The language history maps were represented as posters, books, or power points; these presentations were video-recorded, transcribed, and coded. Our analysis focuses primarily on the language history maps and literacy *trayectorias*.

Mixed-Methods Analysis

We examined the *ASI SOY* items loading on the following ideological factors: Motivation for Teaching Profession; Personal Efficacy; Personal Epistemology; and Cultural Teaching Beliefs (Flores et al., 2010). Descriptive statistics provided us a general profile of *aspirantes'* ideologies. Upon completion of the quantitative analysis, we examined the qualitative data for insights into *aspirantes'* ideologies. Using deductive analysis, we coded candidates' language history maps and literacy *trayectorias* for the following themes: (1) motives for pursuing bilingual teacher education; (2) personal efficacy [problem solver, views of self as learner, confidence in self, perseverance]; (3) personal epistemology [views on how knowledge is constructed, how kids learn, how knowledge is acquired]; and (4) projected cultural responsive teaching beliefs. Using constant-comparison and peer review, our final analysis represents a triangulation of quantitative and qualitative results. Names are pseudonyms and ethnic labels are self-identified. *Aspirantes'* writing and speech in Spanish are in original format and may have errors.

Results

Motives for Pursuing Bilingual Teacher Education

A preliminarily examination on the *ASI SOY* (1=Not at all like me and 7=More like me) reveal three major motives for pursuing teaching: (a) giving back to the community; (b) positive teacher role models and a desire to make a difference; and (c) familial support of *aspirantes'* career choice. A few *aspirantes* (*n* = 8) also selected "other" as their motive for pursuing teaching (see Table 4.1). These self-reported responses indicate *aspirantes'* decisions were based on (a) enjoyment/ love for children; (b) bilingual education teaching profession as a calling; and (c) opportunity to impact children, parents, and society.

While enjoyment/love for children is a prototypical response for pursuing teaching, motives for pursuing bilingual teacher education as a calling clearly support wanting to give back to the community. Also, *aspirantes'* desire to make a difference is validated with their motive to impact children, parents, and society.

Giving Back to the Community

Qualitative data shows participants' desire to give back to the community. *Aspirantes* see their role as helping children improve, retain, and sustain their native Spanish language skills as well as encouraging linguistic and cultural pride. Josefa (age 23, Mexican American, San Antonio native) points to maintaining her own bilingualism and cultural legacy:

> *Mi aprendizaje y desarrollo de dos lenguas ahora me [h]a llevado a seguir mi sueño de ser maestra bilingüe y ayudar a estudiantes mantener su cultura al mantener su lengua natal y a aprender otra lengua que los llevará a tener muchísimas más oportunidades en la vida* [Learning two languages allowed me to realize the dream of becoming a bilingual teacher; to help students maintain their culture and native language; learning another language will give them life opportunities].

Gisela's (age 33, Hispanic, grew up in Mexico) motive recognizes the societal advantages of bilingualism:

Table 4.1 Motives for Pursuing Bilingual Teacher Education

	M	*SD*
1. Family members have been teachers.	2.36	2.25
2. I want to give back to my community.	6.60	0.76
3. A teacher's work schedule will meet my family needs.	4.76	1.85
4. I had a good teacher; therefore I want to make a difference in students' lives.	6.16	1.49
5. My family values my decision to become a teacher.	6.20	1.47
6. Other (Write in response): Why I am considering the teaching profession.		

ser bilingüe tiene sus ventajas. Habrá puertas nuevas y brinda muchas oportunidades para avanzar en esta sociedad. Es por eso que yo pienso que la educación bilingüe es importante para los niños de nuestro futuro [Being bilingual has advantages. It opens doors, offers opportunities to advance. That's why I believe bilingual education is important for our future children].

Positive Teacher Role Model

The majority report good teacher role models in their schooling experiences. Sulema (age 27, Latina, raised in Houston) remembers:

Las maestras fueron para mi un gran apoyo y precisamente por eso decidí estudiar para ser maestra bilingüe [My teachers were very supportive, that's why, I decided to become a bilingual teacher].

Isabela (age 26, Mexican American, San Antonio native) describes her teacher's influence:

Una maestra me tomó debajo de su ala y me inspiró, motivó, y apoyó seguir adelante en mis estudios para realizar mis sueños de hacer maestra bilingüe. Me aseguró que yo mostraba eso, algo especial que se requiere para hacer maestra bilingüe [A teacher took me under her wing; she inspired, motivated, and supported me in my dream of becoming a bilingual teacher. She assured me that I had what it took, that something special required of bilingual teachers].

This quote points to an affective attribute needed to work with children learning two languages, while also navigating different cultural systems and possibly adapting to a new country.

Familial Support of Career Choice

Familial support emerged as important for choosing teaching as a profession. Alicia (age 23, third-generation Mexican American, reared in Central Texas) exemplifies this familial cultural value:

Yo sabía que yo quería ser maestra, y hablé con mis tías que también son maestras y con mi maestra de kinder, y me animaban y me decían que si podía hablar [bien el español] con los niños, que no me desanimara [I knew I wanted to be a teacher. I spoke with my aunts who are teachers and with my kindergarten teacher. They motivated me and would tell me that I could speak (good Spanish) that I should not give up].

While the pursuit for becoming a bilingual teacher may be idiosyncratic, the most common motive was a strong desire to give back to their community. Bilingual teacher role models, supportive family members, and strong personal beliefs buffered motives.

Table 4.2 Personal Efficacy

		M	SD
7.	I believe that words can have more than one meaning.	6.08	1.53
12.	When my friends have problems, they come to me.	6.20	1.0
13.	I am good at resolving conflicts.	6.32	0.90
16.	I manage my problems well.	6.04	1.14
17.	I like challenges.	5.80	1.22
20.	If I try hard, I can learn.	6.32	1.38
30.	I enjoy the language, values, customs, and traditions of the United States.	6.56	0.87

Personal Efficacy

The items measuring personal efficacy display a high degree of agreement among these *aspirantes*, suggesting that they believe they are competent and undaunted by challenges (see Table 4.2). These factors were also evident in the qualitative findings.

Confidence

BLs often become language brokers for their parents (Orellana et al., 2003), which requires the child to competently enter adult conversations in areas such as, financial employment settings, doctor–patient exchanges, and teacher–parent conferences. This role reversal accentuates BLs' confidence and pride, which likely carries on through life. That confidence and pride allowed a candidate to speak up when chastised by her teacher for speaking Spanish: [My teacher told me:] "You are in America, umm speak English." *Y yo le dije:* "You are in El Paso, you can speak both" (Verónica—age 33, Mexican, raised in a border town). Responding to the teacher's English-only ideologies, Verónica defends her bilingualism highlighting the importance of speaking Spanish in El Paso, a border city with a majority Latin@ population.

Perseverance

Aspirantes' literacy *trayectorias* suggest that their perseverance stems from experiences of maintaining and nurturing their native language. Depending on home or schooling experiences, some candidates describe limited opportunities to develop biliteracy. To illustrate, Carmen (age 46, Mexican American, raised in Chicago), while competent in Spanish, felt that English acquisition was an ordeal. Her experiences with a teacher intolerant of her native language are common (González, 1997; Valdés, 2001). Her perseverance and negative experiences is revealed:

> *Para mí aprender a hablar inglés era dificultoso de niña porque se prohibía hablar español cuando yo estaba en la escuela … Mi maestro … no sabía como comunicarse conmigo y ella no toleraba que yo hablara español* [Learning

English as a child was difficult because speaking Spanish was forbidden in school. ... My ... teacher did not know how to communicate with me and she did not tolerate my speaking Spanish].

Traumatic experiences can leave linguistic scars and shameful memories as Gisela recalls:

Mentiría si dijera que me fue fácil aprender el inglés. Batallé mucho para aprender este segundo idioma ... Creo que aprender el inglés es una de las memorias más penosas que tengo de mi educación. Mayormente, culpo al sistema escolar por no haberme brindado la oportunidad de aprender el inglés paso a paso y correctamente [I would be lying if I said it was easy to learn English. I struggled to learn this second language ... I think learning English is one of the most shameful memories of my education. I blame the school for not giving me opportunity to learn English correctly, step by step].

Gisela's *trayectoria* illuminates the isolation that some BLs feel as they struggle to learn English. Now an adult, she holds the school accountable for denying her a quality education—a stance motivating her to persevere despite her early learning traumas.

Some found reclaiming their native Spanish language and acquiring a professional level of Spanish a challenge. Marta (age 31, Latina, raised in Michigan) explains using English, rather than risk making errors in Spanish:

Cuándo yo llegué primero a Tejas, llegué a un pueblo pequeño cerca de la frontera. Era muy diferente ... y todos hablaban español. Entendí el idioma pero yo no lo podría hablar claramente, supe mejor no hacer una conversación en español porque sabía que saldría mal, era seguro de conversar en inglés [When I came to Texas, I arrived in a small bordertown. It was different. Everyone spoke Spanish. I understood but I could not speak it well. I knew it was better not to speak Spanish because it would come out wrong, it was safe to speak English].

Multiple socio-political factors shape and influence heritage language maintenance and loss (Zentella, 2005) including lack of support for bilingual education, hostility toward immigrants, and a monolingual ideology. Many Latin@s are monolingual by the third generation, or before (Zentella, 1997). Thus, second-, third-, fourth-generation candidates fight an uphill battle to retain or learn Spanish. Yet, as future teachers, they must learn academic Spanish (see Chapter 5). Despite challenges, they persevere. Elena (age 44, Hispanic, San Antonio native) indicates:

Con mucho esfuerzo estoy aprendiendo de nuevo el español que las maestras en mis primeros años de escuela me prohibieron. También aprendo a darle su lugar a mi cultura que tanto intentaba esconder ... [With much effort I am learning Spanish that my teachers forbade during my early school years. I am learning to accept my culture that I tried so hard to hide ...].

Table 4.3 Personal Epistemology

		M	SD
8.	When I study, I look for specific facts.	6.08	1.08
9.	I like movies that don't have an ending.	2.20	1.19
10.	I believe that you learn best from experts.	4.29	1.88
11.	For me, a course in study skills would probably be valuable.	5.08	1.58
15.	I don't have a favorite subject.	2.56	1.85
18.	I learn better from my friends than from my teachers.	3.36	1.25
19.	When learning something new, I become anxious.	4.56	1.58
21.	Even when I study hard, learning is difficult for me.	2.56	1.87
22.	I believe successful students learn things quickly.	3.12	1.39
40.	As a future teacher, my role is to make sure that students understand that there is always one right answer.	2.88	2.05

Thus, the educational experiences of these candidates—which include many years of struggle, hardships, and discrimination—strengthen their resolve.

Personal Epistemology

Aspirantes' epistemological notions, how knowledge is acquired and constructed, may indicate how they will approach learning tasks. While candidates recognize the importance of effort and time in the process of learning, they also believe that new learning can lead to anxiety (see Table 4.3). The *ASI SOY* findings also show that *aspirantes* tend to believe that learning is acquired from experts with certainty in focusing on facts when studying. Yet, they do not agree that there is always a singular correct response. We surmise that *aspirantes* have mixed notions of how they acquire knowledge. Considering their belief that knowledge is acquired from experts, this epistemology may actually reflect cultural practices, whereby elders are highly respected and regarded as experts. Upon examining the qualitative data, we further untangle these knowledge sources.

Role of Knowledgeable Others

Sociocultural views of learning and development posit that learning occurs through interactions with more knowledgeable others (Vygotsky, 1978). *Aspirantes'* epistemological beliefs reveal that their learning was mediated through others. *Aspirantes* credit their parents for their language and literacy learning. Karina (age 36, Hispanic, San Antonio native) shares how her parents taught her language: *"Mi madre nos enseñaba el español y mi papa nos hablaba ingles"* [My mother taught us Spanish, my father spoke to us in English]. Gisela expresses how her father supported her oral language and literacy development:

> *Mi papá nos ponía … a escribir palabras de diferentes niveles … Nos ponía a leer frases que encontraba en el periódico o en libros de español y luego nos pedía que*

practicáramos escribiéndolas en nuestros cuadernos [My father had us write words ... He had us read phrases from Spanish newspapers or books; he asked us practice writing in our notebooks].

Candidates highlight their mother's key role in their learning and development. Bertha (age 26, Mexican American, raised in San Diego, California) describes:

Mientras crecía me di cuenta que mi madre fue y siempre [h]a sido una persona muy importante en mi desarollo y durante mi aprendizaje formando la práctica del español e inglés [Growing up, I realized that my mother was and always has been a very important person in my learning and development, she shaped my Spanish and English].

Aspirantes recalled that their mothers included playful elements through literacy and math games. Indeed, Latin@ parents value play in supporting children's development (Riojas-Cortez & Flores, 2004). For example, Juanita (age 22, Mexican American, from the Texas Río Grande Valley) writes:

Cuando éramos chicos mi mamá se sentaba en el piso con mis hermanos y yo a jugar juegos con tarjetas. Las tarjetas tenían retratos de letras, animales, frutas, verduras y otros objetos comunes. Aprendimos el alfabeto y nuestros números [When we were little, my mom played card games with my brothers and me. The cards had pictures of letters, animals, fruit, vegetables, and other common objects. We learned the alphabet and numbers].

Memories from *aspirantes* demonstrate parental creativity and dedication to their children's education—contrary to deficit views that malign Latin@ parents as not caring about their children's learning (Zentella, 2005). Grandparents and relatives also contributed to the *aspirantes'* education through face-to-face and long distance interactions, such as writing.

In addition to family, *aspirantes* also recognize the importance of schools and teachers in the US and Mexico. Karina writes: "*Y puedo ver como mi mamá, la sociedad, y la escuela fueron el instrumento que implanto estas herramientas en mi vida*" [I see how my mom, society, and school were instrumental in arming me with tools for life]. For Karina, her mother's role intertwines with school and society. Others credit formal schooling. Dorotea (age 22, Hispanic, raised in the Texas Río Grande Valley) asserts: "*Como estuve desde chica en escuelas en México pude desenvolver en aprender escribir, hablar, y leer en español correctamente.*" [Because I went to school in Mexico from a young age, I learned to write, speak, and read correctly in Spanish].

Juanita highlights the role of affect in learning and explains how her teacher motivated her to love Spanish and improve biliteracy:

[Y]o no pude desarrollar un apreciación o mi amor para el idioma española hasta que conocí a la señora Marcos, mi maestra de español. ... No solamente me animo a ser bilingüe, sino que tener destrezas de alfabetización en dos idiomas ... [I did not develop appreciation or love for Spanish until I met

Mrs. Marcos, my high school Spanish teacher. She motivated me to become bilingual and develop literacy skills in both languages].

Language, Culture, and Learning Connections

Analysis of *aspirantes'* language history maps demonstrates interconnectedness among language, culture, and learning. This was evident in the use of *dichos* (proverbs), culturally coded axioms taught at an early age, expressing important life lessons. In translating the *dichos* to English, we found no English equivalent; this reinforces the role of language as a cultural tool. Several proclaim learning through *dichos*:

Alicia: *Mi abuelita decía dichos como, "Ya te quedaste sin Juan y sin las gallinas, o el sordo no oye pero compone* [My grandma would say, …].

Julia, age 23, Hispanic, raised in Mexico: *Mi mamá siempre decía, "El que mucho abarca, poco aprieta. Dime con quién andas, y te diré quién eres."* [My mom would say, …].

Like other studies on Latin@s' home pedagogies (Delgado Bernal et al., 2006; Espinoza-Herold, 2007; Riojas-Cortez & Flores, 2009), *aspirantes* express the important life lessons family members provide in the form of cultural axioms. Higher forms of thinking are required to reflect on why a certain behavior needs to be corrected.

Learning in One Language Facilitates Second Language Learning.

Research on second language acquisition argues that language and literacy skills transfer from a first language to the second (Pérez, 2004). As bilinguals, *aspirantes'* experiences illustrate language transfer. Lucía (age 22, Hispanic, who grew up along the US–Mexico border) reveals:

Cuando entré a la universidad y empecé a tomar cursos de teorías de lenguaje y bilingüismo, fui entendiendo, que mis habilidades del inglés se pasan al segundo idioma. Como ya sabía leer y escribir en inglés, y como era buena en eso, fue fácil para mí escribir y leer en español [When I entered the university and began to take classes on language theories, I understood that my English skills transferred to the second language. Since I read and write in English, it was easy to write and read in Spanish].

Others wrote how Spanish helped develop English. Nidia (age 30, Hispanic, from Mexico) explains how cognates and her teacher's simultaneous translation increased her vocabulary:

La maestra Aguilar era bilingüe y nos explicaba todo en español y en inglés. Yo recuerdo que eso me ayudó mucho a desarrollar mi vocabulario en inglés porque algunas palabras suenan casi igual que en español [Ms. Aguilar was bilingual. She explained everything in Spanish and in English. I remember that helped develop my vocabulary in English because some words sound almost the same in Spanish].

Cultural Responsive Teaching Beliefs

The cultural responsive teaching beliefs items imply that *aspirantes* have strong notions regarding the role of the native language and culture in the classroom (see Table 4.4). Their responses reveal positive beliefs in their projected competence and effectiveness. Clearly prevalent is the value given to the belief that children learn over time and are naturally smart. These *aspirantes* value that their students learn facts, which is aligned with their personal epistemological belief about learning.

Developing Linguistic and Cultural Pride

Evident in the *trayectorias* is the value placed on linguistic and cultural pride. Eugenia (age 22, *Puertorriqueña*, raised in the Texas Río Grande Valley) describes her role in the third person:

> *Ella está muy orgullosa de hablar dos idiomas, y le gustaría ayudar a sus futuros estudiantes aprender inglés y español ... Eugenia cree que las maestras deberían enseñarle a sus estudiantes a no avergonzarse de su cultura y su lengua pero al contrario sentirse orgulloso de sus raíces* [She is proud to speak two languages and would like to help her students learn English and Spanish ... Eugenia thinks teachers should teach students to not be ashamed of their culture or home language, and instead, feel pride about their roots].

Similar to Eugenia, Sulema envisions:

> *Mi deseo personal es mostrarles a los niños que se puede hablar inglés sin tener que desechar el español. Quiero que mis estudiantes sepan valorar su lengua natal ... Si el estudiante rechaza su propio idioma jamás sabrá su verdadera*

Table 4.4 Cultural Responsive Teaching Beliefs

	As a future teacher, ...	M	SD
32.	my role is to make sure students learn specific facts.	5.63	1.81
33.	my role is to recognize that children are naturally smart.	5.50	1.53
34.	I will be able to teach all students.	6.42	1.02
35.	my role is to make sure students learn how to look for solutions.	6.67	.70
36.	it is important for me to speak the language of my students.	6.83	.48
37.	I believe students' negative home experiences can be overcome by good teaching.	5.46	1.96
38.	my role is to assure that my students have ethnic pride.	6.42	.97
39.	it is important for me to know the cultural background of my students.	7.00	.00
41.	I believe that children develop their intelligence over time.	6.04	1.43

identidad [My desire is to show children that you can speak English without discarding Spanish. I want my students to appreciate their first language. If students reject their language, they will never know their true identity].

These statements illustrate willingness to teach two languages and desire to promote pride in native language and culture. A few *aspirantes'* project other future beliefs, such as wanting to be like their former teachers who taught them, which is linked to their initial motives for pursuing teaching.

Enthusiasm for Language and Literacy Learning

We found that *aspirantes* want to instill enthusiasm for language and literacy learning. Beatriz (age 24, Mexicana, raised in Mexico) conveys this passion:

> *Yo seguí mi pasión por escribir antes de leer. Como una futura maestra yo quisiera implementar activdades para que los niños aprendan a amar estas habilidades* [I followed my passion for writing before reading. As a teacher I want to plan activities so children can learn to love these abilities].

Carmen's desire to motivate her students stems from her negative, fear-filled educational experiences:

> *¡Qué bonito es poder aprender sin temor! Un día yo también voy a ser maestra y mis experiencias de los años pasados se emplearán en algo positivo ... Esa palabra de miedo la reemplaceré con un sentimiento más noble que es el querer. Me refiero a el querer de ser una buena y efectiva maestra. Mi mayor deseo es que mis futuros estudiantes compartan el entusiasmo de aprender un nuevo idioma* [How wonderful to learn without fear! One day I will be a teacher and my past experiences will be used for something positive ... I will replace fear with a more noble feeling, want. I'm referring to wanting to be a good and effective teacher. My main wish is that my students share my enthusiasm to learn a new language].

Discussion and Conclusion

Aspirantes' ideologies, such as attitudes, dispositions, beliefs, and values, often intersect and mutually influence the ways they process preparation. Our study reveals that membership in culturally and linguistically marginalized communities—both prior to and during preparation—tilts teaching ideologies toward a social justice perspective. *Aspirantes* recognize their role as linguistic and cultural role models and embrace this calling with a deep desire to make a difference in students' lives. They expect to give back to their communities by transforming schooling for BLs. In their preparation program, transformation was experienced firsthand: cultural and linguistic pride, passion for learning in two languages, knowledge and skill in their first language, and participation in a learning community with shared values and beliefs.

An examination of the learning experiences and beliefs of these *aspirantes* as second language learners shows familiarity with pejorative schooling conditions. We uncovered prior family, community, and academic experiences that will likely mediate their views as learners and as future teachers—many of which are helpful for successfully teaching. Negative experiences involving language learning may provide insights of the experiences their future students face. Lived experiences, coupled with theoretical understandings from their preparation, potentially provides candidates with deeper conceptualizations of the role of language as a cultural tool for learning and as a critical societal resource. *Aspirantes* have the capacity to apply their cultural knowledge to the learning-teaching process in communities, which in many cases are similar to their own.

Transforming Teacher Preparation

The zeal with which *aspirantes* enter the university to pursue their goals of becoming teachers may not necessarily be supported, nurtured, or encouraged in traditional bilingual teacher preparation programs (see Chapter 1 and 2); programs should have a conceptual framework as outlined by *Educar* (see Chapter 2). *Aspirantes* may be forced to conform to disempowering traditional experiences, rather than participating in programs that value and apply culturally lived prior knowledge enriched by family and ethnic communities. The vision, curriculum, and field experiences of preparation programs may inadvertently emphasize conformity to a dominant ideology (see Chapter 6). Privileging such official curriculum structured through hegemonic discourses may not adequately prepare candidates. Powerful and meaningful programs allow them to *brotar*—to break through myopic preparation canons.

Results from this study disclose issues that must be considered when designing, implementing, and evaluating programs. First, programs must challenge *aspirantes'* belief systems acquired through their socialization process and influenced by hegemonic dominant cultural discourse. Teacher educators need to explicitly provide *aspirantes* a safe space for revealing past learning experiences, particularly those grounded in home and cultural practices. Because motives, beliefs, and efficacy inform an individual's ideology, they must be unearthed, examined, and reflected upon throughout their program. Exploration of identity and ideology can be addressed in courses examining bilingual language development; cultural diversity, authentic multicultural children's literature; examination of families, communities, and schools; and Spanish for heritage language speakers. These experiences can be mediated through written, visual, and field assignments centered on topics such as language learning and loss, cultural and familial histories, culture and cognition, community resources, and socio-political forces. Second, programs must recognize the centrality of language in teaching and learning. Language is a tool for constructing and mediating knowledge. Programs must encourage *aspirantes* to use their languages and culture(s) as pedagogical tools when selecting instructional strategies and curricular content. Courses must be delivered in Spanish (see Chapter 5). If *aspirantes'* language and culture have been lost or devalued as a result of their prior schooling and societal conditions, we suggest that they explore local Latin@ communities and unearth relevant linguistic and authentic cultural experiences. We must also assist them in recognizing how to apply these linguistic and cultural experiences to the learning-teaching process and help them understand their role in the construction of knowledge (see Chapter 2 and 7). In doing so, *aspirantes* become aware how their past experiences may be mirrored in schools as well as contemporary Latin@ communities.

Bilingual teacher educators must model, scaffold, and motivate *aspirantes* through a program design that constantly monitors, examines, and evaluates candidate ideologies. We argue that one way to achieve this goal is by legitimizing *aspirantes'* cultural and linguistic experiences within curricular content. We recommend that programs include assignments, experiences, and projects to achieve these objectives. Such projects help *aspirantes* become aware of how their ideologies influence how they view children, learning, and teaching.

Research Directions

Given the lack of scholarship in the field of bilingual education teacher preparation, researchers must heed the call and conduct more investigations with a variety of methodologies. Future research should use case, micro-ethnographic, quantitative, and mixed methods for:

- Exploring the connection between *aspirantes'* motives for pursuing bilingual education and their future teaching beliefs.
- Studying *aspirantes'* histories as a tool for tapping into culturally responsive teaching strategies.
- Capturing bilingual teachers' ideological development across time, including during their preparation program and into their first five-years of teaching.
- Documenting the use of culturally responsive teaching strategies to accentuate students' linguistic and cultural pride, competence, and perseverance.
- Examining the relationship among bilingual education teacher ideology, approaches to teaching, and student academic outcome.
- Investigating effective bilingual education teacher programs that develop teachers who can impact students' linguistic, cultural, and cognitive development.
- Researching the use of effective bilingual education teacher preparation strategies for preparing culturally efficacious teachers.

References

Alba, R. (2005). Bright vs. blurred boundaries: Second-generation assimilation and exclusion in France, Germany, and the United States. *Ethnic and Racial Studies, 28*(1), 20–49.

Armaline, W. D., & Hoover, R. L. (1989). Field experience as a vehicle for transformation: Ideology, education, and reflective practice. *Journal of Teacher Education, 40*(2), 42–48.

Ashton, P. T., & Webb, R. B. (1986). *Making a difference: Teacher's sense of self-efficacy and student achievement.* New York: Longman.

Bandura, A. (1993). Perceived self-efficacy, cognitive development and functioning. *Educational Psychologist, 28*(2), 117–148.

Bartolomé, L. I., & Trueba, E. T. (2000). Beyond the politics of schools and the rhetoric of fashionable pedagogies: The significance of teacher ideology. In E. T. Trueba & L. I. Bartolomé (Eds.), *Immigrant voices: In search of educational equity* (pp. 277–292). Lanham, MD: Rowman & Littlefield.

Borko, H., Liston, D., & Whitcomb, J. A. (2007). Apples and fishes: The debate over dispositions in teacher education. *Journal of Teacher Education, 58*(5), 359–364.

Brownlee, J., Purdie, N., & Boulton-Lewis, G. (2001). Changing epistemological beliefs in pre-service teacher education students. *Teaching in Higher Education, 6*(2), 247–268.

Cho, G., & De Castro-Ambrosetti, D. (2005/2006). Is ignorance bliss? Pre-service teachers' attitudes toward multicultural education. *The High School Journal, 89*(2), 24–29.

Creswell, J. W. (2009). *Research design: Qualitative, quantitative and mixed methods* (3rd ed.). Los Angeles: Sage.

Delgado Bernal, D., Elenes, C. A., Godinez, F., & Villenas, S. (Eds.). (2006). *Chicana/Latina education in everyday life: Feminista perspectives on pedagogy and epistemology.* Albany, NY: SUNY.

Espinoza-Herold, M. (2007). Stepping beyond *Sí se puede: Dichos* as a cultural resource in mother–daughter interaction in a Latino family. *Anthropology & Education Quarterly, 38*(3), 260–277.

Flores, B. B. (2001). Bilingual education teachers' beliefs and their relation to self-reported practices. *Bilingual Research Journal, 25*(3), 275–299.

Flores, B. B., & Clark, E. R. (2004). *Normalistas*: A critical examination of *Normalistas* self-conceptualization and teacher efficacy. *Hispanic Journal of Behavioral Sciences, 26*(2), 230–257.

Flores, B. B., Desjean-Perrotta, B., & Steinmetz, L. E. (2004). Teacher efficacy: A comparative study of university and alternatively certified teachers. *ACTION in Teacher Education: Journal for the Association of Teacher Educators, 26*(2), 27–46.

Flores, B. B., Clark, E. R., Claeys, L., & Villarreal, A. (2007). Academy for Teacher Excellence: Recruiting, preparing, and retaining Latino teachers through Learning Communities. *Teacher Education Quarterly, 34*(4), 53–69.

Flores, B. B., Clark, E. R., Guerra, N., Casebeer, C. M., Sánchez, S. V., & Mayall, H. (2010). Measuring the psychosocial characteristics of teacher candidates through the Academic Self-Identity: Self-Observation Yearly (ASI SOY) Inventory. *Hispanic Journal of Behavioral Sciences, 32*(1), 136–163. Retrieved from http://dx.doi.org/10.1177/0739986309353029

García-Nevarez, A. G., Stafford, M. E., & Arias, B. (2005). Arizona elementary teachers' attitudes toward English language learners and the use of Spanish in classroom instruction. *Bilingual Research Journal, 29*(2), 295–316.

Goddard, R. D., Hoy, W. K., & Hoy, A. W. (2000). Collective teacher efficacy: Its meaning, measure, and impact on student achievement. *American Educational Research Journal, 37*(2), 479–507.

González, G. (1997). Culture, language, and the Americanization of Mexican children. In A. Darder, R. Torres, & H. Gutiérrez (Eds.), *Latinos and education: A critical reader* (pp. 158–173). New York: Routledge.

González, N. E., Moll, L., & Amanti, C. (Eds.). (2005). *Funds of knowledge: Theorizing practices in households, communities and classrooms.* Mahwah, NJ: Erlbaum.

Karabenick, S. A., & Clemens-Noda, P. A. (2004). Professional development implications of teachers' beliefs and attitudes toward English language learners. *Bilingual Research Journal, 28*(1), 55–75.

Lin, H. L., Gorrell, J., & Taylor, J. (2002). Influence of culture and education on U.S. and Taiwan preservice teachers' efficacy beliefs. *The Journal of Educational Research, 96*(1), 37–46.

National Comprehensive Center for Teacher Quality and Public Agenda. (2007). *Lessons learned: New teachers talk about their jobs, challenges, and long range plans.* Retrieved from http://www.tqsource.org/publications/LessonsLearned1.pdf

Olsen, L., & Jaramillo, A. (1999). *Turning the tides of exclusion: A guide for educators and advocates for immigrant students.* Oakland, CA: California Tomorrow.

Orellana, M. F., Reynolds, J., Dorner L., & Meza, M. (2003). In other words: Translating or "para-phrasing" as a family literacy practice in immigrant households. *The Reading Research Quarterly, 38*(1), 12–34.

Pajares, F. (1997). Current directions in self-efficacy research. In M. Maehr & P. R. Pintrich (Eds.), *Advances in motivation and achievement* (Vol. 10, pp. 1–49). Greenwich, CT: JAI Press. Retrieved from http://www.des.emory.edu/mfp/effchapter.html

Pérez, B. (2004). *Becoming biliterate: A study of two-way immersion education.* Mahwah, NJ: Erlbaum.

Reyes, M. L., & Garza, E. (2005). Teachers on the border: In their own words. *Journal of Latinos and Education, 4*(3), 153–170.

Riojas-Cortez, M., & Flores, B. B. (2004). *Los padres y los maestros*: Perspectives of play among bilingual stakeholders in public schools. *Advances in Early Education and Day Care, 13,* 267–288.

Riojas-Cortez, M., & Flores, B. B. (2009). Supporting preschoolers' social development in school through funds of knowledge. *The Journal of Early Childhood Research, 7*(2), 185–199.

Romo, H. (2008). The extended border: A case study of San Antonio as a transnational city. In R. Márquez & H. Romo (Eds.), *Transformations of la familia on the US-Mexico border* (pp. 77–104). Notre Dame, IN: Notre Dame Press.

Sánchez, P., & Ek, L. (2008). *Escuchando a las maestras/os:* Immigration politics and Latina/o pre-service educators. *Bilingual Research Journal, 31*(1), 1–24.

Sandoval-Lucero, E. (2006). Recruiting paraeducators in bilingual teaching roles: The importance of support, supervision, and self efficacy. *Bilingual Research Journal, 30*(1), 195–218.

Schommer-Aikins, M. (2004). Explaining the epistemological beliefs system: Introducing the embedded systemic model and coordinated research approach. *Educational Psychologists, 39*(1), 19–29.

Sinclair, C., Dowson, M., & McInerney, D. M. (2006). Motivations to teach: Psychometric perspectives across the first semester of teacher education. *Teachers College Record, 108*(6), 1132–1154.

Swars, S. L. (2005). Examining perceptions of mathematics teaching effectiveness among elementary preservice teachers with differing levels of mathematics teacher efficacy. *Journal of Instructional Psychology, 32*(2), 139–147.

Taylor, R. L., & Wasicsko, M. M. (2000, November 4). *The dispositions to teach.* Paper presented at SRATE, Lexington, Kentucky. Retrieved from http://www.educatordispositions.org/dispositions/The%20Dispositons%20to%20Teach.pdf

Tschannen-Moran, M., & Hoy, A. W. (2001). Teacher efficacy: Capturing an elusive construct. *Teaching and Teacher Education, 17,* 783–805.

US Census Bureau. (2006–2008). American Community Survey: 2006–2008 Three-Year Estimates. Metropolitan statistical area: San Antonio, Texas.

Valdés, G. (2001). *Learning and not learning English: Latino students in American schools.* New York: Teachers College Press.

Villegas, A. M. (2007). Dispositions in teacher education: A look at social justice. *Journal of Teacher Education, 58*(5), 370–380.

Vygotsky, L. (1978). *Mind in society.* Cambridge, MA: Harvard University Press.

Wilkerson, J. (2006, April 20). Measuring teacher dispositions: Morality or standards based. *Teachers' College Record.* Retrieved from http://www.tcrecord.org/.

Zentella, A. C. (1997). *Growing up bilingual: Puerto Rican children in New York.* Malden, MA: Blackwell.

Zentella, A. C. (2005). *Building on strength: Language and literacy in Latino families and communities.* New York: Teachers College Press.

5   Fostering Candidate Spanish Language Development

Michael D. Guerrero
and Concepción M. Valadez

Research on learning confirms the use and development of native language as essential for conceptual, social, and academic growth. Studies substantiate how sustained use and development of children's native language benefits them academically (Gaarder, 1965; Merino, Politzer, & Ramírez, 1979; Thomas & Collier, 2002; Ulibarrí, Spencer, & Rivas, 1981; United Nations Educational Scientific & Cultural Organization, 1953, 2008). Hernández-Chavez (1988) maintains that:

> On a cultural level, language is the symbolic expression of community, encoding a group's values, its folkways and its history. Socially, it is the most powerful means of interaction and communication, and it is through language that an individual or a group seeks and attains participation in society. The denial of a people's development and use of its native tongue is thus a denial of its participation in society and of its very peoplehood.
>
> (p. 45)

Unfortunately, in social practice, sustained native language instruction for bilingual learners (BLs) has proven to be a formidable challenge. While many certified bilingual education teachers are perfectly fluent in all modalities of the Spanish language, a fair number express a sense of tentativeness about being able to deliver instruction across the curriculum in Spanish, and some lack specific skills to do so (Fabelo, 2008; Guerrero, 2003; Sutterby, Ayala, & Murillo, 2005; Valdés, 1989; Waggoner & O'Malley, 1984). This situation exists in spite of long-standing language proficiency standards intended to guide teachers' ability to teach across the curriculum in the child's native language (Center for Applied Linguistics, 1974; National Association for Bilingual Education, 1992; Texas State Board for Educator Certification, 2004). The discrepancy between the official guidelines and the actual performance in practice, points out the distance between the technical concerns and the social status of the issues being addressed (Fishman, 1996; Valadez & Díaz, 2008).

We find this state of affairs particularly frustrating. After more than four decades of preparing bilingual education candidates, we have struggled to prepare them with knowledge and skill to actively engage in the co-construction of knowledge mediated by the child's native language, and in this case, Spanish. We have been lethargic addressing the very Achilles' heel of our profession—recognition that the US as a linguistic society does not value bilingualism and uses language ideologies, policies, deficit thinking, and myths to control social capital (Flores, 2005; Fry & Lowell, 2003; Hernández-Chávez, 1977; McGroarty, 2008; Peñalosa, 1980; Phillipson, 1988; Tollefson & Tsui, 2004). Are we doing bilingual education on someone else's terms? Have we, as Grinberg and Saavedra (2000) failed to transform bilingual education and maintained our own misrecognized existence? Grinberg and Saavedra (p. 420) assert:

> We locate bilingual/ESL education as a settlement within US educational institutions' larger historical agenda of (a) "Americanizing" (Spring 1994, 1997), (b) reproducing a social and cultural system that ultimately perpetuates the interests of the powerful and privileged (Bourdieu & Passerson, 1977) and (c) "docilizing" and disciplining the body and the mind (Foucault, 1979). The legitimization of bilingual/ESL education as an academic field has had disabling consequences because it has controlled resistance against the historical role of deculturalization with US schools (Spring, 1994). Therefore, we contend that it is necessary to keep asking, as urged by Freire (1970a, 1970b, 1985, 1989, & 1994), "In favor of whom are we educating?"

The purpose of this chapter is to come to a better understanding of why we do what we do as we prepare bilingual education candidates to deliver instruction in Spanish across the curriculum. We maintain that while the language related social, political, and economic forces are mighty, we can and must find ways to improve our Spanish language-related teacher preparation practices. If we are to change anything, we have to recognize what needs changing. Moreover, we need a tool and a language for naming what we come to recognize. We need a coherent theory. We have chosen Gee's (2008) theory on ideology in discourses for approaching this goal.

Theoretical Framework

In this section, we briefly synthesize related work from the last decade centered on the acquisition of academic language, and academic English and Spanish in particular. We begin with Guerrero (2003) who maintained that bilingual education teachers acquire academic Spanish by participating in and becoming a member of a community of people, mostly professionals, who use and perpetuate academic Spanish. This is followed by a brief description of Scarcella's (2003) conceptual model of academic English. Valdés (2004), in effect, links the ideas of appropriating an identity to academic language, and academic language to social class and power and to the work of Gee (2008). Gee's theory of discourses is quite complex and requires and merits treatment well beyond the scope of this chapter. The section concludes with calls for a renewed and explicit language role of professors in bilingual education.

We know little about the reasons that might explain why many candidates struggle to acquire academic Spanish (Guerrero, 2003). After reviewing three models (Durgunoglu & Verhoeven, 1998; Hornberger & Skilton-Sylvester, 1998; Merino, Trueba, & Samaniego, 1993) aimed at understanding the process by which people become bilingual/biliterate, the authors settle on the participation metaphor introduced by Pavlenko and Lantolf (2000), borrowed from Sfard (1998). These models, however, offer insight into the process by highlighting the interplay of community, school, and individual variables, political and economic factors, and linguistic processes and power relations.

Sfard (1998) brings a different perspective by focusing attention on how it is that people become members of particular academic communities, in this instance the bilingual education community. Sfard explains that acquiring the ability to communicate in the languages of the community and acting according to its particular norms is paramount for membership. She clarifies how the norms of the community are negotiated over time and in the process of consolidating the community. Candidates would be viewed as newcomers and potential reformers of the practice, while their professors would constitute preservers of its continuity. Candidates and professors would constitute a community with defined language norms where new members are socialized into an academic community. Of course, we may not have much say or control over our language norms as Durgunoglu and Verhoeven (1998) and Hornberger and Skilton-Sylvester (1998) suggest, and we may not even be conscious of them.

Scarcella (2003) synthesized existing knowledge about academic language leading to a useful conceptualization of what academic language entails and how one becomes proficient in its academic register. Scarcella posits that linguistic, cognitive, and socio-cultural/psychological dimensions constitute academic language. Both the linguistic and cognitive dimensions of this model are linked to its socio-cultural/psychological dimension. More elaborate than Sfard (1998), this component entails one's norms, values, beliefs, attitudes, and practices associated with academic language. Building on the work of Gee (1996, 1998, & 2002) and akin to Sfard, Scarcella takes the position that students internalize these attributes through a process of socialization and apprenticeship in the context of schooling. Though Scarcella amply references Gee, she does not delve into an explanation of where the norms, values, attitudes, and practices associated with an academic language of a given academic community originate; nor does she allude to matters of power or language ideologies.

Before addressing these two voids, consider Valdés' (2004) position. Referencing Gee (1990), she suggests that acquiring particular ways of speaking are rooted more in what she calls legitimate participation in dominant practices. It entails communication spheres where those who master the Discourse use academic language naturally, and are then perpetuated in social practices that embody it through apprenticeship. She ties this to candidates' academic Spanish, surmising that being educated primarily in English, have not allowed them to master or be socialized into the academic or supposedly higher variety levels of Spanish. Valdés makes clear that matters of Discourse are tied to issues of power and ideologies, and that minimal scholarship examines the situation of Spanish/English candidates.

Gee (2008) explains that ideologies, such as the English Only movement, emanate from the elite whose interest is to retain and enhance their societal power. Drawing on Marx, Gee (p. 28) reasons that the elite create ideology, a composite of their knowledge, beliefs, and behavior, and are able to enact it by "getting others with less power and status to accept their 'inverted'[view of reality in two ways." One way is by getting intellectuals, such as university professors, to promote their views. The other is by organizing institutions to promote ways of thinking and behaving that serve the interests of those in power. An example is instituting pejorative language policies in schools and exclusively using English as the medium of instruction. These views and ways of thinking and behaving are perpetuated through Discourses. Gee (2008) sums up the essence of Discourse:

> A Discourse is a socially accepted association among ways of using language and other symbolic expressions, of thinking, feeling, believing, valuing, and acting, as well as using various tools, technologies, or props that can be used to identify oneself as a member of a socially meaningful group or "social network," to signal (that one is playing) a socially meaningful "role" or to signal that one is filling a social niche in a distinctively recognizable fashion.
>
> (p. 161)

Gee explains that we have a primary Discourse, which essentially encapsulates our cultural identity as a member of a particular family and community. This includes the vernacular language(s) and literacies acquired through socialization and apprenticeship in the family unit. As individuals venture outside the realm of their immediate environment, they inevitably come into contact with other institutions, such as school and work, which make up society. Gee refers to these as secondary Discourses. They include language and literacy practices and their attendant, attached value. The acquisition of certain secondary Discourses, which he terms as dominant Discourses of White middle-class English, lead to power, status, and money. Discourses can and generally do change over a lifetime, some radically more than others, which might explain shifts to English and heritage language loss.

These theoretical lens and societal, contextual language realities can help us begin to understand why candidates, even certified teachers, express and display linguistic inadequacy in Spanish and literacy practices associated with the secondary Discourse we identify as bilingual education. In many cases, opportunities to acquire the Spanish and literacy practices associated with this secondary Discourse are short-lived, of questionable quality, and devalued in schools. Historically, US mainstream education, including bilingual education, has promoted English acquisition (August & Hakuta, 1997; Bernal-Enríquez, 2000). In spite of the PK-12 linguistic ideological push towards English Only, some candidates manage to hold on to oral Spanish language practices and a few literacy practices, acquired through their primary Discourse; and this is essentially what they bring when entering the academic community of practitioners of the secondary Discourse, bilingual education.

Guerrero and Guerrero (2009) declare that university professors must responsibly, consciously, and actively rectify this situation. We first outline language-related practices that undermine the acquisition, learning, and value of Spanish language and literacy practices, followed by recommendations to eradicate these debilitating beliefs, attitudes, and practices. We aim to promote acquisition of desired language and literacy practices, coupled with associated meta-knowledge and strategies for candidates to make do while "waiting for the revolution" (Gee, 2008, p. 108).

Issues, Controversies, and Problems

We perceive that a pressing issue facing the bilingual education community, that is directly responsible for the candidate preparation, resides with tenured or tenure track professors. We realize that Spanish language development begins very early and during the onset of schooling, and sooner in the home, through apprenticeship into Spanish/English language practices; however, our focus is on professors' languages and literacy habits, practices, norms, and beliefs, since virtually no attention has been paid to their role in the socialization of candidates to the language and literacy practices embedded within the secondary Discourse of bilingual education.

Bilingual Education Professor Language Proficiency

Only a handful of references exist that raise the issue of the Spanish language proficiency of bilingual education professors who are responsible for apprenticing candidates into the valued language and literacy practices defining the academic community. Gaarder (1977, p. 88) makes the following recommendation: "Members of the teaching staff must also be highly literate in the non-English language and fully capable of using it as the exclusive medium of instruction in their classes." Similarly, Calderón and Díaz (1993, p. 66) maintain: "Professors in a teacher preparation program must possess or gain the skills to teach bilingual teachers in Spanish." Collectively, these recommendations suggest that professors may not be able to conduct their duties in and through the medium of Spanish.

Guerrero (1999) points out that job descriptions commonly list ability to teach courses in Spanish as a desired but not necessary qualification. A recent job announcement in the *Chronicle of Education* (2010) included the following qualification for an associate/full professor, "Academic competence in Spanish is highly desired." It would prove insightful to understand why this competence is not required. Additionally, college professors of bilingual education do not have to pass the same Spanish language proficiency test mandated for the candidates they are preparing. While we are not proponents of high-stakes language testing, we wonder why the academy adopts this contradictory practice. The bigger issue is the ways distinct roles of language apprentice and mentorship get blurry, perhaps even reversed, given the possibility that candidates may be more proficient in academic Spanish than professors. This incongruity would not likely occur in US higher education English-mediated instruction.

Construction of New Knowledge in Academic Spanish

Candidates seem to experience what might be called *educatio interrupta* in their apprenticeship into a Spanish-based secondary Discourse associated with formal schooling. It is an established reality that most PK-12 bilingual language programs in the US are transitional and subtractive in nature (August & Hakuta, 1997;

Thomas & Collier, 2002). The problem is more than not having access to linguistic aspects of academic Spanish over a PK-20 span of time; the central issue is the message conveyed that devalues the use of academic Spanish as a valid medium for instruction and construction of new knowledge. By new knowledge, we mean knowledge that might potentially impact or transform the quality of life. Clearly, there is no reason why new knowledge should only be constructed in academic English. Ada (1976) insightfully informs the bilingual education academic community that our native language must be used at the highest academic strata to ensure its prestige and continued existence within our society. Bear in mind that Spanish is among the top five languages in the world, and the US is home to the fifth largest population of Spanish speakers in the world (Lipski, 2008, see Chapter 1).

Teaching Content Area Courses in Academic Spanish

Decades ago, Gaarder (1977) made explicit that candidates and even doctoral students in this field, should have an opportunity to acquire knowledge through the Spanish language medium. Calderón and Díaz (1993) indicate that few candidates report receiving any of their coursework in Spanish. One might infer that it may be partially due to the professors' lack of Spanish language proficiency. However, it could be due to the unavailability of resources, such as textbooks and articles, in academic Spanish. This results in reading about bilingual pedagogy in English, perhaps with some oral Spanish instruction, and then followed by discussion and writing experiences in both Spanish and English. Institutional norms might also discourage or programmatically mitigate the delivery of course content in Spanish. This is common practice when bilingual education candidates are mixed with general education and monolingual ESL certificate candidates, even when only one candidate needs language accommodation. What is peculiar about this occurrence is the ease with which it is justified and how easily we concede even though the English-speaking candidates have an entire PK-20 educational infrastructure, including massive libraries, designed to their monolingual worldview.

Role of Foreign Language Departments

Spanish language course work offered in foreign or modern language departments is often required in most programs. Generally, candidates take some kind of advanced grammar or composition course, or a specific course for this particular population, such as Spanish for the bilingual classroom. Perhaps we engage in this practice because professors of Spanish are perceived as the experts in: the language, teaching language, meeting the differentiated linguistic needs of our candidate, and addressing the limitations in our profession.

This practice seems to suggest that we as bilingual education professors lack Spanish language expertise to meet candidates' Spanish language needs. Further, as candidates successfully complete these language requirements, we presume that their language needs have been met. But just how much do we really know about what happens in foreign language departments with candidates pursuing a bilingual certification, most of whom are female from various Spanish language origin groups which have historically been academically under-served and linguistically marginalized in PK-12 schooling.

Following Gee's (1990) notion of dominant Discourse, Valdés, González, López García, and Márquez (2003) explore the language ideologies embedded in the Discourse of foreign language departments and their teaching of academic Spanish. In the sites studied by this team, several findings emerged that are worthy of contemplation since they relate directly to speakers of Spanish in the US who speak varieties of Spanish similar to bilingual education candidates. The findings showed that: (a) foreign language departments were more focused on teaching Spanish literature than teaching language. When the focus was on the latter, the emphasis was one of standardness/purism and the eradication of vulgar colloquialisms; (b) there were two primary kinds of Spanish language professors, native speakers from Spain and Latin America and Euro-Americans who learned Spanish as a foreign language; and (c) evidence of departmental hierarchy of language varieties, revealed that the Spanish spoken by US ethnic minorities was the least valued due in part to this group's politically subordinated position. As might logically follow, these researchers report that Spanish language faculty believed speakers of US varieties of Spanish had insurmountable academic Spanish language challenges, and negative faculty attitudes toward this group was prevalent.

Field-Based Courses and Student Teaching

Candidates are required to fulfill a certain number of hours in bilingual classrooms during their preparation. The purpose varies from observing, to assisting with, and delivering instruction. The potential merits of experiencing the role of teacher as an apprentice cannot be overstated. The challenge for faculty and administrators engaged in preparation is finding adequate mentors and spaces for the apprentices so candidates can experience how Spanish language is used to advance bilingual, social, cognitive, and academic development of BLs (García, Kleifgen, & Falchi, 2008).

Locating mentors and spaces pose a serious challenge for the preparation programs. More critically, these field-based experiences may expose candidates to subtractive language norms, values, beliefs, attitudes, and practices of teachers who may undermine the additive language orientation professors are trying to instill in candidates, albeit in English. Thus, the native language theory professors propagate conflicts with the language practices enacted by teachers and observed by candidates. This can lead to the most bizarre linguistic rationalizations among bilingual faculty, including positions such as— it is good for candidates to see bad teaching; teaching strategies can compensate for a lack of facility in the school register; or teachers' Spanish language proficiency does not matter since few language programs are additive.

Testing Academic Spanish Language Proficiency

The entire discussion rests on the assumption that candidates' ability to teach in academic Spanish is critical to BLs' schooling achievement, which is at the core of our ideology. The looming question is—How proficient is proficient enough and what do we do to promote and monitor said proficiency? In most instances, candidates are deemed proficient if they pass a Spanish language proficiency test once in their career. Seidner (1981), however, observed that there was a lack of consensus regarding the nature of language fluency, though candidates were expected to be fluent in the target language. Grant (1997) revealed the wide variation in tests in terms of how candidates' oral Spanish language and literacy skills are measured across the 17 states that use them. Guerrero (2000) argues that little is known about these tests' validity and the social consequences associated with their use (Messick, 1989). Empirically, we know little about how language proficient teachers should be; yet, we rely on language tests of questionable validity to make this judgment.

Summary

There is little doubt that we have painted a dismal picture of the secondary Discourse that concerns Spanish language and literacy practices embedded within preparation programs. Of course, not all issues exist at every preparation site to the same degree, and challenges other than language can be identified. However, we are doing bilingual education on someone else's terms by not practicing and perpetuating the development of high levels of Spanish language in our candidates. As scholars and intellectuals, we must not unwittingly perpetuate the English Only language ideologies of the elite. Of interest is that Hernández-Chávez (1977) made such indictments so long ago.

Solutions and Recommendations

We can weaken the hegemonic grip of English within our preparation programs and begin to redefine this dimension of our professional Discourse. Our position is that everything revolves around the construction of new knowledge published in Spanish. This requires a major shift in our language practices. If we as scholars do not value the use of Spanish in academic publications, we fail to demonstrate this value through our own actions. Thus, we should not be surprised if our candidates follow suit.

We must reach a point in our scholarly activity where we automatically elect to create new knowledge in Spanish as often as we do in English. This is feasible because some individuals already have the language skills. This activity should create the opportunity for professors to develop their literacy skills in Spanish. The production of joint publications could take the form of apprenticeships, with the more skilled writer, perhaps a graduate or doctoral candidate, modeling and scaffolding written discourse in academic Spanish for the less capable.

New knowledge published in Spanish provides sorely needed tools and reading materials for candidates. These resources have potential to gradually elevate the prestige of Spanish language in the US, as well as the Spanish-speaking world. We cannot continue to prepare candidates without a foundational text written in Spanish. Clearly, we have the capacity to produce these materials. With the availability of written texts and media in Spanish, preparation programs can be infused with listening, reading, and writing activities in Spanish. This would help create the daily social context for the professor and candidates to use the Spanish language for a genuine social purpose, the acquisition of knowledge.

Of course, having tools to teach courses in Spanish is of little consequence, if professors cannot conduct all aspects of instruction in Spanish. Preparation programs need to take stock of their Spanish language capital and ensure that those who can teach in Spanish are given the opportunity to do so. Faculty who feel tentative about their ability to fulfill this obligation, and who desire to teach in the program, should develop a professional development plan that will allow them to acquire language proficiency. New hires should be required to demonstrate their ability to teach in the target heritage language.

The long-standing practice of relying on other members of the academic community to address the language needs of candidates is worthy of re-examination. Professors of Spanish must demonstrate commitment to social justice and to working collaboratively with colleges of education to alleviate the historical pattern of underachievement among BLs. Clearly, the discussion with our well-intentioned colleagues must be predicated on the nature of the speech of the candidates who arrive at their door, seeking to be teachers. The variations of the Spanish they bring should be the base for building the language skills they will need for their task of adding the school register to their own repertoire and, in turn to their students (Valadez & Díaz, 2008). The acquisition of the formal features of the Spanish language will, nonetheless, more readily be acquired over time and in and through the active use of the language within the preparation curriculum as a whole. Again, this points back to the need for professors to be able to provide such feedback and the tools for mediating learning.

We maintain that assessment and measurement of the kinds of language and literacy practices and skills candidates possess are central to BLs' achievement. We would encourage faculty to take and pass the same language proficiency tests as their candidates. A clearer sense of the linguistic benchmark mandated by the state, local education agency, higher education institution, department or program will likely lead to reflection, discussion, and hopefully, needed action. Faculty must then ask themselves if the kinds of opportunities candidates have in their programs are sufficient to meet mandated benchmarks. Perhaps more importantly, faculty must understand what needed language and literacy practices and skills might be lacking from the mandated language assessment and plan to address these voids.

More complex is addressing and mitigating the subtractive language and literacy practices candidates might experience during field placements and student teaching. At the very least, candidates should have the opportunity, early on, to appropriate meta-knowledge about the linguistic tension between theory and practice by identifying, examining, naming, and interrogating these linguistic contradictions. This must become a recurring theme throughout their preparation. As a starting point, we suggest that candidates develop, analyze, and reflect upon their own bilingual development. Of course, coming to a deeper understanding of the power of English language ideologies, and how they have come to roost in our own bilingual education Discourse, must begin with bilingual education professors.

Implications for the Improvement of Practice

We recognize that transforming what we have become accustomed to doing in a depreciatory sociopolitical context where bilingual education is devalued is no simple undertaking, especially if we are unable or unwilling to recognize and address this challenge. Program faculty must collectively evaluate the Spanish language issues raised in this chapter within their respective programs, milieus, and academic communities. Hopefully, such an evaluation will generate comfortable conversations about the value and multiple uses of Spanish within preparation programs. It might be difficult to acknowledge our own Spanish language shortcomings in a Discourse, which may have been managed and legitimized. An *Educar* program (see Chapter 2) is characterized by the omnipresent values and uses of both languages. Professors, candidates, and BLs are at the very core of shifting Discourse from Spanish as a bridge to English to bilingualism and biliteracy as the foundation of legitimate and meaningful schooling for all children.

Drawing from Gee (2008), we believe that professors, acting locally, regionally, nationally, and globally, have the professional and moral obligation to initiate a transformation, to actively resist the encroachment of English on our preparation practices, by consciously and methodically laying out a plan of action to address the concerns raised in this chapter and in this text. Society is slowly realizing the impoverishing limitations of monolingualism (Meisel, 2007). Let the first step in this act of resistance be the publication of an article, a book chapter, a book, a monograph, a textbook, or media document in the Spanish language from each of us, individually or collectively, who share responsibility of preparing bilingual education candidates. No other stakeholder in the bilingual education community really has this responsibility or is better positioned to fulfill it. In the final analysis, we concur wholeheartedly with Flores (2005, p. 93) who states:

> We must resist and continue to right the wrongs; we must prevail and plant the seeds for generations to come; we must unite in our efforts to construct and maintain a just society; we must act or we will perish by our own lack of courage, by our own collusion, or by our own will to remain as part of the status quo.

Future Research Directions

Based on the issues outlined in this chapter, we would encourage faculty, graduate students, and doctoral candidates to consider the following research topics. The overarching goal of this research agenda must be the improvement of instruction for BLs. We recommend qualitative and or quantitative inquiry into:

- Language ideologies of university teaching faculty and instructors involved in the candidate preparation.
- Candidates' perceptions of intersection of popular registers of the Spanish language and the registers of formal school Spanish.
- Studies of career-long development of additional language(s) of professors and instructors involved in candidate preparation.

- Challenges and language strategies used by faculty in developing candidate language skill for academic subject matter instruction in Spanish.
- Relationship of foreign language departments with candidate preparation.
- Relationships among field-based courses and student teaching in terms of instruction in Spanish.
- Validity of state mandated language tests and their relationship to the language used for effective teaching, and
- Spanish language experiences of candidates in relation to test performance and BL achievement.

References

Ada, A. (1976). Editor's introduction. *Journal of the National Association for Bilingual Education, 1*, 1.

August, D., & Hakuta, K. (1997). *Improving schooling for language minority children: A research agenda.* Washington, DC: National Academy Press.

Bernal-Enríquez, Y. (2000). *Factores socio-históricos en la pérdida del español del suroeste de los Estados Unidos y sus implicaciones para la revitalización.* In A. Roca (Ed.), *Research on Spanish in the US* (pp. 121–136). Somerville, MA: Cascadilla Press.

Bourdieu, P., & Passerson, J. (1977). *Reproduction in education, society, and culture.* London: Sage.

Calderón, M., & Díaz, E. (1993). Retooling teacher preparation programs to embrace Latino realities in schools. In R. Castro & Y. Ingle (Eds.), *Reshaping teacher education in the Southwest: A response to the needs of Latino students and teachers* (pp. 51–70). Claremont, CA: Tomas Rivera Center.

Center for Applied Linguistics. (1974). *Guidelines for the preparation and certification of teachers of bilingual/bicultural education.* Arlington, VA.

Chronicle of Higher Education. (2010). Retrieved from http://chronicle.com/jobs/0000625697-01

Durgunoglu, A., & Verhoeven, L. (1998). Multilingualism and literacy development across different cultures. In A. Durgunoglu & L. Verhoeven (Eds.), *Literacy development in a multilingual context: Cross cultural perspectives* (pp. 289–298). Mahwah, NJ: Erlbaum.

Fabelo, D. (2008). *Academic Spanish during mathematics instruction: The case of novice bilingual education teachers in elementary classrooms.* Doctoral dissertation. University of Texas, Austin.

Fishman, J. A. (1996). *In praise of beloved language: A comparative view of positive ethnolinguistic consciousness.* New York: Mouton de Gruyter.

Flores, B. (2005). The intellectual presence of the deficit view of Spanish-speaking children in the educational literature during the 20th century. In P. Pedraza & M., Rivera (Eds.), *Latino education: An agenda for community action research* (pp. 75–98). Mahwah, NJ: Erlbaum.

Foucault, M. (1979). *Discipline and punish: The birth of the prison.* New York: Vintage.

Freire, P. (1970a). Cultural action for freedom. *Harvard Educational Review, 40*(2), 205–225.

Freire, P. (1970b). *Pedagogy of the oppressed.* New York: Continuum.

Freire, P. (1985). *The politics of education: Culture, power, and liberation.* New York: Bergin & Garvey.

Freire, P. (1989). *Learning to question: A pedagogy of liberation.* New York: Continuum.

Freire, P. (1994). *Pedagogy of hope: Reliving pedagogy of the oppressed.* New York: Continuum.

Fry, R., & Lowell, B. (2003). The value of bilingualism in the US labor market. *Industrial and Labor Relations Review, 57*(1), 128–140.

Gaarder, A. (1965).Teaching the bilingual child: Research, development and policy. *Modern Language Journal, 49*(3), 165–175.

Gaarder, A. (1977). *Bilingual schooling and the survival of Spanish in the United States.* Rowley, MA: Newbury.

García, O., Kleifgen, J., & Falchi, L. (2008). *From English language learners to emergent bilinguals.* NewYork: Teachers College, Columbia University.

Gee, J. (1990). *Social linguistics and literacies: Ideologies in discourses.* London: Falmer Press.

Gee, J. (1996). *Social linguistics and literacies: Ideologies in discourses* (2nd ed.). London: Taylor & Francis.

Gee, J. (1998). *What is literacy? Negotiating academic literacies: Teaching and learning across languages and cultures.* Mahwah, NJ: Erlbaum.

Gee, J. (2002). Literacies, identities, and discourses. In M. Schleppegrell & M. C. Colombi (Eds.), *Developing advanced literacy in first and second languages* (pp. 159–176). Mahwah, NJ: Erlbaum.

Gee, J. (2008). *Social linguistics and literacies: Ideology in discourses* (3rd ed.). New York: Routledge.

Grant, L. (1997). Testing the language proficiency of bilingual teachers: Arizona's Spanish proficiency test. *Language Testing, 14*(1), 23–46.

Grinberg, J., & Saavedra, E. (2000). The constitution of bilingual/ESL education as a disciplinary practice: Genealogical explorations. *Review of Educational Research, 70*(4), 419–441.

Guerrero, M. (1999). *Spanish language proficiency of bilingual education teachers.* Center for Bilingual Education and Research Explorations in Bi-national Education. Arizona State University, Project Alianza.

Guerrero, M. (2000). The unified validity of the four skills exam. *Language Testing, 17*(4), 397–421.

Guerrero, M. (2003). Acquiring and participation in the use of academic Spanish: Four novice Latina bilingual education teachers' stories. *Journal of Latinos and Education, 2*(3), 159–181.

Guerrero, M., & Guerrero, M. (2009). El (sub)desarrollo del español académico entre los maestros bilingües: ¿Cuestión de poder? *Journal of Latinos and Education, 8*(1), 55–66.

Hernández-Chávez, E. (1977). Meaningful bilingual bicultural education: A fairytale. *Journal of the National Association for Bilingual Education, 1*(3), 49–54.

Hernández-Chávez, E. (1988). Language policy and language rights in the United States: Issues in bilingualism. In J. Cummins & T. Skutnabb-Kangas (Eds.), *Minority education: From shame to struggle.* London: Multilingual Matters.

Hornberger, N., & Skilton-Sylvester, E. (1998). *Revisiting the continua of biliteracy: International and critical perspectives.* Paper presented at the Annual Meeting of the American Educational Research Association. (ERIC Document Reproduction Service No. ED 421–863), San Diego, CA.

Lipski, J. (2008). *Varieties of Spanish in the US.* Washington, DC: Georgetown University Press.

McGroarty, M. (2008). The political matrix of linguistic ideologies. In B. Spolsky & F. Hult (Eds.), *The handbook of educational linguistics* (pp. 98–112). Malden, MA: Blackwell.

Meisel, J. (2007). The bilingual child. In T. Bhatia & W. Ritchie (Eds.), *Handbook of bilingualism.* Malden, MA: Blackwell.

Merino, B., Politzer, R., & Ramírez, A. (1979). The relationship of teachers' Spanish proficiency to pupils' achievement. *NABE Journal, 3*(2), 21–37.

Merino, B., Trueba, E., & Samaniego, F. (1993). Towards a framework for the study of the maintenance of the home language in language minority students. In B. Merino, E.

Trueba, & F. Samaniego (Eds.), *Language and culture in learning: Teaching Spanish to native speakers of Spanish* (pp. 5–25). Washington, DC: Falmer.

Messick, S. (1989). Meaning and values in test validation: The science and ethics of assessment. *Educational Researcher, 18*(2), 5–11.

National Association for Bilingual Education. (1992). *Professional standards for the preparation of bilingual/multicultural teachers.* Washington, DC.

Pavlenko, A., & Lantolf, J. (2000). Second language learning as participation and the (re) construction of selves. In A. Pavlenko & J. Lantolf (Eds.), *Sociocultural theory and second language learning* (pp. 155–177). Oxford: Oxford University Press.

Peñalosa, F. (1980). Chicano bilingualism and the world system. In R. Padilla (Ed.), *Theory in bilingual education: Ethnoperspectives in bilingual education research* (Vol. 2, pp. 3–17). Ypsilanti, MI: Eastern Michigan University Press.

Phillipson, R. (1988). Linguicism: Structures and ideologies in linguistic imperialism. In T. Skutnabb-Kangas (Ed.), *Minority education: From shame to struggle* (pp. 339–358). Bristol, UK: Multilingual Matters.

Scarcella, R. (2003). *Academic English: A conceptual framework* (Technical Report 2003-1). University of California Linguistic Minority Research Institute.

Seidner, S. (1981). Language assessment at post-secondary institutions. In R. Padilla (Ed.), *Ethnoperspectives in bilingual education research* (Vol. 3, pp. 368–380). Ypsilanti, MI: Eastern Michigan University Press.

Sfard, A. (1998). On two metaphors for learning and the dangers of choosing just one. *Educational Researcher, 2*(27), 4–13.

Spring, J. (1994). *Deculturalization and the struggle for equality: A brief history of the education of dominated cultures in the United States.* New York: McGraw Hill.

Spring, J. (1997). The American school, 1642–1996 (4th ed.). New York: McGraw Hill.

Sutterby, J., Ayala, J., & Murillo, S. (2005). *El sendero torcido al español*: The development of bilingual teachers' Spanish language proficiency. *Bilingual Research Journal, 29*(2), 435–452.

Texas State Board for Educator Certification. (2004). *Bilingual target language proficiency standards.* Austin, TX.

Thomas, W., & Collier, W. (2002). *A national study of school effectiveness for language minority students' long-term academic achievement.* Santa Cruz, CA: Center for Research Education, Diversity and Excellence, UC, Santa Cruz.

Tollefson, J., & Tsui, A. (Eds.). (2004). *Medium of instruction policies: Which agenda? Whose agenda?* Mahwah, NJ: Erlbaum.

Ulibarrí, D., Spencer, M., & Rivas, G. (1981). Language proficiency and academic achievement: A study of language proficiency tests and their relationship to school ratings as predictors of academic achievement. *National Association for Bilingual Education Journal, 5*(3), 47–80.

United Nations Educational Scientific & Cultural Organization. (1953). *The use of vernacular languages in education.* Monographs of Fundamental Education VIII. Paris: IFMRP.

United Nations Educational Scientific & Cultural Organization. (2008). *Mother tongue matters: Local language as a key to effective learning.* Paris: UNESCO.

Valadez, C., & Díaz, M. A. (2008). *El profesor principiante en las aulas escolares en EEUU: Retos y posibilidades.* In C. Marcelo (Ed.), *Profesores principiantes e inserción a la docencia.* Barcelona: OCTAEDRO.

Valdés, G. (1989). Testing bilingual proficiency for specialized occupations: Issues and implications. In B. R. Gifford (Ed.), *Test policy and test performance: Education, language, and culture* (pp. 207–229). Norwell, MA: Kluwer.

Valdés, G. (2004). Between support and marginalization: The development of academic language in language minority children. *Journal of Bilingual Education & Bilingualism, 7*(1–2), 102–132.

Valdés, G., González, S., López García, D., & Márquez, P. (2003). Language ideology: The case of Spanish in departments of foreign languages. *Anthropology & Education Quarterly, 34*(1), 3–26.

Waggoner, D., & O'Malley, M. (1984). Teachers of limited English proficient children in the United States. *Journal of the National Association for Bilingual Education, 9*(3), 25–42.

6 Diversity Coursework

Developing Cultural Competency

Rosa Hernández Sheets, Blanca Araujo,
Gloria Calderon, and John Indiatsi

Multicultural courses required in most teacher preparation programs since the 1970s yield negligible improvement in student learning outcomes. This coursework, often socio-political in nature and generally disconnected from sociocultural learning theory, appears to encourage social change, promote advocacy, and sermonize hope. The curricular content rarely helps *aspirantes*/candidates make meaning of what is needed to develop cultural competency. Sheets (2003, p. 117) reminds us that while we may

> inspire, we have not demonstrated the capacity to educate a professoriate who can prepare preservice candidates to succeed in diverse settings, nor have we developed teacher preparation programs that understand how to select programmatic content, experiences and strategies needed to help [them] … apply cultural and language dimensions to curriculum and practice.

However, along with instructional and programmatic weaknesses in preparation programs, we acknowledge that other factors contribute, such as *aspirante* ideological positions, PK-12 school culture, assessment requirements, and curricular mandates.

Taking into consideration the role of multicultural coursework, consider, that in most institutions, issues of diversity are neither incorporated throughout nor embraced by the majority of professors. Instructors of record are assigned to teach these courses own diversity problems. Those teaching other courses position themselves to disregard multicultural concerns. In academe, accountability for *aspirante* satisfaction with course content and delivery resides with the professor. Individuals teaching required diversity courses, often, are forced to survive under conditions characterized by multiple levels of resistance. When problems arise, support from colleagues and administration is generally tentative, somewhat unpredictable, and always inconsistent. So, it is within this socio-political context of higher education that bilingual preparation programs, themselves under siege, must develop meaningful diversity coursework.

In spite of known institutional constraints, multiculturalists argue that diversity coursework has potential to minimize results of the dominant socio-political ideology shaping how *aspirantes* conceptualize the meaning of culture, view who is capable of learning, understand how to learn to teach, frame pedagogical curricular knowledge, and define good teaching (Gay, 2000; Hollins, 2008; Shkedi & Nisan, 2006). Theoretically, diversity coursework facilitates *aspirantes'* acknowledgement and deconstruction of previously held damaging assumptions about the capabilities and entitlements of ethnic minority and poor children. Potentially, diversity coursework promotes greater understandings of diversity pedagogy (Sheets, 2005); and, most importantly, imparts knowledge and skill to improve BLs' learning outcomes.

This chapter suggests a knowledge base to help guide, plan, design, and evaluate curriculum in diversity courses; and, discusses its role in bilingual preparation programs. Since we presume that *aspirantes* are prepared to work with children in settings designed to maintain existing socio-political conditions, we begin with a discussion on ideology. We follow with a suggested framework for diversity curriculum, implications for transforming practice, and conclude with recommendations for research.

Literature

This section begins with definition and discussion on ideology. Next, a brief research of the literature on diversity coursework in general, is followed by the paucity of research examining diversity coursework for *aspirantes.*

Ideology

Ideology is defined as "visionary theorizing; a systematic body of concepts; a manner or the content of thinking characteristic of an individual, group, or culture; the integrated assertions, theories and aims that constitute a sociopolitical program" (Webster, 1976, p. 568). Ideologies can be viewed as an organized set of beliefs, attitudes, ideas, opinions, assumptions, and theories supporting particular educational, social, and political viewpoints. Individuals and groups, purposefully or inadvertently, use ideologies to select and maintain personal attitudes, purposes, and goals. Ideology provides internal, consistent, habitual thinking patterns enabling beliefs and values to fit tightly together into a total, often unconscious, mental structure (Shkedi & Nisan, 2006). Shkedi and Nisan (2006) explain that ideologies do "not require external endorsement or sanction" because they "possess a priori authority and are self-validating" (p. 689).

In a culturally diverse society, the ideological positions of the dominant cultural group often prevail in institutions, such as schools, the work place, and government (Hollins, 2008). Dominating ideologies organize institutions so that the group holding power perpetuates and sustains maximum control over people with minimal conflict (Lye, 1997). Since a goal is to avoid conflict, the ideological position or the subsequent control of the content of thinking may, for some, seem invisible or unnoticeable. Lye (1997) points out that groups do not deliberately plan to oppress people or to:

> alter their consciousness (although this can happen), but rather [it is] a matter of how the dominant institutions in society work through values, conceptions of the world, and symbol systems, in order to legitimize the current order.
>
> (p. 12)

In any given society, the legitimization of how the world should work including ways to think, which ideas to adopt, and what knowledge is valued are accomplished through the teaching of its young. Concepts, valued by the majority, are repeatedly ingrained in symbols and practices until they become part of the current thinking and understanding of what is natural. Thus, in a diverse society, the dominant ideology is perpetrated, assisted, preserved, and nourished by established institutions, such as schools, under the control of the dominating culture (Hollins, 2008).

Ideology, when viewed as a teacher belief system, is integrated into an educational philosophy that guides specific principles that strengthen and affirm a belief system. This belief system is continually confirmed by robust convictions systematically integrated in attitudes, assumptions, and knowledge (Meighan, 1981; Shkedi & Nisan, 2006; Van Dijk, 1998). They steer *aspirantes'* thinking, judgment, and receptiveness to knowledge. To illustrate, if *aspirantes* believe that bilingual learners (BLs) should speak English, they may judge native Spanish speakers as linguistically deficient, and may choose to resist required ESL courses. As teachers, they may take an exam to obtain an ESL endorsement to enhance job opportunities, while simultaneously ignoring or resisting opportunities to advance understandings of second language pedagogy. It is important to acknowledge *aspirantes'* sets of beliefs, habits of mind, and unsubstantiated assumptions regulating their access to pedagogical knowledge and curriculum (see Chapter 4). Instructors must acknowledge that *aspirantes'* ideology influences attitudes about their expertise, as well as how they conceptualize learning to teach and teaching.

Aspirantes' preconceived notions about student characteristics, the nature of curriculum, and what determines good teaching are difficult to modify. They, inadvertently or purposefully, discount information contradicting their worldview. Unwittingly, their potential to gain knowledge and culturally competent teaching strategies is subordinated to their ideological position. Although some work suggests *aspirante* change at the completion of particular coursework (Cochran-Smith, 1991; Sleeter, 2001), we are not convinced that extremely personal, deeply embedded ideological positions can be changed through a single diversity course. For this reason, the *Educar* model incorporates diversity issues throughout.

We maintain that an ideology can be exposed, acknowledged, and brought to consciousness. *Aspirantes* can self-challenge and self-modify previously held reactions. They can begin to grasp how they routinely alter and reject principles of diversity in ways to fit their own narratives, to conform to familiar spaces, or to accommodate intolerable situations. Consider *aspirante* rejection of teacher responsibility for student learning. Scholars explain that dominant ideological beliefs emphasize that individuals are responsible for their own achievement and success (Bartolomé, 2004; Farley, 2000). This orientation alleges that everyone, including BLs and children living in high-poverty neighborhoods with substandard schools, have equal schooling opportunities. This belief is perpetuated by an ideology of independence and individualism, a conviction that individuals control their own destiny (Hollins, 2008). If *aspirantes* believe that the system is fair for everyone; they reason that underserved children have schooling opportunities equal to White and middle-class students. These *aspirantes,* especially if they believe that they worked hard to achieve, might tend to shun personal responsibility for student learning. Dismissing possible shortcomings of knowledge and skill, they can readily justify blaming children, parents, and their communities. They rationalize that societal, political, health, economic, and schooling conditions are consequential to children who live in particular geographic zip codes; and, that these socio-public deficiencies, not schooling policies and practices, impinge on student access to schooling opportunities. These *aspirantes* may silently or openly oppose programs designed to compensate for the lack of schooling opportunities available to students marginalized by economic living conditions beyond their control. A non-suspect agenda may include a "why can't you be like me" attitude or "I was poor and didn't speak English when I went to school; but, I worked hard" singular point of reference which can distant teachers from their own kind. This nearly impenetrable disassociation, present within a student and teacher shared ethnicity, obstructs culturally competency development.

Conceptual literature advocating reform, suggests that *aspirantes,* regardless of ethnic backgrounds or linguistic heritage, tend to unconsciously hold beliefs reflecting damaging dominant ideologies upholding negative judgments of the intellectual potential of ethnically diverse children (Gay, 2000). While scholarship has not linked the improvement of student learning outcomes to *aspirante* ideology, teacher educators must be conscious that *aspirantes*, who are predisposed to see schooling as fair, may conclude that parents and students are negligent and irresponsible. Although *aspirante* ideology is only one component of curricular content in diversity coursework, we view it as an introductory step towards the development of pedagogical cultural competence.

Diversity Coursework

There are differences in program policies, practices, and curricular experiences for general education candidates and those specially prepared for BLs. In terms of diversity coursework, *aspirantes* take specially designed multicultural courses within their own programs; or, they enroll in multicultural courses with general candidates depending on their program's policy. In the *Educar* model, *aspirantes* take diversity course(s) within the bilingual program. This course is viewed as foundational; therefore, the expertise of the instructor of record, its sequence within the program, and its curricular content are critical to program vision (see Chapter 1). In this chapter, we separate the scholarship addressing diversity coursework in generalist and bilingual programs.

While many of the diversity concerns found in generalist programs are applicable to bilingual teacher preparation and English as a Second Language (ESL) models; we concede that some may not be germane, may manifest themselves in different ways, or both. Obviously, issues involving general candidate characteristics may typify both generalist and monolingual candidates preparing to teach BLs; however, for the most part, ethnic, linguistic, and economic attributes and lived experiences present in the majority of bilingual *aspirantes* may not mirror those of the general White middle-class candidate population. Other concerns, such as the status, sequence, substance, and structure of diversity coursework; the quality, expertise, and status of instructors of record; as well as integration of diversity content throughout the program are likely pertinent.

General Education Diversity Coursework

While there is a considerable body of scholarship on the role of diversity coursework in generalist preparation programs, most is promotional and conceptual, rather than empirical (Sheets, 2003). Available empirical studies focus on candidate predispositions, beliefs, characteristics; methodological flaws; and, issues regarding the skill and knowledge of teacher educators (Hollins & Guzman, 2005; Sheets & Chew, 2002). Hollins and Guzman (2005) critique the overabundance of self-studies utilizing unreliable instruments. Other scholars examine program concerns, such as course sequencing within the program and limitations of single-course requirements; however, the majority of the work concentrates on personal characteristics, limited experiential knowledge, and problematic resistance of the predominantly White, female, monolingual, middle-class candidate population (Hollins & Guzman, 2005; Sleeter, 2001; Zumwalt & Craig, 2005). Some point out the inadequacies of the majority White professoriate who mirror deficiencies similar to the candidate population; or, detail instructors' lack of academic preparation and teaching experience with diverse student populations (Ladson-Billings, 2005; Sheets, 2003; Sheets & Chew, 2002).

Bilingual Education Diversity Coursework

The dearth of empirical research examining diversity coursework for bilingual candidates soon became apparent. Regardless of different descriptors and direct examination of journals' table of contents, the studies we found focused on White candidates in general programs. The limited scope in the review of literature in this section exemplifies this scarcity.

The de la Piedra (2007) action research study, addressing candidates' ideological issues, took place near the Mexican border. This self-study examined how Mexican-origin candidates ($n = 30$) responded to a service-learning family-community project. Course goals challenged candidate-attitude toward Mexican-origin families to help them acknowledge how ideology can support cultural deficit perspectives. Finding showed that candidates: experienced conceptual change in defining parental involvement; made connections between their life experiences and those of students and parents; and linked theory to practice.

The Sheets and Chew (2002) qualitative study, in San Francisco, examined 32 female Cantonese/English Chinese American bilingual candidates' perception of diversity course value taught by seven different instructors, of which only three had specific academic preparation in diversity. All took the course outside the bilingual program; thus, they were enrolled in one of the seven sections mixed with candidates from the general program. Findings included: perceiving White candidate dominance of classroom dialogue and resistance as major barriers to knowledge gain; acknowledging the complexity of implementing multicultural education; questioning personal schooling experiences; accepting personal lack of knowledge of other cultural groups; and, recognizing the psychological and academic benefits of ethnic studies since diversity courses offered minimal cultural content specific to Chinese American bilingual children.

Suggested Framework for Diversity Coursework

In the *Educar* model, instructors of record are aware of the role and contribution of diversity courses to the program. The curricular content in these courses gives *aspirantes* multiple opportunities to: challenge damaging mainstream social and educational ideologies, conceptualize cultural competency, and understand the developmental nature of learning how to teach BLs. Since a goal of *Educar* is to prepare *aspirantes* with knowledge and skill to facilitate learning, diversity courses address sociocultural learning theory. They are positioned at the beginning of the program, so the knowledge gained is connected, expanded, and applied in subsequent content methods courses and field experiences.

Suggested Diversity Curriculum

Gay (2000) describes specific teaching techniques aimed at raising candidate consciousness and advancing acceptance of diversity. Other instructors, in self-study, qualitative research designs, describe personal pedagogical strategies to combat candidate resistance (Cochran-Smith, 1995; Ladson-Billings, 1991; Tatum, 1992). In this section, we present a way to organize candidate and doctoral diversity course content as a development process to reinforce and encourage cultural competency progression. While this curriculum, based on the first authors' university teaching experiences, is not collaboratively designed or empirically tested, it does provide insight to sample course content.

Aspirante Diversity Course

Since the course is conceptualized as a process, three distinct parts encourage movement from deep understandings of diversity pedagogical theory (Sheets, 2005) to its application in practice.

PART I

The first part introduces key concepts, which are continually reinforced throughout the course. These include: ideological positions, teacher responsibility for student learning, culture and cognition connections, and operational definitions of terminology. *Aspirantes* become aware that cultural competence is a journey rather than a destination. Topics for the first three or four sessions focus on issues such as the purpose of schooling, dominant cultural influences in schooling, the role of one's personal conceptual framework guiding classroom decisions, teacher identity, and most importantly, the difference between teaching as performance versus teaching as facilitating learning. An overview of three major learning theories, behaviorism, developmentalism, and sociocultural learning theory introduces the second part of the course. *Aspirantes* analyze the strengths and limitations in learning theories, examine their relationship to culture and cognition, and observe how these theories look in practice.

PART II

The second part makes explicit linkages among sociocultural learning theory (Cole, 1995; Hatano & Wertsch, 2001; Kozulin, 2002; Vygotsky, 1978); teacher type typology (Hollins, 2008); and, diversity pedagogical dimensions (Sheets, 2005). *Aspirantes* are given multiple opportunities to conceptualize the ways these theories overlap and intersect and how application mediates and facilitates instruction in particular situations and settings.

PART III

Application of diversity pedagogy theory and sociocultural learning theory to practice and movement in teacher type is the focus of the third part of the course. Experiences in the final part of the course deliberately connect theory to practice. In small self-selected groups, using Hollins' (2008) typology, sociocultural theory, and the diversity pedagogy dimensions (Sheets, 2005), they observe and discuss classroom policies, conditions, and curriculum containing or missing these elements. *Aspirantes* experience lesson plan design, with a specific student population in mind, incorporating sociocultural learning theory and diversity pedagogy beginning with Type I and ending with group efforts to design Type III lessons (Hollins, 2008). *Aspirantes* realize that learning to teach is developmental, requires time, expects commitment, demands effort, and involves skill development. Candidates plan their journey, visualize and contextualize knowledge, and focus on ways to develop culturally responsive pedagogical skills incorporating a conceptual framework that integrates their own cultural knowledge and knowledge of other cultures.

Curriculum for Graduate Course(s)

The curricular content for a graduate diversity course(s) responds to the needs of graduate students who generally have academic concentrations in areas other than cultural diversity; and, who may be interested in becoming teacher educators. Since many graduate students teach undergraduate diversity courses or may be required to teach diversity courses as teacher educator regardless of their area of specialization, we discuss a foundational graduate diversity course. This course begins with the precursors of multicultural education and follows with the origin, purpose, disciplinary orientation, and ideological positions of four diversity theoretical perspectives: multicultural education, critical pedagogy, critical race theory, and diversity pedagogy. It also explores the relationship among schooling issues and their implications to the preparation of university professors, educational researchers, curriculum specialists, and school administrators.

Divided into five parts, the first section examines the early scholarship between the 1940s and 1960s. Prior to 1940, children from ethnic minority groups did not appear in the literature. They were neither participants in the studies conducted during this era, nor were their schooling conditions of concern. Scholars between the 1940s and 1960s were White race-conscious liberals, sociologists, and psychologists. They produced a potent body of controversial work, whose legacy, because of its wide distribution, prominence of its authors, and federal funding, continues to influence current thinking and theoretical frameworks guiding schooling programs designed for ethnic minority and poor students (Sheets, 2006, unpublished manuscript). This early scholarship includes: work from a sociological perspective describing ethnic minority and poor children as pathological; research advancing genetic inferiority; and, studies promoting a cultural deficit model. This damaging image of ethnic minority and poor children along with the *Civil Rights Movement* of the 1960s were precursors to the visionary educational diversity ideologies emerging in the late 1960s and continuing today.

The next four sections introduce, examine, and analyze the following diversity ideologies: multicultural education (e.g., James Banks, Geneva Gay, and Carl Grant), critical pedagogy (e.g., Paulo Freire, Henry Giroux, and Peter McLaren), critical race theory (e.g., Gloria Ladson-Billings, William Tate, and Richard Delgado), and diversity pedagogy (e.g., Rosa Hernández Sheets).

Awareness of this knowledge base allows graduate students to understand the historical and socio-political background influencing the genesis of the diversity scholarship. Throughout the course, they realize that their knowledge of diversity scholarship is emerging and developmental. They understand their responsibility, as future teacher educators, to connect diversity ideologies to classroom practice. They are asked to begin with small steps and continually move forward when challenged, both as individuals and as educators; and, to recognize ways in which their service can disadvantage or benefit children. Truly aware that becoming a culturally responsive educator requires relentless commitment, high investment of time and energy, and taking ownership of their development and skill, their journey continues. *¡Poco a poco se anda lejos!*

Transforming Teacher Preparation

The purpose of this chapter is to help current and future teacher educators facilitate *aspirantes'* learning in diversity coursework. Clearly, a rhetorical mission statement or inferred acceptance of diversity is inadequate. Teacher educators must realize the limitations in coursework laden with socio-political rhetoric, positioning children as victims of an oppressive society, or repeated calls for social justice devoid of learning theory and instructional strategies. Likewise, course content exclusively focusing on the needs of White middle-class candidates is neither relevant to *aspirantes* nor does it advance pedagogical cultural knowledge. A substantive, systemic transformative program change explicitly acknowledging connections between culture and cognition and one that purposefully prepares *aspirantes* to contextualize and mediate instruction is needed.

Diversity courses must link what Hollins (2008) calls the "deep meaning of culture in schooling" with cognition. This can rarely be accomplished in programs if we continue to hire small numbers of faculty with diversity expertise in bilingual departments; or, if program administrators assume that faculty with expertise in bilingual education or membership in an ethnic minority group automatically means that they have knowledge and skill to design, teach, and evaluate *aspirantes'* learning in diversity courses. Perhaps the lack of academically trained bilingual education professors in diversity are reasons why programs are exclusively language dominated, at the expense of other diversity pedagogical dimensions;

or, why the scholarship in this area is virtually nonexistent. At times, this language supremacy serves to minimize language as a powerful cultural tool and may result in subordinating language to mere translations of existing dominant culture instructional methods and content.

We do not question nor diminish the critical role bilingualism plays in the schooling of BLs nor in the preparation of *aspirantes* for BLs. Acknowledging the strong relationship between bilingualism and cognition, we realize its significant connection to BLs' academic performance and interpersonal relationships in classrooms. Along with grammar and vocabulary, a language has strong cultural components, including "distinctive verbal customs, patterns of thought, and styles of communication" (Sheets, 2005, p. 108). Since student–teacher and student–student interpersonal relationships and active student participation are at the heart of mediated instruction, *aspirantes* must understand how to sustain and promote heritage language growth. However, we also contend that other diversity pedagogical dimensions must be deemed relevant.

Another critical issue is the preparation of bilingual education teacher educators as diversity instructors. It is ultimately the teacher educators' responsibility to create and sustain emotional, cultural, and cognitive conditions in diversity coursework and field experiences that enable *aspirantes* to learn. It is evident from the foregoing discussion that teacher educators and *aspirantes'* ideologies often determine how they perceive curricular content, characterize BLs' academic potential, conceptualize learning, understand learning how to teach, and comprehend teaching about teaching. Social ideology formation is deeply rooted in the socio-political and dominant societal cultural frames (Hollins, 2008). These misguided orientations provide rationale for BLs' lack of achievement, which are often disassociated with teacher cultural competency. Therefore, to effectively prepare *aspirantes*, doctoral programs preparing teacher educators ought to consider enhancing awareness of sociocultural learning theory and diversity pedagogies. They also can provide opportunity for reflection and deconstruction of dominant ideologies that perpetuate inequitable schooling conditions for the emerging majority bilingual student populations.

Thus, program effectiveness requires a shift in vision, policies, and practices. Towards this end, programs ought to be structured and anchored on a knowledge base that breaks away from tradition. Teacher educators who effectively connect culture and cognition actualize theory to practice and create learning conditions that uphold *aspirante* responsibility for BLs learning. These programs embrace new ideas that encourage *aspirantes* to begin and continue their journey toward cultural competence.

Research Directions

Generally, research on the development of *aspirantes'* cultural competency is needed in both the conceptual and empirical scholarship. Issues of the multiple dimensions of diversity, as an essential component of preparation, is lacking in the discussion of exemplary programs. We suggest that future research directions respond to this need and address the promising contributions of diversity coursework. While research in bilingual education teacher preparation addresses specific programmatic aspects, such as: language assessment and development (Sutterby, Ayala, & Murillo, 2005) and recruitment/retention (Flores, Clark, Villarreal, & Claeys, 2007), missing in the scholarship is research on the role and value of diversity coursework. Tangentially, some studies may address cultural diversity, but few center on diversity coursework for *aspirantes*.

Second, issues regarding *aspirantes'* characteristics, cultural awareness, and ideological positions require further exploration. As identified in this chapter, these factors play a critical role in their conceptualization of the learning–teaching process. Therefore, to strengthen cultural foundational coursework, research connecting *aspirantes'* characteristics, cultural awareness, and ideological positions need to be explored in relation to the application of cultural pedagogical knowledge to the schooling context.

Lastly, teacher educators need access to research-based information on best practices in diversity coursework for *aspirantes*. An extensive search of the literature showed an embarrassing scantiness of research in this area. Theoretical aspects of diversity pedagogy are documented (Sheets, 2009); however, not much is known about *aspirantes'* knowledge and ability to apply diversity pedagogy or any other diversity ideology to practice. We encourage further exploration and evaluation of curricular frameworks for diversity coursework. It is our belief, that diversity coursework in preparation programs, as they exist today, are not built on any well thought out and carefully formulated framework. Rather, it seems that bits and pieces of diversity ideas garnered by course required textbooks, interests, and proclivities of assigned instructors dictate curricular content. Programs need comprehensive frameworks that take into account all the cultural dimensions through which learning, learning how to teach, and teaching about teaching is constructed.

References

Bartolomé, L. I. (2004). Critical pedagogy and teacher education: Radicalizing prospective teachers. *Teacher Education Quarterly, 31*(1), 97–122.

Cochran-Smith, M. (1991). Learning to teach against the grain. *Harvard Educational Review, 61*(3), 279–310.

Cochran-Smith, M. (1995). Uncertain allies: Understanding the boundaries of race and teaching. *Harvard Educational Review, 65*(4), 541–570.

Cole, M. (1995). The zone of proximal development: Where culture and cognition create each other (pp. 146–161). In J. V. Wertsch, (Ed.), *Culture, communication and cognition: Vygotskian perspectives*. New York: Cambridge University Press.

de la Piedra, M. (2007). Making connections: Bilingual pre-service teachers' service-learning with Spanish-speaking parents living along the U.S./Mexico border. *TABE Journal, 9*(2). 98–114.

Farley, J. E. (2000). *Majority-minority relations* (4th ed). Upper Saddle River, NJ: Prentice Hall.

Flores, B. B., Clark, E. R., Villarreal, A., & Claeys, L. (2007, Fall). Academy for teacher excellence: Recruiting, preparing, and retaining Latino teachers through learning communities. *Teacher Education Quarterly, 34*(4), 53–69.

Gay, G. (2000). *Culturally responsive teaching: Theory, research, and practice*. New York: Teachers College Press.

Hatano, G., & Wertsch, J. V. (2001). Sociocultural approaches to cognitive development: The constitution of culture in mind. *Human Development, 44*, 77–83.

Hollins, E. R. (2008). *Culture in school learning: Revealing the deep meaning of culture* (2nd ed.). New York: Routledge.

Hollins, E. R., & Guzman, M. T. (2005). Research on preparing teachers for diverse populations. In M. Cochran-Smith & K. M. Zeichner (Eds.), *Studying teacher education: The report of the AERA panel on research and teacher education* (pp. 477–548). Mahwah, NJ: Erlbaum/AERA.

Kozulin, A. (2002). Sociocultural theory and the mediated learning experience. *School Psychology International, 23*(1), 7–35.

Ladson-Billings, G. (1991). Like lighting in a bottle: Attempting to capture the pedagogical excellence of successful teachers of Black students. *International Journal of Qualitative Studies in Education, 3*(4), 335–344.

Ladson-Billings, G. (2005). Is the team alright? *Journal of Teacher Education, 56*(3), 229–234.

Lye, J. (1997). *Ideology: A brief guide*. Retrieved from http://www.brocku.ca/english/jlye/ideology.html

Meighan, R. (1981). *A sociology of education*. London: Holt, Rinehart and Winston.

Sheets, R. H. (2003). Competency vs. good intentions: Diversity ideologies and teacher competency. *International Journal of Qualitative Studies in Education, 16*(1), 111–120.

Sheets, R. H. (2005). *Diversity pedagogy: Examining the role of culture in the teaching-learning process*. Boston: Allyn & Bacon.

Sheets, R. H. (2006). *Ideology*. Unpublished manuscript.

Sheets, R. H. (2009). What is diversity pedagogy? *Multicultural Education, 16*(3), 11–17.

Sheets, R. H., & Chew, L. (2002). Absent from the research, present in our classrooms: Preparing culturally responsive Chinese American teachers. *Journal of Teacher Education, 53*(2), 123–137.

Shkedi, A., & Nisan, M. (2006). Teachers' cultural ideology: Patterns of curriculum and teaching culturally valued texts. *Teachers College Record, 108*(4), 677–725.

Sleeter, C. E. (2001). Preparing teachers for culturally diverse schools: Research and the overwhelming presence of whiteness. *Journal of Teacher Education, 52*(2), 94–106.

Sutterby, J. A., Ayala, J., & Murillo, S. (2005). *El sendero torcido al español* [The twisted path to Spanish]: The development of bilingual teachers' Spanish-language proficiency. *Bilingual Research Journal, 29*(2), 435–452.

Tatum, B. D. (1992). Talking about race, learning about racism: The implication of racial identity development theory in the classroom. *Harvard Educational Review, 62*(1), 1–24.

Van Dijk, T. A. (1998). *Ideology: A multidisciplinary approach*. London: Sage.

Vygotsky, L. (1962). *Thought and language*. Cambridge, MA: MIT Press.

Vygotsky, L. (1978). *Mind in society: The development of higher psychological processes*. M. Cole, V. John-Steiner, S. Scribner & E. Souberman (Eds. & Trans.), Cambridge, MA: Harvard University Press.

Webster's New Collegiate Dictionary. (1976). Springfield, MA: Merriam.

Zumwalt, K., & Craig, E. (2005). Teachers' characteristics: Research on the indicators of quality. In M. Cochran-Smith & K. M. Zeichner (Eds.), *Studying teacher education: The report of the AERA panel on research and teacher preparation* (pp. 157–260). Mahwah, NJ: AERA/Erlbaum.

7 Crisálida

A Metaphor for Bilingual Education Teacher Preparation

María Torres-Guzmán and Thao Tran

In science we learned that the butterfly's journey consists of four complex metamorphosis stages—the egg, the caterpillar, then caterpillar in a chrysalis, and *voilà*, we have a butterfly. We use the complexity of the butterfly's journey for scientific thinking (Berliner, 1990) and to crystallize (Hubbard & Power, 2003) our understandings about teacher candidate identity development and the transformative possibilities of bilingual teacher education programs in this process.

The literature identifies levels of bilingual education teacher competencies (Canales & Ruiz-Escalante, 1992) as a starting point for analyzing the potential structures within a program. In promising research studies on cultural diversity and preparation, Hollins and Torres-Guzman (2005) found this scholarship fails to examine connections between preparation programs with candidacy or readiness. The identification of components, as the case of the butterfly, does not illustrate nor acknowledge the process of knowledge transmission or transformation within preparation programs. We agree with Flores (2001) that studies on components also neglect looking at the candidate's transformative development through self-reporting practices. Thus, we examine preparation through the lens of candidates' self-reports of their own development.

The journey of becoming a bilingual education teacher can be paralleled to the constant shedding of skins that occurs in the metamorphosis, that is, the constant becoming of their identities (Hall, 1997) in the on-going cultivation of skills, knowledge, and persona. We view these processes up close, as transformative instances or moments occurring in the day-to-day lives of candidates; and as such, we make distinctions between the traditional definitions of transformation as solely large, socially significant qualitative changes. We believe that by doing so we are able to focus on the agency of the individual in their own development within the context of daily life practices in their communities of practice.

In this chapter, the phenomenon of identity development of candidates is explored as it occurred within the preparation program. The purpose is to examine the process of identity development and practices of candidates as they encounter disruption—internally and externally triggered—and engage in agency. We conclude with a discussion of research directions in this field.

Theoretical Framework

The process of becoming a butterfly is a useful metaphor for preparation if we view "learning to teach as the process of forming an identity as a teacher" (Clarke, 2008, p. 53). We take from Clarke the theory of "identity development as part of a broader theory of learning, meaning, practice and community" and we use, as he does, the concepts of discourse, identity, and community of practice.

Both Vygotsky (1962) and Halliday (1973) view languages and cultures as shaping and being shaped by individual/community discourses and practices. They view the relationship of language and individual/community as dynamic and locate polyphonic discourses and meanings of practices in the use of language. Identity development of teaching, within this relationship is socially and culturally constituted, continuously recreated, and situated within fluid boundaries (see Chapter 3). Through the examination of the discourses of candidates, we get at both identity and development.

The second aspect of the theory of learning/teaching is the concept of community of practice (Lave & Wenger, 1990), where the relationship of the individual in the group is emphasized, as it is in community where the individual ideas and the social norms of speaking and behaving are established. This concept illustrates how candidates reproduce, sustain, and transform both identities and communities through their engagement in the acts of teaching in schooling where more than one language and associated cultures are used for learning; through alignment of norms of believing, acting, judging, and evaluating the social and instructional needs of bilingual learners (BLs); and through imagining self, others in the profession, students, parents, and communities as multilingual speakers and learners aspiring educational attainment and achievement. Sociocultural theory, thus, helps us examine the candidate ongoing development as an individual within the social practices and discourses of the teaching community as created within institutions, such as preparation programs, and the broader bilingual community.

The third theoretical element is the perspective of language in the Halliday (1973) sense of social semiotic. In this view, discourse is supplemented by detailed linguistic instances of candidates' "utterances and interactions as construing the ideational content of their systems of knowledge and belief, the interpersonal relations of their community, and their intrapersonal identities" (Clarke, 2008, p. 39). We add to Clarke's framework three theoretical propositions related to the field of bi/multilingualism.

From the theory of language facilitation (Cummins, 1996; Hakuta, 1986), we take the understanding that language and culture of group membership or identity is key to the acquisition of a second language and its associated culture and, more importantly, for learning. This theory has been central to the broader bilingual community and its development as a field. It helps us to give language(s) and culture(s) a space not just as a social semiotic, but also as object of inquiry within the community of practice of bilingual teachers.

From a critical sociocultural perspective (Lewis, Enciso, & Moje, 2007), we take the understandings of the study of multiple languages, cultures, literacies, and identities and how they are defined. It calls for the inclusion of differences in perspectives. The inclusion of difference is critical to learning in multiple languages in schools. We do not just want to pose questions about how the shifts in candidate identity (Lave, 1996; Gee, 2001) occur; we want to specifically highlight moments of conflict, disjuncture, or difference within the candidates' comparative discourse about language and culture and their practices within multilingual settings and how these become spaces for learning.

The last notion is that of transcultural repositioning (Guerra, 2007), defined as a set of rhetorical practices associated with identity formation that ethnic minority group members are more likely to have greater opportunity of experiencing than the members of a privileged group. Our current understanding, being that the negotiation of identities are socio-historically situated and that repositioning the self is also about the pain of language loss and the struggle for maintenance in an era that privileges language intolerance and monolingualism (Pavlenko, 2003). The ethnic minority individual is likely to navigate the distinct cultural worlds they come from and inhabit as comparative discourses. This comparative discourse shows up as constitutive elements of their identity. We propose that in *Educar* programs (see Chapter 2), the array of experiences of repositioning of self in different socio-political and linguistic environments strengthen candidates' abilities to facilitate moments of transcultural repositioning within the space of teaching. Our experience is that while all candidates preparing to become bilingual education teachers already have transcultural experiences, some of the repositioning necessarily occurs during their preparation. Both dominant and ethnic minority groups are confronted with understanding their own ethnocentric ways while trying to embrace new identities in relation to their students and to understand that all humans are capable of learning.

Thus, we propose that programs are the *crisálida* (chrysalis), the institutional context through which candidates reposition themselves transculturally— linguistically, culturally, and socially—in relation to what is the central activity of their community of practice. That is, understanding substantively the role of language and culture in learning, not just by understanding the language; but by going beyond to understand the challenges of access, language, cultural and pedagogic equity, and social justices for themselves and their students (Nieto, 2000). It is a place of becoming within the life of an individual candidate and within their sociohistorical times. At this stage, the full-fledged teacher identity has not emerged.

Methodological Consideration

This study focuses on a teacher education graduate program. We collected the student writing of a subset of 15 fellowship recipients from whom we required applications, study group participation, community service, electronic portfolios, and end-of-year evaluations. We use discourse analysis to explore: (a) how they saw their own past experiences and subjectivities as incorporated or shut out of their transcultural repositioning in relation to the activity of learning, (b) how different identities were recognized by other bilingual student teachers, teachers in the field, and teacher educators in the program, (c) what cultural models or ways of knowing (Gee, 1996) were invoked in the program or classes and how these models, and associated discourses, framed their transcultural repositioning, identities, and opportunities for agency, and (d) what moments of disruption and agency, that is, strategic making and remaking of self and sometimes the material conditions surrounding the self, were afforded in social exchanges within the program/profession. We wanted to examine how transformation occurs, if and when it does, by examining the discourse of the candidates.

Findings

Pulling from the Past into the Present

As stated above, aspiring-to-be-teachers are in constant positioning and repositioning of self as they envision the self as teacher in bilingual teaching environments. We understand they come to the act of envisioning themselves as bilingual teachers with many prior experiences as social beings. They have prior schooling experiences in and from which they observed the acts of teaching from a distant-yet-affected position of learner. From pre-school through undergraduate, candidates have observed and felt a diversity of models of teaching. In a sense, they are continuing a process that is familiar to them but there is a significant difference at this point. The distinction is centered on their capacity of choice and freedom.

All candidates included in this study had prior learning/teaching and personal experiences that caused disruption/dissonance in their life's trajectory and motivated them to become bilingual teachers (see Chapter 4). They were asked to share how their life experiences informed their educational philosophy, personal values, and beliefs. We chose to highlight the examples of previous encounters and experiences with educational, social, and economic injustices. Abby Xiang, a Chinese American candidate, expressed the following in her writing:

> When I was in ESL program seven years ago, I did not have the privilege to learn English in a dual language program. I would never forget the experiences of struggling to maintain my native language as I try to fit in American life. At the time, I told myself that no ESL students should ever repeat my path. Language could, but should never be a block for students to learn.
>
> (Fall 2008 Application)

Her personal experience as a BL helped inform Abby's job as the coordinator for a community ESL program and her choice to study in the bilingual program. At some level, every candidate goes through the struggle of learning a second language, but the circumstances or sociocultural context of learning the second language can vary.

Some choose to teach in bilingual settings due to exposure to injustices, as Michael proposed:

> Through my experience in the Bilingual Education classroom as a K-8 grade substitute teacher in XY District 100 (in IL), I saw many bilingual elementary school students thrown into majority language classrooms prematurely. This caused them to gradually lose their Spanish reading, writing, and speaking skills and fall way behind in the majority language classrooms. As a result

of this experience, I have strong convictions about the endless benefits of an enrichment dual language program both for English Language Learners and for the majority English population in which both languages are embraced and developed upon.

Michael's experience of being a White male teacher in a bilingual Spanish classroom facilitated his conviction of the importance of being an advocate for a program that maintained the student's native language while developing the second language. Positionalities emerging from social class, race, and gender have always been a place of contention in the classrooms, particularly in urban and public school settings.

Similarly, Rachel, self-identified Asian American/Spanish bilingual, gives insight into her understanding of language as non-native to the Paraguayan culture. She articulated the dissonance she saw in the statuses of majority/minority languages while volunteering as a teacher:

> In Paraguay, there are two recognized languages in the country: *Español* and Guarani. Although it was expected for teachers and students to speak primarily *Español* at school and Guarani at home, rural schools mainly spoke and taught in Guarani while schools in the towns or cities conducted school in *Español*. Guarani is Paraguay's indigenous language that is more expressive in meaning and more comfortable when spoken. On the other hand, *Español* was viewed as the educated language and only spoken in the capital or major cities. In schools, it was necessary to learn to read and write in both. This account of bilingualism allowed me to realize how important it is to maintain a home language for the history, values, and morals that were connected to it and involve the "educated" language for another status and reputation given in society.

She learned that while social tensions are likely to exist around language, as a teacher she could support students to value Guarani language. Rachel's understanding of the political and social discourse regarding high- and low-language varieties helped her learn how to negotiate herself as learner and teacher.

While these candidates speak different languages and have varied ethnic backgrounds, what runs through their discourse as common is that they drew from key incidents in their own lived linguistic and cultural experiences to understand the dynamics—the incorporation or shutting out of their transcultural repositioning in relation to the activity of learning and larger context of what it means to be a student in a multilingual educational setting. Furthermore, in examining their writing, we have come to see the constitutive comparative nature of their discourse, whether it is self to an imagined other, privileged self to less-privileged, and status differences outside self. We also understood how their two years in the program allowed them to be part of a community of practice with a discourse that, while at times disruptive, conflictual, or different, allowed the possibilities of channeling personal convictions and experiences into new experiences that could make a difference in that they were brought to consciousness and converted into a knowledge resource from which they could think about their roles as teachers for BLs.

Recognizing Different Identities

We approached identity development within a community of practice, as it is manifested in candidates' discursive manner. By doing so, we realized that they are involved in constant processing and interacting with self and others. Three themes emerged with respect to how candidates recognized themselves and were recognized by others.

The first theme is what we call authentication, identified within as the process of conscious self-definition. All the students, Chinese- or Spanish-speaking, were concerned about developing their abilities in the languages with which they identified ethnically and culturally, other than English. This concern, however, was not just related to self; it was related to their professional aspirations. They understood that if they were not academically proficient in the language of the children they were to serve, they could be a detriment to the student's success. They were not only able to define who they were; they were able to express how their identities were discursively verified (Bucholtz & Hall, 2005) through their understanding of the relation of and with language and learning in the bilingual teaching community of practice.

Moments and processes of authentication were not only tied to self-definition but to the profession of choice. Ida, self-identified as biracial (White/Latina) and bilingual (Spanish/English), is a case in point. Her two years in the program offered her opportunities to experience both disruptive moments and discursive processes. In much of her written work, particularly in the final evaluation and reflection of her learning, she referred to her Spanish language development as pivotal to her development as a teacher:

> As someone who speaks Spanish, I regret not having the opportunity to practice and develop my Spanish academically in elementary school. I only started developing my Spanish in an academic setting once I reached high school and not truly until I reached college. Now as a student who has worked with bilingual students in … NY … I have learned that bilingual programs are not just to teach students a second language, but also to help students think "outside the box" and make them more flexible linguistically and academically in their future, whatever it may be …

Through the process of authentication, candidates constantly repositioned themselves—they played with the ability to situate themselves while maintaining a view of self as enduring the process (Trueba, 1999) of transformation, and they also played with the multiplicity, fragmentation, and hybridity of their transcultural repositioning process. Debbie shows how she positions her work with language minority communities, first within the context of nationalist identity and gradually building her narrative in a self-defining way to say who she is:

> Just like a nationalist fights for his or her country, a Universalist fights for humanity. I'm an American and Peruvian citizen, though I grew up in Latin America, India and Europe and did not live in the United States until I started as an undergraduate at New York University. I have made a strong

commitment to use my written, verbal and advocacy skills for educational and social projects in Ecuador, New York City and India … If we don't tell their stories, then no one will, and my ambition as a teacher is to foster and create tools with which these stories can be shared and ultimately valued.

(Debbie, Spring 2009 Application)

The second theme the discourse raised was related to the dynamic nature of development and transformation. We examined the shifts in thinking that occur during interaction with others that inform the candidate's identity development and transformation. We saw the process as an intersubjectivity achieved through social and cultural interaction (Bucholtz & Hall, 2005). The interactions with others entailed interactions with all social and cultural categories, such as their teaching and learning institutions, peers, communities, students, and family. These social interactions, at the same time, lead candidates into self-discoveries.

All the candidates underwent shifts in thinking, and identity, at some point during the program. We focus on Sebastian, a bilingual Spanish teacher candidate in the South Bronx, as he illustrates the comparative discourse and the dynamism of the process very poignantly. Sebastian self-identifies as a Mexican American from California and as a major advocate for the field of bilingual/bicultural education. His identity and lived experiences propelled and committed him to the field. In first grade, his mother pulled him out of a bilingual class and put him in a regular classroom for fear that he would not be successful (Sebastian, spring 2008 application). Since he joined us in 2007, he has flourished as a leader within his school. He had been a charter schoolteacher in Los Angeles of which he states:

After the passing of Proposition 227, I have not seen a successful program in place in the LA metropolitan area, even though there are many, many English Language Learners and regular education students that could benefit greatly from it. It seems that there are families and communities, including those of first-generation immigrants, which are confused about how successful bilingual education has been or can be.

His own early experience with bilingual education and his experiences in teaching in Los Angeles and in New York repositioned him as an advocate and a leader. Of his leadership role, he wrote:

At my middle school, we began planning the development of a dual language program that would begin in the 2008–2009 school year. After many meetings, reading, and discussion, we came up with a theory-based model and defined steps to begin the Dual Language Enrichment *Program/Programa de Enriquecimiento de Dos Idiomas* at MS 223. The program focuses on high expectations, communication with families, and academic rigor, always leading from a bilingual and bicultural lens. I see myself as a teacher leader in my middle school and at Teachers College.

We can see shifts of his thinking and identity as a teacher and in his understanding of the relationship between language, culture, and learning.

Interestingly, the two geographically different experiences encompass his life and teaching narratives as comparative, and his interactions as fluid. Sebastian shows that shifts and reposition of ourselves are never based on a relationship with one isolated entity, such as the school or an individual, but rather that of constant interaction and intersubjectivities with numerous, overlapping entities. While a major starting point in his life leaving the bilingual learning environment because of the sociocultural stigmatization of bilingual education, the multiple interactions within the field helped him recognize who he wants to be within the field.

The third theme is related to what Freire (2001) would call the incompleteness, the never-ending, on-going nature of identity development and transformation. Everyone in this group created an e-portfolio of their educational philosophy, teaching, and learning practices. The questions running through their work were about their development as teachers, for example: "Am I a better teacher if I know x, y and z?" What type of training practices, as well as theories, do I need to prepare me to be a bilingual educator? How do I look at my other personal goals in relation to my goal of being a better bilingual educator? Is studying for this MA enough? What else do I need? One Chinese candidate wrote,

> At this moment, I realize studying at Teachers College does not necessarily make me a good teacher. Even if I read many papers and journals to catch up with these experienced guys in theories, I will never truly know how to be a good teacher until I experience teaching in person.
>
> (Mei Mei, Fall 2008 Application)

Delving closer into their work, we learned that the questions above may have driven and guided them at the beginning of their candidacy, but that they were only triggers. Encounters and collaboration with others allowed them to redefine and refine their questions, to reposition themselves and to create opportunities of transformation not only for self but also for others. Jin Xin (Spring 2009 Application), a Chinese bilingual candidate shared how this occurred for her:

> Passionate about student organizations, I joined AMES and soon created a Language Exchange program that provided a dynamic network as well as a constant platform for students with interests in learning or improving oral proficiency of second languages.

Another example of this on-going transformation and incompleteness of being was articulated by Kacey, who self-identifies as White, bilingual in Spanish and English, as she attempts to define her own learning and teaching moments. She describes moments where she felt her development as collaboration.

> Another area of my work in which collaboration played an integral role was the Teaching BLs Conference. At first, I felt slightly overwhelmed by the task of presenting at the conference, among many of my professors. However, after brainstorming with [one of them], I felt that I had a more focused theme to present. Additionally, after bringing our ideas back to a program meeting, I felt

affirmed and clearer about the ideas we had generated due to the thoughtful feedback I received from the staff and my fellow colleagues. Our monthly meetings also served as a time for me to discuss the roadblocks I faced in my own classroom and for the other members to help me see a multitude of ways to get around, through, or over those obstacles.

The pattern we found was that candidates, Chinese- and Spanish-speaking, engaged in identity development and in the process of transforming into a bilingual teacher, as making conscious choices and self-defining around issues of culture, language, and learning while engaged with others. We found the recognition of self as including different identities at different moments requires authentication, constant reflection for self-improvement, and acceptance of the incompleteness of being. In addition to bringing in their experiences and subjectivities to the process of becoming a teacher, the candidates, through a comparative narrative, spoke consciously about the shifts in their thinking and practices, they tended to describe their repositioning, transcultural and otherwise, in relation to multiple others, as both situational and enduring across multiple situations.

Cultural Ways of Knowing

In the preparation programs, candidates begin to envision themselves in the future, by career choice, as a full-fledged practicing teacher within a community of practice. It is from the program context when the initiation into teaching requires a transcultural repositioning of self in relation to BLs, to knowledge about learning, to curriculum and instruction, and to institutional language policies and practices in a conscious way. Many found the coursework, both its theoretical and practical sense, to be a major facilitating point in teaching them how to frame their development as bilingual teachers. We found two poignant themes ran through the narratives.

The first theme focused on how they applied the theoretical knowledge gained from classes in their own classroom practice. The theoretical knowledge they invoked, however, was not traditional second language acquisition theory, but the sociocultural and sociolinguistic framework of bilingual education. For example, in the foundations of bilingual education class, candidates are taught about both the psycholinguistic and sociolinguistic aspect of bilingualism. At the end of the course, they are not only aware about the difference between interlanguage/intralanguage transfer, but also the political, social, and cultural implications behind the term bilingualism. Kacey stated:

Through my *Tiene Vuelta* community service hours, I applied my theoretical knowledge within the practical setting of a ninth grade math class in a low-income high school in Brooklyn. This experience challenged me to understand the needs of ELLs in a broader context. In choosing this area of service, I also confronted the effect of students' socio-economic status on how their language needs are perceived and addressed within a school setting.

(Kacey, Spring 2009 Application)

Like many candidates in the program, Kacey also struggles with her process of perfecting her Spanish to the level of fluency. Similar to others, she acknowledges the importance of gaining fluency to help the academic success of her students, but through her coursework and community building activities in the program, she realized that she is able to develop other knowledge that would make her a good bilingual educator as well:

> For example, through my explorations of what kinds of literature was authentic, culturally relevant, and appropriate for our library, I not only became more familiar with the types and authors of children's literature that were available in Spanish, but I also became a more astute evaluator of quality children's literature in Spanish.

Seeking out authentic and appropriate reading materials is an endeavor every teacher experiences. Kacey and her other colleagues realized while creating a bilingual children's library for the program that finding appropriate bilingual materials is more challenging than the mainstream teacher, since children's literature in Spanish and Chinese are scarce in the US. Additionally, just because a book is in Spanish does not mean it is appropriate for a first grader to read.

Coursework also helped candidates with their classroom cultural practice. This is the second theme that emerged. Candidates experienced first-hand how the social and political aspects of bilingual education affected their own classroom. Instead of having daily bureaucracy paralyze their teaching practices, they appeared to take more ownership of their practices and were able to look at their teaching development beyond those challenges. In Jackie, a self-identified Latina, we see emergent understandings of a larger discourse of bilingual education:

> During those tutoring sessions, I became aware of some of the political aspects of bilingual education and these insights helped me better understand my first semester classes, particularly, Foundations of Bilingual Education and Cross-Cultural Communication and Classroom Ecology. Additionally, I was able to practice some of the skills I learned about in TESOL Methods K-6, particularly language assessments and Language Experience Approach teaching strategies. As a first semester student without experience leading my own classroom, the real-life experience tutoring in a classroom in New York helped me feel more connected to my studies and kept me motivated.
>
> (Jackie, Spring 2008 Self-reflection Paper)

Ida, also saw the development of her teaching practices based on her understanding of students' learning abilities and styles. For her, the discourse involved the day-to-day practice of working with the students. She volunteered to stay after school and work with one male student in a South Bronx middle school for one semester. After struggling to understand how to teach him to enjoy learning, she was able to shift her own ways of knowing, seeing into his perspective:

> When we were working together, I could really see a difference in the student during regular class time. I don't know if it was him just getting acclimated to

the class before the other students arrived, but I think it was that we were able to work on work that not only interested him, but in which he was central to the thinking and figuring out process. I thought that the poem, "Where I am from" was a great example of how the student was engaged in school work ... I also addressed his love of geography and we would talk about the countries that our families were from in both English and Spanish. He could go on for hours about the topic and would always mention it throughout the day on the days we worked with the atlas.

(Ida, Fall 2008 Final Evaluation)

While classes in the program informed understandings, the pattern, when they were able to put theories into practice, showed a clear shift or repositioning of their own cultural mode of knowledge. While this new shift allowed them to be creative and confident in their identities as candidates in the program and teachers of BLs, it also shaped and was shaped by their agency as they created new meanings for motivation and hope for their career and for the field.

Disruption and Agency

Our last question was a concern. We wanted to identify moments of disruption and agency, particularly in the strategic making and remaking of the self, but we were concerned about being able to capture them adequately. We realized that while we could not capture the significant critical moments for all candidates, both disruption and agency were themes running through the first three questions. These two aspects of transformation, disruption and agency, were like the two faces of a coin, although our tendency was to focus on one or the other, as if they could be separated. For example, we were privy of the "aha" moment when a teacher finally realized, while standing in front of her third-grade class, why she became a bilingual teacher in the first place. If we only examined this moment, we realized, it would be adhering to a definition of transformation as only what could be. We realized that since transformation is dependent on where the individuals are and how they interconnect with broader social issues, where they are coming from and what they define as oppression; a disruption or a place of departure is critical as well. Both need to be highlighted. We realize that when they decide to commit to a person, a relationship, an activity, and especially to their life's work, it does not occur instantaneously, instead, it is a process, experienced and reflected upon from awhile back.

Taking the issue of commitment as a place in the process, which would highlight both the disruption and agency relationship, we looked at discourse in reflections as moments when and where they made the strategic shift within the field and in their life when they made the commitment. We asked them to trace not just their growth as an educator and as a person, but the discomforts or disruptions that they experienced before they got to a moment of agency.

Ida is illustrative of the pattern found. She provided various anecdotes regarding her experience in the program and in her teaching. As she grappled with Spanish fluency, multiple commitments to family and jobs and, particularly, commitment to the program for two years, she voiced frustration with the process. Yet, she noted in her final evaluation that the required reflective process was absolutely necessary for her to realize her commitment:

> I know that it is difficult for me to participate in program activities because of my school, student teaching, and work commitments, but I feel it is a necessary part of my life because I have learned a lot about things that happen in the different aspects of being an educator … Another area in which I have grown is being reflective about my work. Being able to fill out these reflections at the end of the semesters has enabled me to put down on paper and look at how and why I have done things and make suggestions for my future work. In the past, I never really thought about what I had done and how I could make it better. Now, I always look at my past work, consider the situation I was in, and think about how I could make it more successful.

Many other candidates spoke about the importance of the reflection process during their program as a way of understanding their growth. Sebastian and Yvonne, both self-identified as Mexican-American, stated that being in the program had been a result of personal initiative for their life's work. Other students, such as Jackie and Kacey, felt the program helped them see the need to commit themselves to reach out and connect with others. Jackie wrote the following about her fellowship study group:

> Interacting with … [colleagues] … has helped me understand the diversity of experiences in our program and the value of coming together to share our perspectives, hopes, and frustrations in affecting change in our classrooms and communities. As a returning … [student], I feel that … this year I could help new … students … feel welcome in our group as we draw on past programs and study groups to move onward this semester. I also hope to draw on the momentum of last semester and encourage all participants to bring a sense of ownership to our commitment to the … program.

Kacey also spoke to her commitment to reach out and connect to others within the school setting in the following writing:

> Once again, I turned to the community. I first connected with individual parents through phone calls and frequent written notes. I listened to both what was happening with their children and what was happening with them. As the trust in our relationship grew, I learned more about their cultures and family histories. I asked them to share information and resources about their cultural traditions and holidays so that our class community could reflect their values.

In summary, we found that process of reflection assisted in the process of identity development as teachers and in the verbalization of their struggles, disruptions and agency, as they commit to the field. Their commitment went beyond the program, classroom, and community of teachers in the field; it was ultimately to the children and school communities.

Conclusions

Inquiries on transformation center on the relationship between the process and the nature of who we are as we go through and are confronted by new situations. The chrysalis/*crisálida* we have come to understand as a phase and a process depending on the protective needs of the caterpillar—the beautiful jade green shell hardens or softens around the ribbed body of the caterpillar. We learned that in the chrysalis, we could start to see the caterpillar evolving to take a fuller body. It becomes a nesting place, a place that pumps life and energy into the butterfly. It served as a metaphor for the preparation program as we see individuals evolving and taking on the role of teacher; we see it as a safe place from which individuals work their aspirations and dreams into realities of classrooms and embodiment of theories.

Within, we have discussed the repositioning, as Guerra (2007) proposes, of the teachers to be as largely transcultural in nature, where we see multiplicity, fragmentation, and hybridity. One of the ways this occurred was in the comparative nature of life narratives. Whether choosing the profession, creating authentic views of self, committing to constant improvement as a professional, putting into practice what they learned in theory, creating classroom cultures of learning, and reflecting, and committing themselves to the professional field and the communities they serve, there was always some level of comparison with their own past or in relation with their internal dialogue with others. Furthermore, the shifts in learning and identity formation, as Lave (1996) and Gee (2001) propose as two parallel journeys are at some point the same, such that new identities move along with new forms of knowledge, and participation, and positioning.

The time and space of shifts in identity development is individually determined. We found that the different components constituting programs, such as coursework, fieldwork, language and cultural development, reflection and inquiry, understanding and acting on social justice and equity, vary as to when and how they become a cause or context for the identity development and transformation of bilingual teachers. These shifts are accompanied both by some level of disruption and agency.

Thus, our focus on the process permitted us to capture where the potential for new possibilities are born and take shape. When studying teacher identity development as a process, we contend that it would be possible to understand how teachers develop voice (Nevárez-La Torre, 1999), what might influence their teaching at different points in their development (Flores, 2001), and how social justice curriculum can be realized in their classrooms (Nieto, 2000). We believe that by examining programs as a process of assisting candidates to develop identities as teachers of BLs, we will be able to rethink programs so that the questions candidates begin to ask are not about what do I do the first day but what are the differences in social organizations that might inhibit or promote learning (Gutierrez, 2009) or what do I learn from being exposed to the families of my students that I can bring into the conversation with my students (Téllez, 2002), or what funds of knowledge or learning strategies from the child's home and community can I incorporate in the curriculum (González, Moll, & Amanti, 2005)?

Transforming Teacher Preparation

As we conclude, we would like to strongly recommend that programs:

1 Promote reflections that reveal how candidates are assuming their roles as teachers and what is triggering shifts in their views.
2 Collect and analyze reflection data for the purpose of program development that is inclusive of the immediate and long-term needs of candidates.
3 Share analyzed data with candidates so it permits them to understand how they can pull from their past as an intellectual resource that can assist them to envision themselves as future teachers.
4 Share with students the importance of theory and its role in the process of transformation, shifting identities, and practices.
5 Promote professional development among faculty through the analysis of data on candidate identity development.

Research Directions

As teacher educators we suffer, like teachers in schools, instructional isolation. We teach our courses in almost complete seclusion from others. Faculty may come together for administrative and programmatic work, but rarely stop to view their work from the standpoint of process and, less frequently, from the perspective of identity development. For us, it was instructive to analyze the data from this framework and to understand candidate discourse, partially generated by us.

We were able to see how it is a natural tendency to make judgments about candidates as capable or incapable, when we looked at components, but we also saw different and more exciting possibilities if we looked at them as unfinished, as someone in the process of authentication and becoming. Thus, we felt that we need to promote research that:

1 Focuses on the process candidates undertake to become bilingual education teachers;
2 Engages in comparative analysis across national and international bilingual teacher education programs to better understand what is unique to a specific program and what is constitutive to programs, in general; and
3 Promotes nationally and internationally communication on bi/multilingual teacher education and candidate and teacher identity.

We propose that our findings, while limited to one program, can help others conceptualize, name, and study the process their candidates undertake to become teachers. We know that programs are constrained by state mandates, but whatever these may be and however we might organize courses and fieldwork experiences, it would benefit us to know how candidates reposition themselves, transculturally in relation to the students and community they will serve.

References

Berliner, D. C. (1990). If the metaphor fits, why not wear it?: The teacher as executive. *Theory into Practice, 29*(2), 85–93.

Bucholtz, M., & Hall, K. (2005). Identity and interaction: A sociocultural linguistic approach. *Discourse Studies, 7*(4–5), 585–614.

Canales, J., & Ruiz-Escalante, J. A. (1992). *A pedagogical framework for bilingual education teacher preparation programs.* Retrieved from http://www.ncbe.gwu.edu/ncbepubs/symposia/third/canales.htm

Clarke, M. (2008). *Language teacher identities: Co-constructing discourse and communities.* Clevedon, UK: Multilingual Matters.

Cummins, J. (1996). *Negotiating identities: Education for empowerment in a diverse society.* Los Angeles: California Association for Bilingual Education.

Flores, B. B. (2001). Bilingual education teachers' beliefs and their relation to self-reported practices. *Bilingual Research Journal, 25*(3), 1–23.

Freire, P. (2001). *Pedagogy of freedom: Ethics, democracy, and civic courage.* Lanham, MD: Rowman & Littlefield.

Gee, J. P. (1996). *Social linguistics and literacies: Ideology in discourses.* Bristol, PA: Taylor & Francis.

Gee, J. P. (2001). Identity as an analytic lens for research in education. *Review of Research in Education, 25,* 99–125.

Gonzalez, N., Moll, L. C., & Amanti, C. (2005). *Funds of knowledge: Theorizing practice in households and classrooms.* Mahwah, NJ: Erlbaum.

Guerra, J. C. (2007). Out of the valley: Transcultural repositioning as a rhetorical practice in ethnographic research and other aspects of everyday life. In C. Lewis, P. Encino, & E. B. Moje (Eds.), *Reframing sociocultural research in literacy* (pp. 137–162). Mahwah, NJ: Erlbaum.

Gutierrez, K. (2009). *University-community partnerships and technology-based learning of youths in after-school settings.* Presented at the American Educational Research Association Annual Meeting, San Diego, CA.

Hakuta, K. (1986). *Mirror of language: The debate on bilingualism.* New York: Basic Books.

Hall, S. (1997). Old and new identities, old and new ethnicities. In A. King, (Ed.), *Culture, globalization and the world system: Contemporary conditions for the representation of identity* (pp. 41–69). Minneapolis: University of Minnesota Press.

Halliday, M. A. K. (1973), *Explorations in the functions of language* (Dilin İşlevlerinde Keşifler). London: Edward Arnold.

Hollins, E., & Torres-Guzman, M. E. (2005). Research on preparing teachers for diverse populations. In M. Cochran-Smith & K. Zeichner (Eds.), *Studying teacher education: The report of the AERA panel on research and teacher education* (pp. 477–548). Mahwah, NJ: Erlbaum/AERA.

Hubbard, R. S., & Power, B. M. (2003). *The art of classroom inquiry: A handbook for teacher researchers.* Portsmouth, NH: Heinemann.

Lave, J. (1996). Teaching, as learning, in practice. *Mind, Culture, and Activity, 3*(3), 149–164.

Lave, J., & Wenger, E. (1990). *Situated learning: Legitimate peripheral participation.* Cambridge: Cambridge University Press.

Lewis, C., Enciso, P., & Moje, E. B. (2007). *Reframing sociocultural research on literacy: Identity, agency and power.* Mahwah, NJ: Erlbaum.

Nevárez-La Torre, A. A. (1999). Developing voice: Teacher-research in bilingual classrooms. *Bilingual Research Journal, 23*(4), 451-470.

Nieto, S. (2000). *Affirming diversity.* New York: Longman.

Pavlenko, A. (2003). The making of an American: Negotiation of identities at the turn of the twentieth century. In A. Pavlenko & A. Blackledge (Eds.), *Negotiation of identities in multilingual contexts* (pp. 34–67). Clevedon, UK: Multilingual Matters.

Téllez, K. (2002). Multicultural education as subtext. *Multicultural Perspectives, 4*(2), 21–26.

Trueba, H. T. (1999). *Latinos unidos: From cultural diversity to the politics of solidarity*. New York: Rowman & Littlefield.

Vygotsky, L. (1962). *Thought and language*. Cambridge, MA: MIT Press.

Part III

Praxis

A critical bicultural pedagogy can emerge within a social context where teachers
are ground in a commitment to both individual and social empowerment.

Antonia Darder. (1991). *Culture and power in the classroom:
A critical foundation for bicultural education.* Westport, CT:
Bergin & Garvey, p. 127.

8 *El Aprendizaje por Medio del Juego*

Bilingual Early Childhood Settings

Mari Riojas-Cortez and Iliana Alanís

¿Quiénes Son los Niños?

Census projections for the youngest children suggest that by 2050 Latin@s under the age of five will number 8.6 million compared with Whites numbering 12.3 million (U.S. Census Bureau, 2004); many of them growing up as Bilingual Learners (BLs). Quality early childhood programs, particularly prekindergarten (Pre-K), with well-prepared teachers are therefore necessary to meet the needs of this changing demographics (see Chapter 1). Important to note, however, that quality early childhood programs for this population are often defined as "intervention programs" because the focus is on increasing the cognitive and social emotional development of young preschoolers. The problem with the word "intervention" is that it assumes there is something wrong with the children and that is why intervention is needed. Studies such as one conducted by Fuller et al. (2009) describe young BLs as lacking in cognitive skills and, therefore, in need of immediate intervention.

Many states, such as Texas, primarily offer Pre-K programs for children who are: second language learners, homeless, low-income or dependents of a military active-duty parent. Interestingly, Oklahoma, Georgia, and New York have strong initiatives to create universal Pre-K programs to serve all children. Over 38 states that provide funding for half-day Pre-K experienced a 40% enrollment increase over the last five years (Barnett, Hustedt, Hawkinson, & Robin, 2006). The increase in Pre-K programs creates a need to recruit and prepare early childhood bilingual teachers. Institutions of higher education must address the preparation of Pre-K bilingual education candidates.

How teachers engage children in early childhood settings is largely determined by the shared philosophy that children learn by engaging them in developmentally appropriate practices (DAP) such as play in which children are actively co-constructing knowledge. Teacher preparation programs must ensure that bilingual early childhood teacher candidates are prepared with the tools for creating a child-centered ecology. This can be accomplished through course work focusing on bilingual early childhood education and emphasizing the importance of play theory for learning and teaching.

Play Theory for Learning and Development

A strong well-defined philosophy regarding how children learn allows bilingual early childhood teacher candidates to create contexts that are supportive of young children's learning. It is vital to understand that play begins at birth (Lillemyr, 2009) and children come with a variety of play experiences depending on their cultural background. We support socioconstructivism as well as culturally and developmentally appropriate practices (CDAP), acknowledging that children use their culture as a learning tool and interact through play to make learning meaningful. Observing play allows candidates to learn more about children's cognitive, cultural, linguistic, socio-emotional, and physical development. Play is particularly important for young BLs, since often they are marginalized from playful learning opportunities (Long, Volk, & Gregory, 2007).

While creating a child-centered, play-based, active-learning environment defines Pre-K classroom practice, many teachers do not associate play with learning academic skills. A strong body of literature establishes the importance of play for learning. Recent studies found that symbolic substitution related to sociodramatic play as a strong predictor for early reading and math skills (Hanline, Milton, & Phelps, 2008). This scholarship further supports that candidates need a strong play theoretical foundation to substantiate the role of play for BLs. For example, understanding the different categories of play can assist candidates in selecting appropriate areas and materials to enhance children's developmental linguistic, social, and academic skills.

Yet, after an intensive search of major universities across the US that offered bilingual education programs, we found that almost no program of study included a course in play or early childhood development. Additionally, the coursework that was offered focused exclusively on language and identity issues. For teachers of young children, it is important that they understand how language and identity are intertwined within the different developmental areas including emotional, social, cognitive, physical, and cultural.

In this chapter, we identify four objectives in the preparation of bilingual Pre-K candidates:

1 Understanding play theory and valuing the importance of play for children's acquisition of concepts and skills related to academic, linguistic, and social development.
2 Recognizing the role of play for learning and teaching in bilingual settings.
3 Creating play environments in the bilingual education classrooms.
4 Identifying issues that prevent Pre-K teachers from offering play environments.

Theoretical Framework

Socioconstructivists believe that learning is socially mediated and rooted in a specific cultural and historical context (Munzó & Rueda, 2001). This theory, based on Vygotsky's (1978) premise that children's mental, linguistic, and social development is supported by more competent others through social interactions within a social context. Thus, children learn through interactions with more knowledgeable persons, creating a cognitive and developmental zone of proximal development (ZPD) (Vygotsky, 1978). In the ZPD, learning is scaffolded to provide a foundation to support development of complex skills and concepts (Tharp & Gallimore, 1989). This foundation includes the prior knowledge needed to understand new concepts and the assistance required to assimilate or accommodate new knowledge with existing knowledge. As teachers scaffold children's learning, they allow them to gain higher levels of understanding (Morrison, 2008). The ZPD is constantly moving and changing, as children's understandings are refined through assistance and scaffolding by others (Morrison, 2008).

The experiences and skills bilingual young children bring to school are the critical resources of prior knowledge used to make connections with new concepts (Munzó & Rueda, 2001). This depends on teacher skill to relate new concepts to children's funds of knowledge (Moll, Amanti, Neff, & González, 1992). When teachers promote social interaction through play, children learn and develop knowledge from one another. They integrate cultural knowledge and make connections to the children's personal experiences.

Socioconstructivism and Play Theory

Vygostky (1978) believes that play is an important medium to develop social skills through the ZPD. Bodrova and Leong (2003) explain that Vygotsky viewed play as foundational for later learning. When children play, they deepen conceptual understandings and develop language through the negotiation process with others (Morrison, 2008). Engaging in different types of play, such as constructive and sociodramatic play, enhances children's cognitive skills.

Cognition and Play

Early childhood theorists, such as Piaget, Vygotsky, Erikson, and Bruner have established the importance of play for children's development. They concur that play allows children to perform different cognitive tasks such as problem solving, cause and effect, and comprehension. Pre-K children develop cognitive skills such as reasoning, perception, numeracy, memory, and language through play.

Constructive play with blocks, art materials, or sand and water, children work with others, practice spatial-temporal and analytic skills, and acquire concepts (Cohen & Uhry, 2007), as well as develop mathematical abilities (Glaister & Glaister, 2007; Miyakawa, Kamii, & Nagahiro, 2005; Wolfgang, Stannard, & Jones, 2001).

The types of blocks found in Pre-K classrooms vary, depending on the teacher's understanding of the importance of block play or on available resources. Block play allows children to utilize and enhance cognitive, social, motor, and linguistic skills (Santrock, 2004; Stroud, 1995). During block play children use cognitive skills including imagination, logical reasoning, problem-solving, sorting, and classifying (Johnson, Christie, & Wardle, 2006). Researchers also indicate that block play enhances discourse development (Wellhousen & Kieff, 2001). Riojas-Cortez (2001) found that Latino children who engage in block play use their culture to communicate thoughts by creating scenarios reflecting their funds of knowledge.

To help children create complex scenarios and enhance cognitive skills, the teacher can include reusable materials (Johnson et al., 2006) and add culturally relevant materials to the block center. Teachers can guide children through their ZPD and help them move to the next developmental level as they play using appropriate materials in block play.

Wooden blocks are often kept from Pre-K classrooms because many teachers feel they make too much noise and it takes too long to put them away. Other teachers simply do not see the value of block play (Tunks, 2008). Some prefer Lego because these take less space. Unfortunately, instead of focusing on developing children's cognitive skills, some Pre-K teachers concentrate on classroom management.

Through block play, teachers can see the influence of gender roles and cultural differences. As a bilingual Pre-K teacher, the first author often noticed that girls did not choose block play. When asked why, girls stated, "*mi mamá no me deja jugar con cosas que son de niños*" [my mother does not let me to play with boy's things]. Tokarz (2008) emphasizes the need to encourage girls to play with blocks to increase their language, cognitive, and social skills. Candidates should learn how to promote block play since children not only build structures; but, engage in dramatic play scenarios that develop language skills and reinforce dual language skills.

Cognitive abilities related to mathematical skill development can be taught or practiced by manipulatives. An appropriate activity for basic number concepts is the use of counters in math centers. For instance, if teachers are teaching a unit on self or family, they can add items or counters such as buttons. The game can use a sewing kit box—*la cajita de costura*. In the *cajita*, the children will find familiar items making play culturally relevant. Items can include buttons, thimbles (*dedales*) or thread spools or any item that children recognize. This game not only enhances cognitive and linguistic development, including counting and adding, but it also promotes imaginative play through culturally relevant resources. Consequently, teacher educators must provide examples of play as a tool for learning if candidates are to understand the significance of block and manipulative play.

Language and Play

Language development is a complex process. Young BLs have different levels of native language and English proficiency and with varying speech abilities. While some BLs have extensive vocabularies, others may use baby talk or decide not to speak, and for some, speech is incomprehensible. Consequently, teachers often have misconceptions about BLs' level of language proficiency. They refer to children, who do not have high proficiency in academic Spanish or English, as "having no language." Others judge BLs who code switch as confused. Such descriptions reveal conflicting ideological orientations regarding the nature of BLs' dual language development. Sometimes, in an effort to help BLs develop language, teacher talk becomes the dominant classroom focus rather than facilitating meaningful language events (Linfords, 1999).

A very important part of Pre-K classrooms is circle time, an instructional time centered on children's language. Teachers, who utilize circle time effectively, allow children to engage in meaningful language through playful interaction. For instance, Riojas-Cortez (2001) described a kindergarten teacher who used circle time to provide opportunities for student talk. This teacher guided children through routine activities such as calendar, attendance, and weather. On one occasion, children pretended to be the teacher when taking attendance; they discovered an equal number of boys and girls. Since this had never happened before, the children initiated a discussion on how to solve this problem. The teacher used this teachable moment to help children identify what *igual que* or "equals to" meant. As a result, these interactions yielded growth in math vocabulary and concepts.

Circle time provides opportunity to enhance cultural knowledge and promote second language learning (DeBey & Bombard, 2007) through nursery rhymes and songs. *Versitos,* such as *Tortillitas para Mamá* and *Pollito Asado,* create a nurturing culture, because these include an important family member in the child's life and, consequently are familiar to many young BLs. The song *Pin Pon* discusses self-help skills. It describes a little boy doll who listens to his parents and follows directions on appropriate ways to take care of himself such as: combing hair, brushing teeth, washing face, eating, and going to sleep. Many children's books and CDs include these traditional songs, which should be shared in preparation programs.

Traditional indoor and outdoor games also engage children in playful language. Many children in Mexico and other Latin American countries play *Los elefantes, A la víbora de la mar,* and *La rueda de San Miguel.* Riojas-Cortez and Flores (2009) discovered that many Mexican American parents were not familiar with such games and wondered why they were never taught in school. This is an example of cultural loss, which happens as families assimilate and acculturate. Thus, it is important that candidates learn these games. The first author was elated to see a dual-language first-grade teacher playing *Doña Blanca* during recess with ethnically diverse children. The game not only enhanced BLs' language development, but also promoted new cultural experiences for children not familiar with the game.

Another playful language-based activity for children during circle time is story time/*tiempo de contar cuentos.* It is important for candidates to understand that story time can involve reading to children (Alanís, 2007). Examples of appropriate literature for bilingual Pre-K classrooms include books that are not direct translations from English, but are written by Latin@ authors who bring young BLs cultural experiences in texts such as *Pelitos*/Hairs by Sandra Cisneros (1997), *Una canasta para tía* by Pat Mora (1997), *El árbol de Navidad* by Alma Flor Ada (1997). Candidates can become skillful oral storytellers (Alanís, 2007). Storytelling can occur during circle time, but can also be an outdoor activity. Teachers can select shaded outside areas to read, re-tell, or create their own stories. Parents can be invited during storytelling time. Riojas-Cortez, Flores, Smith, and Clark (2003) found that parents engaged in storytelling with their children used simple materials such as stuffed animals. Home literacy practices dispel the deficit perspective that young BLs experience few if any literacy interactions and activities at home (Riojas-Cortez, Flores, & Clark, 2003).

Play spaces provide opportunities for children to negotiate and practice literacy through their cultural lens (Wohlwend, 2008). For example, during sociodramatic play, children can create scenarios, use language to negotiate meaning and process (Garvey, 1990), and participate in various activities associated with their and others' cultural heritage (Morrison, 2008). In a *Casita* center, children can explore gender roles, cultural norms, and language patterns through playful interactions resembling those found in their environment. Children can create stories related to their home practices, thus utilizing funds of knowledge (Riojas-Cortez, 2001). It is through sociodramatic play that children learn early literacy skills, such as creating stories with characters, settings, plots, and solutions, and developed with the beginning, middle, and end. Reifel and Nicholson (2008) suggest that Pre-K teachers expand children's learning by documenting the stories created during play and sharing them with other children. Thompson (2008) maintains that dramatic play allows BLs to practice concepts they know and understand in their first language as well as communicate with others in the second language.

Outdoor Play

David Elkind (2001, 2003, 2006, 2007), a renowned child psychologist, has been advocating children-play for decades. He acknowledges that children need to play in a variety of settings for different purposes. Some educators may confuse outdoor play with recess, which is a traditional way of looking at children playing outside on the playground. In Pre-K classrooms, outdoor play benefits children by allowing them to: a) interact with one another to develop linguistic skills, b) negotiate relationships that enhances socioemotional skills, c) learn about nature to promote cognitive skills, d) practice self-regulation, and e) use locomotor skills which increases physical skills. Sometimes teachers want to add academic objectives to outdoor play, hence dictating children-actions rather than allowing choice. For example, Giles and Wellhousen (2005) describe teacher-tested activities that integrate reading and writing on the playground. Although these activities are well intentioned, the purpose of outdoor play is thwarted and children are not able to develop holistically during play.

In the public schools, recess seems to be the only opportunity for play. Unfortunately, teachers often use recess as a tool to shape young children's desired behavior and sometimes principals do not recognize the value of play. In a conversation with a school principal, who worked with a large population of young BLs, she proudly noted that her school did not have recess, "all the time is dedicated to academics" she said. Many young children in bilingual classrooms experience the same situation. In conversations conducted with bilingual early childhood teachers during classroom observations regarding outdoor play, many have indicated that they do not include outdoor play in their lesson plans because they are not required to do so. The first author's observations of bilingual early childhood classrooms also show that many of the teachers would mention the need for children to "go to the playground" to release energy and once the children were outside it was time for the teachers to socialize with one another.

Unfortunately, a literature search regarding BLs and outdoor play yielded no articles or books; the only topic was on young BLs' sedentary lifestyles and obesity. To break the cycle of misconceptions regarding outdoor play, teacher educators must discuss the positive effects of physical development on academic development. It is important to provide examples of how physical play, the development of gross motor skills needed to support fine motor skills, prepares children for academic learning by establishing the fine motor skill development.

The majority of research conducted regarding outdoor play focuses on environment and playgrounds (Frost, Brown, & Sutterby, 2004; Keeler, 2003). Although both topics are important, outdoor play also allows young children to engage in pretend play. According to Perry (2003), outdoor play allows children to experiment with different language and cognitive skills such as cause and effect, interaction, verbalization of a plan, and negotiation. Teacher educators must provide candidates with knowledge to engage children in physical play for specific purposes, such as practicing gross motor and fine motor skills.

Creating Play Environments in the Bilingual Classroom

Given the role of play on development, knowing how to create playful learning environments is critical for young BLs. Teachers have to consider the logistics and organization of the learning areas, what materials to include, and the relationship of learning areas to each other. Effective Pre-K teachers also consider that BLs learn best when teachers incorporate community linguistic and cultural resources including bringing families into classrooms where they are valued as experts (Riojas-Cortez, Flores, & Clark, 2003; Volk & Long, 2005). To create CDAP environments where play is the main learning mechanism, teachers, candidates, and teacher educators must understand essential areas to include in the classroom such as large space for circle time and games, small areas for learning centers, outdoor areas for motor play, and how to represent the children's culture throughout the classroom environment.

Learning Centers Support Play

Learning centers in Pre-K settings provide child-directed activities focused on learning needs and interests of young children (Morrison, 2008). Centers can promote children's social and language skills, but only if the teacher understands how centers benefit young children's development. Centers yielding rich language growth include housekeeping (*la casita*), blocks (*los bloques*), literacy (*alfabetización*), art (*arte*), and sand and water (*arena y agua*). *La casita* and *los bloques,* in particular, support sociodramatic play episodes where teachers can observe a variety of cognitive and linguistic skills as well as incorporation of children's funds of knowledge (Riojas-Cortez, 2001). Pre-K centers encourage child-initiated learning that promotes cognitive, language, motor, linguistic, and social development appropriate for young BLs.

Issues and Controversies Preventing Play-Based Classrooms

Clearly, there are many benefits for bilingual teacher candidates to learn about play theory and the role of play in children's development. We contend that there are however, several reasons that teacher preparation programs and teachers do not focus on play in the early childhood classroom. We discuss some of these in this next section.

Standards-Based Movement

Historically, Pre-K programs served to socialize children to the "rules of school" and to enhance their socio-emotional development (Fuller, Bridges, & Pai, 2007). Rather than focusing on development, the standards-based movement has pushed-down the academic curriculum. During recent times, the purpose of Pre-K is to provide children with academic, social, and behavioral skills necessary for kindergarten with a major focus on developing literacy and numeracy skills (Morrison, 2008, Strickland & Riley-Ayers, 2006). This academic focus has shaped, influenced and transformed Pre-K curricula and the activities of Pre-K children, particularly BLs. Preschools for BLs are standardized with scripted teaching, viewed as more practical due to unprepared preschool staff (Fuller et al., 2007). This shift has resulted in the reduction of play in Pre-K and its disappearance in kindergarten. Interestingly, many affluent preschools with White middle class populations continue to offer a play-based curriculum, where tests are not even considered. Conversely, in programs with low-income BL populations, there is a focus on letters and numbers through drills and memorization. Many Pre-K teachers believe this rote learning will help children perform well on district or state-mandated tests.

High-Stakes Testing

The standards-based movement has increased standardized testing in the early grades (Alliance for Childhood, 2009). The practice of testing four-year-olds and standardized preschool curricula is changing Pre-K education into an extension of K-12 schooling with pressures of accountability (Valdez & Fránquiz, 2010). Teachers working with four-year-olds are required to use instructional time to test children on basic skills so that teachers can identify the children that are "falling behind and require intervention" (M. Rosales, personal communication). This results in the narrowing of the preschool curriculum with little time left for unstructured playtime and recess (Wood, 2004). Conversations with Pre-K teachers reveal frustration with the amount of testing time. One Pre-K teacher commented, "We spend about two weeks just testing the children. No instruction, just testing."

Consequently, teachers are consumed with standardized testing and remediation instead of structuring indoor and outdoor playful learning opportunities for young children. In Texas, for example, districts that need financial assistance for their Pre-K programs are encouraged to participate in grants that focus on literacy readiness skills. Participating programs must use a state-mandated test, which may not be aligned with the Pre-K curriculum (Pre-K Directors, personal conversations). The focus on testing in Pre-K is troublesome because it often promotes excessive use of worksheets to benchmarking children's progress.

School Culture

School practices reveal misunderstandings of the benefits of play. For many administrators and experienced teachers (Bodrova & Leong, 2003), play is not allowed in academic settings because it is not compatible with schooling goals. A large number of programs receiving Early Reading First or Reading First federal grants serve BLs. These grants require Pre-K classrooms to have learning centers; however, the centers are primarily focused on discrete literacy skills such as letter recognition, phonemic awareness, letter writing, and word writing. There are no provisions for the centers yielding the most oral language such as housekeeping or blocks, and many administrators have asked teachers to remove such centers. Opportunity for meaningful play is not present in these Pre-K classrooms.

It is imperative that preparation programs teach candidates to become advocates of play for learning and teaching. Otherwise new teachers will erroneously rely on prescriptive teaching that does not allow a play-based curriculum to develop cognitive, social, linguistic, and physical skills in children. Additionally, preparation programs must show candidates how to comply with school administrators' requirements while at the same time providing opportunities for play in the classroom.

Transforming Teacher Preparation

We began this chapter by discussing the political nature of Pre-K education and its impact on Pre-K teachers, candidates, and children. We argued for the need to incorporate more playful learning opportunities to develop children holistically through CDAP. We focused on young BLs who come to school with prior experiences and skills that are often ignored or marginalized. Subsequently, we identified the need for Pre-K candidates to develop a strong philosophical view of play as the main source of learning and teaching for BLs.

Pre-K candidates must have a clear understanding of CDAP practices that promote social, emotional, linguistic, and cognitive development. As we prepare candidates to change existing paradigms, they must first understand the schooling obstacles, and know how to devise strategies to overcome such limitations. Since there are many competing philosophies bombarding new teachers, without strong sociocultural theoretical underpinnings, candidates may fall into the trap of "doing what has always been done" even when they know it is ineffective.

Teacher educators must be play advocates, have a paradigm shift, and be willing to *educar para transformar*. We must stop focusing coursework on how to teach children to read and count; instead we should emphasize play theory and its role of play in development. Faculty must infuse more culturally and developmentally appropriate practices in all areas of their teacher preparation program (Spodek & Saracho, 1990), not just in multicultural coursework. One strategy is to increase candidates' field experiences in diverse Pre-K settings, where the majority are BLs.

Research Directions

Research on BLs' play in classrooms related to learning and teaching is needed. Suggestions for future research examining complex topics or themes are listed below:

- Since culture shapes the way children learn, think, understand the world and interpret experiences; how do candidates and teachers respond to cultural and linguistic differences when structuring play environments?

- How does the incorporation of culturally relevant play in preparation programs impact candidate and teacher effectiveness and influence learning outcomes for BLs?
- While play is important in Pre-K curriculum, we remain unsure of how different strategies facilitating skills for BLs in various content areas influence specific aspects of development; therefore, how does play, within very specific content areas, influence social, linguistic, and academic development for BLs?
- As teachers face increased political pressure, we must examine how Pre-K candidates and teachers respond to such pressures and how they resist structures that threaten to create oppressive environments for young children. Thus, how do candidates and teachers negotiate the standards movement, high-stakes testing, and practices in Pre-K?
- What specific knowledge, skills, and experiences provide candidates the tools to resist discourse supporting standardized movements, testing, and administrative demands?

References

Ada, A. F. (1997). *El árbol de navidad/The Christmas tree*. New York: Hyperion.

Alanís, I. (2007). Developing literacy through culturally relevant texts. *Social Studies and the Young Learner, 19*(3) 29–32.

Alliance for Childhood. (2009). *Crisis in the kindergarten: Why children need to play in school*. Available from: www.allianceforchildhood.rog

Barnett, S., Hustedt, J. T., Hawkinson, L. E., & Robin, K. B. (2006). *The state of preschool 2006: State preschool yearbook*. New Brunswick, NJ: The National Institute for Early Education Research.

Bodrova, E., & Leong, D. J. (2003). Chopsticks and counting chips. Do play and foundational skills need to compete for the teachers' attention in a Pre-K classroom? *Young Children, 58*(3), 10–17.

Cisneros, S. (1997). *Hairs/Pelitos*. New York: Random House.

Cohen, L., & Uhry, J. (2007). Young children's discourse strategies during block play: A Bakhtinian approach. *Journal of Research in Childhood Education: An International Journal of Research on the Education of Children, Infancy through Early Adolescence, 21*, 302–315.

DeBey, M., & Bombard, D. (2007). An approach to second-language learning and cultural understanding. *Young Children, 62*(2), 88–93.

Elkind, D. (2001). *The hurried child: Growing up too fast too soon*. Cambridge, MA: Perseus.

Elkind, D. (2003). Thanks for the memory: The lasting value of true play. *Young Children, 58*(3), 46–51.

Elkind, D. (2006). The value of outdoor play. *Exchange, 171*, 6–8, 10–11.

Elkind, D. (2007). *The power of play: How spontaneous, imaginative activities lead to happier, healthier children*. Cambridge, MA: Da Capo Lifelong.

Frost, J., Brown, P. S., & Sutterby, J. A. (2004). The developmental benefits of playgrounds. *Childhood Education, 81*(1), 42–44.

Fuller, B., Bridges, M., & Pai, S. (2007). *Standardized childhood: The political and cultural struggle over early education*. Stanford, CA: Stanford University Press. Fuller, B., Bridges, M., Bein, E., Jang, H., Jung, S., Rabe-Hesketh, S., Halfon, N., & Kuo, A. (2009). The health and cognitive growth of Latino toddlers: At risk or immigrant paradox? *Maternal Child Health Journal, 13*, 755–768.

Garvey, C. (1990). *Play.* Cambridge, MA: Harvard University Press.

Giles, R. M., & Wellhousen, K. (2005). Reading, writing, and running: Literacy learning on the playground. *The Reading Teacher, 59*(3), 283–285.

Glaister, A. E., & Glaister, P. (2007). Math is just child's play in disguise. *Mathematics in School, 36*(1), 8–9.

Hanline, M. F., Milton, S., & Phelps, P. C. (2008). A longitudinal study exploring the relationship of representational levels of three aspects of preschool sociodramatic play and early academic skills. *Journal of Research in Childhood Education, 23*(1), 19–28.

Johnson, J. E., Christie, J. F., & Wardle, F. (2006). *Play, development and early education.* Upper Saddle River, NJ: Pearson.

Keeler, R. (2003). *Creating outdoor play environments for the soul.* Redmond, WA: Exchange Press.

Lillemyr, O. F. (2009). *Taking play seriously: Children and play in early childhood education—An exciting challenge.* Charlotte, NC: Information Age Publishing, Inc.

Linfords, J. (1999). *Children's inquiry: Using language to make sense of the world.* New York: Teachers College Press.

Long, S., Volk, D., & Gregory, E. (2007). Intentionality and expertise: Learning from observations of children at play in multilingual, multicultural contexts. *Anthropology & Education Quarterly, 38*(3), 239–259.

Miyakawa, Y., Kamii, C., & Nagahiro, M. (2005). The development of logico-mathematical thinking at ages 1–3 in play with block and an incline. *Journal of Research in Childhood Education, 19*(4), 292–301.

Moll, L. C., Amanti, C., Neff, D., & González, N. (1992). *Funds of knowledge: Learning from language minority households.* Retrieved from http://www.cal.org/resources/Digest/ncrcds01.html

Mora, P. (1997). *Una canasta de cumpleaños para tía.* New York: Aladdin Paperbacks.

Morrison, G. S. (2008). *Fundamentals of early childhood education.* Upper Saddle River, NJ: Pearson Merrill.

Munzó, L. D., & Rueda, R. S. (2001). Professional roles, caring, and scaffolds: Latino teachers' and paraeducators' interactions with Latino students. *American Journal of Education, 109*(4), 438–471.

Perry, J. P. (2003). Making sense of outdoor pretend play. *Young Children, 58*(3), 26–30.

Reifel, S., & Nicholson, S. (2008). Documenting children's play stories to enhance learning. *Exchange, 30*(6), 43–46.

Riojas-Cortez, M. (2001). Preschoolers' funds of knowledge displayed through sociodramatic play episodes in a bilingual classroom. *Early Childhood Education Journal, 29*(1), 35–40.

Riojas-Cortez, M., & Flores, B. B. (2009). *Sin olvidar a los padres:* Families as collaborators within the school and university partnership. *Journal of Latinos and Education, 8*(3), 231–239.

Riojas-Cortez, M., Flores, B. B., Smith, H. L., & Clark, E. R. (2003). *Cuéntame un cuento:* Bridging family literacy with school literacy. *Language Arts, 81*(1), 62–71.

Santrock, J. (2004). *Children.* Dubuque, IA: Brown & Benchmark.

Spodek, B., & Saracho, O. (1990). *Early childhood teacher preparation.* New York: Teachers College Press.

Strickland, D., & Riley-Ayers, S. (2006, April). Early literacy: Policy and practice in the preschool years. *A Preschool Policy Brief, 10.* Retrieved from http://nieer.org/resources/policybrief/10.pdf

Stroud, J. (1995). Block play: Building a foundation for literacy. *Early Childhood Education Journal, 23*(1), 9–13.

Tharp, R. G., & Gallimore, R. (1989). *Rousing minds to life: Teaching, learning, and schooling in social context.* New York: Cambridge University Press.

Thompson, S. (2008). Appreciating diversity through children's stories and language development. *Early Childhood Research and Practice, 10*(1). Retrieved from http://ecrp. uiuc.edu/v10n1/thompson.html

Tokarz, B. (2008). Block play: It's not just for boys anymore—strategies for encouraging girls' block play. *Exchange, 181,* 68–71.

Tunks, W. K. (2008). Block play: Practical suggestions for common dilemmas. *Dimensions of Early Childhood, 37*(1), 3–7.

US Census Bureau. (2004). *Hispanic and Asian American Americans increasing faster than overall population.* Retrieved from http://www.census.gov/Press-Release/www/releases/ archives/race/001839.html

Valdez, V. E., & Fránquiz, M. E. (2010). Latin@s in early childhood education: Issues, practices, and future directions. In E. G. Murillo, Jr., S. A. Villenas, R. Trinidad-Galvan, & J. S. Muñoz (Eds.) (pp. 474–487), *Handbook of Latinos and education: Theory, research and practice.* New York: Routledge.

Volk, D., & Long, S. (2005). Challenging myths of the deficit perspective: Honoring children's literacy resources. *Young Children, 60*(6), 12–19.

Vygotsky, L. S. (1978). *Mind in society.* Cambridge, MA: Harvard University Press.

Wellhousen, K., & Kieff, J. (2001). *A constructivist's approach to block play in early childhood.* Albany, NY: Delmar.

Wohlwend, K. (2008). Kindergarten as nexus of practice: A mediated discourse analysis of reading, writing, play, and design in an early literacy apprenticeship. *Reading Research Quarterly, 43*(4), 332–334.

Wolfgang, C. H., Stannard, L. L., & Jones, I. (2001). Block play performance among preschoolers as a predictor of later school achievement in mathematics. *Journal of Research in Childhood Education, 15*(2), 173–180.

Wood, G. (2004). A view from the field: NCLB's effects on classrooms and schools. In D. Meier & G. Wood (Eds.). (pp. 33–52) *Many children left behind.* Boston: Beacon Press.

9 Dynamic Biliteracy

Teacher Knowledge and Practice

Bertha Pérez and Mary Esther Huerta

Teachers are crucial to biliteracy development, yet empirical findings about the knowledge, competencies, and beliefs needed by candidates and teachers to scaffold and develop biliteracy are scarce. Many teacher preparation programs use state credentialing mandates outlining the knowledge and competencies needed to teach literacy, but there is little consensus and limited studies of the effectiveness of this criteria (Risko et al., 2008). Additionally, state mandates focus narrowly on literacy while bilingual teacher education candidates need to be prepared to teach both literacy and biliteracy.

Moll and Arnot-Hopffer (2005) studied sociocultural competencies and Jiménez (2000) examined children's biliteracy development. While both suggest biliteracy competencies for candidates, most programs have not incorporated this research to preparation curriculum. This chapter draws from bilingual teacher education, biliteracy, and second language research to address the knowledge bases for effective candidate biliteracy preparation. Biliteracy is viewed as one continuous dynamic "unitary process" (García, 2000; Jiménez, 2000). We examine how Spanish/English bilingual learners (BLs) learn to read, write, and think in both languages. We agree, "teacher education is a matter of developing technical competence of subject matter [literacy/biliteracy] but also sociocultural competence in working with the diversity of students …" (Moll & Arnot-Hopffer, 2005, p. 244).

Theoretical Framework

Preparation on biliteracy from a sociocultural perspective includes reading, writing, and problem solving within linguistic, culturally specific settings that embraces personal history, distinctive lived experiences, and engagements with the surrounding culture (Gee, 1991; Giroux, 2009). In this section, we discuss a sociocultural perspective for bilingual education teacher preparation and introduce the Model for Dynamic Biliteracy Development (MDBD). Our conceptualization of biliteracy and biliteracy teacher education is based on scholarly work (Huerta, 2005; Pérez, 1996, 1998, 2004; Soto-Huerta, 2010).

Sociocultural Perspective

A sociocultural perspective (Vygotsky, 1986) is widely used as a framework for literacy (Gee, 1991, 2000; Heath, 1983) and biliteracy (Jiménez, 2000; Pérez, 2004). This perspective is particularly suited in bilingual contexts because it views learning as culturally mediated through social interactions and languages. Sociocultural theory allows us to study how teacher–student and peer interactions influence biliteracy development. We define biliteracy as the use of or creation of text, written or oral, for thinking, reflecting, and problem-solving within a sociocultural, and bilingual context. This situates biliteracy development as a cultural practice.

Bilingual Education Teacher Preparation for Biliteracy

In the US where bilingual education is still considered compensatory (García, 2009), few Latin@ BLs achieve biliteracy. In other countries, biliteracy is an intentional educational outcome linked to the social elite or to global commerce (De Jong, 1996). At a policy level, becoming biliterate depends on existing laws, legislated policies, and national/regional political climates (Crawford, 2000; see Chapter 15). Biliteracy takes different routes depending on language program: BLs in transitional or immersion programs may learn to read in the first language and then apply and transfer skills in English, while BLs in dual-language programs often read both languages simultaneously.

Programs preparing candidates often depend on the commitment of institutional resources. A quality program includes: hiring competent professors, who are scholars and practitioners; sustaining relationships with model school sites for field practice; securing mentoring experiences for candidates and novice teachers (Pérez, 2004; see Chapter 1 and 2). Imbued in all these considerations are socio-political standpoints that either value or undervalue the development of competent and capable candidates with skills in developing literacies across multiple languages (Skilton-Sylvester, 2003).

Biliteracy preparation requires more than courses, readings, assignments, and field experiences. Candidate development is a dynamic and complex process of acquiring pedagogical skills, experiencing change and growth, requiring examination of beliefs and assumptions, as well as the development of problem-solving and reflexive decision-making skills (Flores, Kheen, & Pérez 2002; Pérez et al., 2003; see Chapter 4 and 7). Ginsburg and Clift (1990) argue for analysis of broader social contexts beyond the "pedagogical techniques and texts and materials within the program" (p. 451). Beyond knowledge and pedagogy, candidates must develop high levels of biliteracy to utilize metalinguistic and metacognitive skills needed to teach across languages. Teacher educators must be aware of candidates' literacy skills and cultural practices to guide personal biliteracy development and understandings of how this knowledge influences approaches to biliteracy (Flores et al., 2002). The knowledge base includes a critical examination of the teaching-learning process of Latin@ BLs and other bilinguals who successfully develop biliteracy. The following studies should be fundamental readings for biliteracy candidates.

Jiménez (2001) and Soto-Huerta (2010) studied how teachers mediated learning contexts that allowed, encouraged, and led BLs to acquire English and gain knowledge of the mainstream culture while maintaining and strengthening their first language and culture. These findings, supported by other studies, found that biliteracy development requires access to high levels of first language literacy (Pérez, 2004), availability of multiple texts in the spoken languages (August et al., 2006; Delgado-Gaitán & Trueba, 1991), and exposure to expert readers and writers of that language (Purcell-Gates, 2007). García (2000) reviewed bilingual reading research of children from several language backgrounds in different settings to understand how native language influences second language literacy. In these studies, the native-language reading measures were stronger predictors of second-language reading than measures of second-language oral proficiency. For older students, second-language oral proficiency measures were stronger predictors of second-language reading than performance on native-language reading measures. Proctor et al. (2005) reported how first-language vocabulary was the strongest predictor of fourth-grade English reading scores. Research on dual language programs provides additional evidence for the role of native-language in biliteracy development. Genesee et al. (2005), Lindholm-Leary (2003), and Pérez (2004) outline guiding principles for teaching in bilingual contexts to attain high levels of biliteracy.

Model for Dynamic Biliteracy Development (MDBD)

We conceptualize the MDBD (Huerta, 2005) building on prior research (Pérez, 2004; García, 1998; Jiménez et al. 1996; Jiménez, 2000, 2001, 2002) to illustrate the comprehensive, dynamic, multidimensional, and reiterative processes that candidates must learn to develop biliteracy while synthesizing complex biliteracy processes (see Figure 9.1). MDBD defines the act of reading as a symbolic, sociocultural situated cycle encompassing a complex range of biculturalism, bilingualism, background experiences, cognitive processes, imaginative and affective expressions, and abilities.

The model considers that BLs develop biliteracy through multiple configurations, meaning-making cycle, domains of knowledge, and levels of competencies. This cycle interacts bi-directionally with the six MDBD components to illustrate how the readers create and recreate the text. The cycle begins with engagement, and is reiterative as the reader proceeds to word level meaning, synthetic meaning, and interpretation. The components are complementary and can occur simultaneous. They include: language inputs, instructional inputs, literacy knowledge, literacy outputs, academic literacy, and affective support.

Language Inputs

Language inputs has three critical dimensions: child's background knowledge, parent literacy practices, and cultural literacy practices. The strong relationship between oral-language development and first-language literacy (Bialystok et al., 2005; Heath, 1983) require that candidates learn how home/community language practices contribute to literacy development and influence learning to read and write in two languages (Flores et al., 2002; Moll & Arnot-Hopffer, 2005; Pérez et

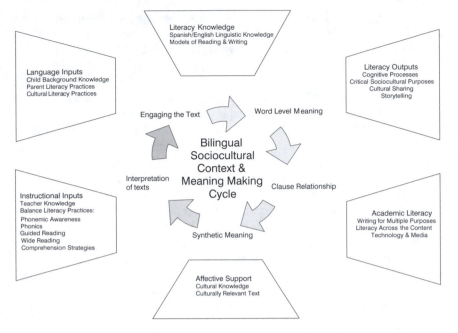

Figure 9.1 Model for Dynamic Biliteracy Development

al., 2003). From these studies, we glean how candidates' own language and literacy development impacts how they incorporate culture, background knowledge, and home literacy practices in teaching. Similarly, studies of children's biliteracy practices, elaborated below, discuss what BLs bring to literacy events.

CHILDREN'S BACKGROUND KNOWLEDGE

Culture and native-language represent cultural capital (Bourdieu, 1977), which, can be used to integrate new learning since it uses prior knowledge and influences ways of talking, acting, learning, and socializing (McLaren, 2009). For example, when BLs read the word *caramel,* cultural background knowledge helps them define the term. The word also includes context: the cultural, sensory, and affective responses experienced in the first encounter with *caramel.*

MDBD situates BLs' cultural background knowledge and first-language as primary inputs for literacy learning. Therefore, candidates should implement multiple pedagogical language strategies to identify and integrate background knowledge. They must discover how family members transmit cultural values, beliefs, and literacy practices to their children through home discourse and intimate discussions (Heath, 1983). Each family's cultural background mediates particular literacy experiences, which creates variability in biliteracy practices.

PARENT LITERACY PRACTICES

Candidates should be prepared to expect a range of variability of literacy practices among Mexican heritage parents (Duke & Purcell-Gates, 2003). Parents define what counts as literacy through practices and expectations. Candidates should acknowledge parental expectations and definitions of literacy. To illustrate, research on Mexican American parents reveal different views on schooling and literacy development (Delgado-Gaitán, 2004; Ramírez, 2003; Valdés, 1996). Some parents believe that good teaching relies on worksheets while others advocate inquiry processes. Some support native-language instruction; others want more English. To advance BLs' academic success, candidates must acquire effective biliteracy pedagogy for BLs and develop culturally sensitive strategies to mediate differences between parental views and schooling expectations.

CULTURAL LITERACY PRACTICES

What children read and how they discuss and interpret texts and word meanings are strongly determined by their cultural connections and the context of the literacy event (Au, 2006; Fitzgerald & Graves, 2004; García, 2000; Pérez, 2004). Au (2006) studied teachers' cultural practices around texts in Hawaiian schools and Pérez (2004) examined teachers' biliteracy practices in Sanish/English dual-language programs. Both studies found that children performed at higher reading levels when texts incorporated the learners' prior knowledge and experiences. Other studies of cultural literacy practices in multicultural, multilingual communities support strategies that value children's historical and cultural knowledge (Heath, 1983; Li, 2008; Moll et al., 1992; Purcell-Gates, 2007).

Attention to background knowledge and cultural referents is also important for older children. Older Mexican American children utilized a variety of reading comprehension strategies to understand a text once they identified the underlying cultural constructs (Jiménez, 2000). Jiménez et al. (1996) showed that struggling middle-school BLs improved fluency when instruction focused on the oral, rapid rereading of culturally familiar English texts. Candidates must examine how both familiar and new cultural elements in texts potentially facilitate or impede comprehension.

Instructional Inputs

The second component of MDBD focuses on candidate/teacher knowledge and the importance of balancing literacy practices such as phonemic awareness, phonics, guided reading, wide reading, and comprehension approaches in instruction. Additionally, MDBD proposes that teacher educators, candidates, and teachers become aware of the hidden curriculum defining power structures which imposes patterns of behaviors and ways of teaching in classrooms that may devalue biliteracy development.

TEACHER KNOWLEDGE

Teacher input may vary depending on individual knowledge of and concern with self-image, agency, materials, procedures, management, accountability, language, literacy processes, and individual student learning. A number of studies report that teachers and candidates experience developmental processes (see Chapter 4), beginning with self-image issues, leading to issues of curriculum and classroom management, and eventual evolvement to application of sociocultural theory (Achinstein et al., 2004; Flores et al., 2002; Pérez et al., 2003). According to Escamilla (2006), bilingual/ESL teacher educators often fail to examine "assumptions … of reading and writing research … these assumptions also include the widespread beliefs that reading processes in a second language may not be significantly different from those in the first language" (pp. 230–231).

BALANCED LITERACY PRACTICES

Literature on biliteracy examines learners and learning, context and purpose, curriculum and pedagogy in both bilingual and monolingual settings (Bernhardt, 2000; García, 2000). The findings support practices balanced among decoding, word level skills, meaning-making, and purposeful reading that includes enjoyment, learning, seeking information on the Internet, or sending text messages. MDBD promotes balanced literacy practices that incorporates how children learn to read, write, and problem solve in two languages. Special attention is given throughout this discussion on the need for candidates and teachers to be knowledgeable about and learn how to facilitate the transfer of linguistic skills and strategies between languages. Common literacy practices include:

1. Phonological Awareness. The current use of phonological awareness requires candidates to have strong first and second language linguistic knowledge. Phonological awareness is language specific; however, some studies found that a child's basic understanding of the function of the phonemic systems transfer from one language to another language, as in the case of Spanish and English. (Bialystok, McBride-Chang, & Luk, 2005)

2. Phonics. Knowledge of phonics in both target languages is essential. While the National Reading Panel Report (2000) reported that phonics could be an efficient tool for reading success, phonics is most effective when it emerges as a needed skill within the context of reading (Allington, 2006). Teacher educators teach candidates how phonics rules vary and how they are language specific. For example, teaching rime may be efficient in English but less effective for teaching Spanish words; and, the silent *e* rule in English does not apply to Spanish, just as the silent *h* in Spanish is not relevant in English.

3. Guided Reading. Candidates must learn to group readers with differing levels of literacy in each language, analyze how small group-guided reading influences reading performance in each language, and use informal assessments during guided reading. Formative data from Informal Reading Inventories (IRIs) and running records assess reading performance (Pérez & Torres-Guzman, 2002) and identify gaps in skills and strategies to help

teachers distinguish between what readers can do and what they are figuring out (Walpole & McKenna, 2006). Unlike other assessments, these tools provide clues about readers' attempts to acquire given skills or strategies. Using culturally relevant texts to assess skills potentially generates more accurate performance outcomes.

4. Wide Reading. Engaged reading depends on the degree of correlation between student background knowledge, preferences, cultural repertoire, and the texts read. For BLs, wide and frequent reading in a variety of genres enhances vocabulary development and improves comprehension (Proctor et al., 2005). Candidates must develop skills to evaluate, select, and use culturally relevant texts to provide ample access to a wide range of quality literature at readability levels in both languages.

5. Comprehension Strategies. Teacher educators need to explicitly teach about the association between metacognitive knowledge and comprehension strategies. Classroom instruction, however, typically targets a limited set of strategies (Afflerbach, Pearson, & Paris, 2008). Jiménez et al. (1996) identified four strategies that BLs in their sample used: questioning, rereading, evaluating, and monitoring comprehension. They found that efficient readers transferred knowledge, skills, and strategies across languages, and used translation and cognates during semantic processing.

Literacy Knowledge

The third component in MDBD concentrates on the Spanish/English linguistic knowledge of candidates and BLs as well as understandings of the various models of reading and writing:

SPANISH/ENGLISH LINGUISTIC KNOWLEDGE

Wong-Fillmore and Snow (2000) suggest that linguistic knowledge is essential, yet many preparation programs fail to develop this competency. They suggest that "an understanding of linguistics can help teachers see that the discourse patterns they value are aspects of their own cultures and backgrounds; they are neither universal nor inherently more valid than other possible patterns" (p. 5). Grosjean (1998) used the term "bilingual view" to describe changes when competences in two languages materialize. Candidates must learn two language systems, study the implications of knowing two languages, and seek possibilities of transfer to minimize interference to gain positive biliteracy outcomes (see Chapter 5). García (2000) found that Spanish phonological awareness and word recognition significantly predicted a BLs' English word recognition; and, that a key predictor of BLs' second-language reading was their ability to transfer specific linguistic skills. Bernhardt (2000) showed that BLs' reading comprehension represents a composite knowledge of the first-language, first-language literacy, and awareness of the linguistic overlaps between languages.

Candidates can learn how BLs use cognates. In an interview with Huerta (2005), Marta, a proficient Spanish reader at the beginning stages of English acquisition is able to define "acids" after reading a fourth-grade English science passage:

R: *¿Supiste el significado de la palabra* "acid"? (Did you already know the meaning of the word "acid"?)

MARTA: *Acido, sí. Lo usamos en casa. Usamos Ajax para limpiar el fregador.* (Acid yes. We use it at home. We use Ajax to clean our kitchen sink.).

Marta connected acid in English to *ácido* in Spanish, showing ability to draw meaning from text that was not language specific but based on a cross-linguistic transfer (García, 1998; Hardin, 2001; Huerta, 2005; Jiménez et al., 1996), and demonstrating skill to use cognates during semantic processing (Bernhardt, 2000; Hancin-Bhatt & Nagy, 1994; Jiménez et al., 1996). Explicit instruction of linguistic patterns, orthographic overlaps, and the application of morphology context sustains BLs' ability to draw inferences about academic words. This requires candidates to know the principles of first- and second-language acquisition and linguistic elements, such as discourse/text structures, and phonology/morphology systems of both languages. This knowledge base can help them organize biliteracy curriculum, implement reading interventions, and distinguish second-language reading performance from cognitive impairment.

MODELS OF READING AND WRITING

Two reading models—psycholinguistic and socio-cognitive—are most commonly used in schools. We suggest blending the two to advance biliteracy development (Pérez, 2004). The psycholinguistic model (Rayner & Pollatsek, 1989) begins with orthographic and phonological processing, whereas the socio-cognitive model (Scribner & Cole, 1981) proceeds from the whole text to the processing of linguistic elements. Reading instruction, based on this model, provides explicit and systematic instruction of linguistic elements to attain automaticity of language processing (Camilli, Wolfe, & Smith, 2006). The socio-cognitive model begins with students reading texts of their interest, with instruction about linguistic and textual elements presented when the student encounters difficulties. Both models require candidates to provide systematic and explicit instruction, which depends on having substantial knowledge of each language and a competency to teach a particular skill when needed or during guided reading lessons (Mathes et al., 2005).

Candidates should be able to guide writing development in both Spanish and English. Clay (2001), Ferreiro (1997) and Heath (1983) show that writing is supported through wide interaction with texts as well as engaging in personal writing. Writing development can best be supported with processes that include listening, reading, and discussing authentic literature (Chamot, 2009). Unlike a struggling monolingual writer, BLs in the early stages of second-language acquisition rely on available sounds, linguistic representations, and symbols of the first-language. Second-language writing instruction must offer BLs ample opportunities to write for personal expressive purposes and always with a focus on meaning-making. Candidates should know inventive spelling, code switching, stages of writing and how to encourage these. At the beginning stages of English writing, only a few pieces should reach the editing stage and the forms chosen for correction should be limited to those that impede meaning. Anderson (2005) found that academic writing competency occurred when BLs' goals included mastery of planning, monitoring, revising, and retrieving.

Literacy Outputs

This component includes cognitive processes, critical sociocultural purposes, cultural sharing, and storytelling. Variability in literacy outputs among BLs are not only a result of cognitive processes, but can be dependent on the teacher's knowledge and competencies in making school literacy accessible, transparent, successful, and efficient. Learner variability may be based on contexts that shift, cultural practices that define reading/writing purposes, the genre of texts, the type of structure used to produce written text, and switching between languages based on a particular literacy event.

COGNITIVE PROCESSES

The "Matthew effect" exemplifies how cognition, motivation, and affect are connected to reading attainment, and describes how repeated success enables better readers to further improve over time while poor readers struggle to find the key to successful reading (Stanovich, 1986). Successful reading triggers reinforcing cognitive processes that enable the storing of information into long-term memory (Perfetti & Bell, 1991). Bernhardt (2000) summarized the differences in reading processes of second-language readers stating:

> The mere existence of a *first*-language (regardless of whether it is only oral, or oral and literate) renders the *second*-language reading process considerably different from the first-language reading process, because of the nature of information stored in memory (p. 112, italics in original) … second-language readers come to the process of second-language reading with representations in memory that possess varying degrees of usefulness and relatedness for processing [of English texts].
>
> (p. 113)

Candidates must learn how to provide BLs with reading experiences that insure success by making literacy experiences transparent, by talking about and describing the cognitive process involved in literacy tasks.

CRITICAL SOCIOCULTURAL PURPOSES

First conceptualized by Vygotsky (1986), the sociocultural perspective has been widely used as a framework for understanding literacy practices, as the theoretical framework for research on biliteracy development, and for inquiry of teacher development. The sociocultural perspective views all learning as mediated by culture, social interactions, and language. Through a sociocultural lens, we can examine candidates', teachers' and children's interactions with others, with texts, and with their biliteracy skills. The MDBD model situates biliteracy development as cultural practice, focused on the central role of social interactions, and cultural tools, such as language and texts used by a community to teach, learn, and solve problems.

Children tell stories to recount past events, thus becoming active participants in literacy events through discourse (Heath, 1983; Valdés, 1996). Primary discourse, the ways language is used and valued in homes/community, provide essential linguistic cues that enable children to distinguish which story elements are valued, the level of importance given to details, how to sequence events, and ways of retelling (Heath, 1983). Another approach is the use of wordless books (Clay, 2001), which allows children to narrate stories through illustrations. Candidate can identify children's cultural ways of using language to create narratives. More sophisticated wordless books can be used with older students to assess language development through cultural ways of narrating.

Academic Literacy

In the MDBD, academic literacy focuses on three areas: writing for multiple purposes, literacy across the content, and technology and media.

WRITING FOR MULTIPLE PURPOSES

Clay (2001), Ferreiro (1997), and Heath (1983) show that writing is supported through wide interaction with texts and genres, as well as engage in personal writing. Writing development also depends on listening, reading, and discussing culturally relevant literature (Chamot, 2009). Teacher educators and candidates should explore research describing the developmental phases of writing where inventive spelling or code switching and language hybridity (Pérez, 2004) are indicators of second-language acquisition. Anderson (2005) found that academic writing competency occurred when bilingual writers' goals included mastery of planning, monitoring, revising, and retrieving.

LITERACY ACROSS THE CONTENT

Academic literacy can be demanding because of expository texts used in mathematics, social studies, and science. The semantic load of expository text may challenge BLs' comprehension. Candidates need to evaluate literacy demands of content texts. However, since there is a high-frequency of cognates in expository texts, the explicit instruction of cognates and Latin/Greek roots can aid Spanish/English BLs to efficiently engage academic literacy. Additionally, candidates must know how to guide BLs' understandings of the genres used in different content areas.

TECHNOLOGY AND MEDIA

The spectrum of electronic media (Eskey, 2005) such as using numbers on the keypad of a cellular telephone to access letters to generate text messages can be another form of literacy.

Affective Support

An important component of MDBD is the intersection of cultural knowledge and the affective domain. This domain was traditionally associated only with motivation. Jiménez' (2000) study of Spanish/English BLs illustrates the importance of cultural identity in literacy use. Environmental print use (Sulzby & Teale, 1991) is an example of how informal knowledge stimulates young children to read and write. Environmental print also plays a strong cultural and affective role in biliteracy practices of teens and adults (Kalmar, 2000).

CULTURAL KNOWLEDGE

Balanced biliteracy preparation programs adjust to include understandings of the relationship between cultural background knowledge and reading achievement. Readers use cultural background knowledge to construct a representation of words or referents (Oakhill, Garnham, & Reynolds, 2005), and to interpret teachers' expectations around texts. Research in bilingual contexts makes evident the need for activation and engagement of prior knowledge (Droop & Verhoeven, 1998). Candidates must learn to analyze how prior knowledge can scaffold the content load of texts, develop strategies that allow BLs access to a wide range of genres, and ensure that reading and writing tasks are relevant.

Most readers create their own meaning during reading, often different from the author's intent and generally based on the reader's own purpose. This is especially the case when cultural referents differ between the author and reader. Langer et al. (1990) found a wide range of text interpretation based on BLs' prior knowledge. Candidates must discern how cultural knowledge generates alternate interpretations. Capacity to guide the meaning-making process helps BLs draw relevant cultural knowledge during reading to support reasonable interpretations. Moreover, definition of interpretation of texts (Bernhardt, 2000) that considers cultural knowledge is broader than the ways school literacy defines reading comprehension.

CULTURALLY RELEVANT TEXT

Candidates must develop knowledge about the pivotal role culturally relevant texts have in enhancing fluency and comprehension (Jiménez, 2000). Reading texts about familiar topics enable BLs to engage in the complex reading process, understand content, and perceive the value assigned to the native culture. Moreover, by connecting cultural knowledge, BLs can draw inferences leading to comprehension. Huerta (2005) reported how fourth-grade BLs responded to comprehension questions after reading about a birthday celebration. Since the text was not illustrated, students drew from their cultural knowledge to generate relevant inferences.

Q1:   What do you think the mother is doing during the birthday party?
REINA: Letting the kids get in line to hit the *piñata* one by one.
ARIEL: Getting the food ready.
JAVIER: Talking to the people at the party.
Q2:   Why is that you can't see the *piñata* when you are trying to hit it? (Expected response: A handkerchief covers the person's eyes.)
MARI: Because it's more fun having your eyes covered with a handkerchief, cause you're going to miss, and the fun (of trying to hit the *piñata*) will last a little bit more.

Culturally relevant texts also hold implications for the whole meaning-making cycle, including providing access to vocabulary and linguistic features. For example, candidates can investigate how using a culturally relevant text facilitates phonemic awareness. BLs can be guided to isolate and blend phonemes using culturally familiar sounds. Teacher programs can explore the multiple implications of using culturally relevant texts.

Transforming Teacher Preparation

While implications for candidate preparation is embedded throughout, we argue for the benefits of a comprehensive model. The limited space allocated to biliteracy in most programs and the central role that literacy plays in all learning, demand that teacher educators and candidates have a holistic understanding of biliteracy processes. The intricate ways that literacy is culturally bound and socially mediated must be studied. The role of literacy in learning across the content areas is a goal not only within itself but also influences life-long learning. The decisive role that biliteracy plays in the academic achievement of BLs requires that candidates be knowledgeable and skillful. This is especially crucial during times of repressive accountability standards that impose "a uniform reading curriculum ... and ... direct instruction in" (Sunderman, Tracey, Kim, & Orfield, 2004, p. 234).

We suggest the MDBD as a framework for biliteracy candidate preparation. While the model is designed as content in a literacy course for candidates who plan to teach BLs, all teachers can benefit from this content. MDBD supposes that candidate learning takes place in sociocultural, socio-cognitive activities as they engage in clinical experiences in bilingual settings. MDBD embodies a dynamic and transformative approach to biliteracy.

Research Directions

Continued research on biliteracy is vital to the development of the next generation of bilingual education teachers. While questions about candidates' belief systems and their effect on decision-making contribute to a growing body of evidence, beliefs about biliteracy must be investigated. Research can inform knowledge and competencies within multiple contexts that teachers must possess to provide responsive teaching. The knowledge of linguistic features of both languages that candidates must possess must be examined as well as how candidates develop skills to access information about BLs' background knowledge; assessment tools and skills that more accurately evaluate BLs' biliteracy development; and, the overall effect of teacher knowledge of the reading and writing processes on biliteracy instruction and attainment.

References

Achinstein, B., Ogawa, R. T., & Speiglman, A. (2004). Are we creating separate and unequal tracks of teachers? The effects of state policy, local conditions, and teacher characteristics on new teacher socialization. *American Educational Research Journal, 41*(3), 557–560.

Afflerbach, P., Pearson, P. D., & Paris, S. G. (2008). Clarifying differences between reading skills and reading strategies. *The Reading Teacher*, 61(5), 364–373.

Allington, R. (2006). Reading lessons and federal policy making: An overview and introduction to the special issue. *The Elementary School Journal, 107*(1), 3–15.

Anderson, N. J. (2005). L2 learning strategies. In E. Hinkel (Ed.), *Handbook of research in second language teaching and learning* (pp. 757–771). Mahwah, NJ: Erlbaum.

Au, K. H. (2006). *Multicultural issues and literacy achievement*. Mahwah, NJ: Erlbaum.

August, D., Francis, D. J., Hsu, H. A., & Snow, C. E. (2006). Assessing reading comprehension in bilinguals. *The Elementary School Journal, 107*(2), 221–238.

Bernhardt, E. B. (2000). Second language reading as a case study of reading scholarship in the 20th century. In M. L. Kamil, P. B. Mosenthal, P. D. Pearson, & R. Barr. (Eds.), *Handbook of reading research* (Vol. III, pp. 791–811). Mahwah, NJ: Erlbaum.

Bialystok, E., McBride-Chang, C., & Luk, G. (2005). Bilingualism, language proficiency, and learning to read in two writing systems. *Journal of Educational Psychology, 97,* 580–590.

Bourdieu, P. (1977). Cultural reproduction and social reproduction. In J. Karabel & A. H. Halsey (Eds.), *Power and ideology in education*. New York: Oxford University Press.

Camilli, G., Wolfe, P. M., & Smith, M. L. (2006). Meta-analysis and reading policy: Perspectives on teaching children to read. *The Elementary School Journal, 107*, 27–36.

Chamot, A. U. (2009). *The CALLA handbook: Implementing the cognitive academic language learning approach* (2nd ed.). White Plains, NY: Pearson.

Clay, M. M. (2001). *Change over time in children's literacy development*. Portsmouth, NH: Heinemann.

Crawford, J. (2000). *At war with diversity: US language policy in an age of anxiety*. Buffalo, NY: Multilingual Matters.

De Jong, E. (1996). Integrating language minority education in elementary schools. Unpublished doctoral dissertation, Boston University

Delgado-Gaitán, C. (2004). *Involving Latino families in schools: Raising student achievement through home-school partnerships*. Thousand Oaks, CA: Corwin.

Delgado-Gaitán, C., & Trueba, H. (1991). *Crossing cultural borders: Education for immigrant families in America*. London: Falmer.

Droop, M., & Verhoeven, L. (1998). Background knowledge, linguistic complexity and second-language reading comprehension. *Journal of Literacy Research, 30*(2), 253–271.

Duke, N. K., & Purcell-Gates, V. (2003). Genres at home and at school: Bridging the known to the new. *Reading Teacher, 57*(1), 30–37.

Durkin, D. (1978–1979). What classroom observations reveal about reading comprehension instruction. *Reading Research Quarterly, 14,* 481–533.

Eskey, D. E. (2005). Reading in a second language. In E. Hinkel (Ed.), *Handbook of research in second language teaching and learning* (pp. 563–579). Mahwah, NJ: Erlbaum.

Escamilla, K. (2006). Semilingualism applied to the literacy behaviors of Spanish-speaking emerging bilingual biliteracy or emerging biliteracy? *Teachers College Record, 108*(11), 2329–2353.

Ferreiro, E. (1997). *Alfabetización: Teoría y práctica* (5th ed.). Coyoacán, México, D. F.: Siglo Veintiuno Editores.

Fitzgerald, J., & Graves, M. F. (2004). *Scaffolding reading experiences for English-language learners.* Norwood, MA: Christopher-Gordon.

Flores, B. B., Kheen, S., & Pérez, B. (2002). Critical need for bilingual education teachers: The potentiality of *normalistas* and paraprofessionals. *Bilingual Research Journal, 26*(3), 501–524.

García, G. E. (1998). Mexican-American bilingual students' metacognitive reading strategies: What's transferred, unique, problematic? *National Reading Conference Yearbook, 47,* 253–263.

García, G. E. (2000). Bilingual children's reading. In M. L. Kamil, P. B. Mosenthal, P. D. Pearson, & R. Barr (Eds.), *Handbook of reading research* (Vol. III, pp. 813–884). Mahwah, NJ: Erlbaum.

García, O. (2009). *Bilingual education in the 21st century: A global perspective.* Malden, MA: Blackwell.

Gee, J. (1991). Socio-cultural approaches to literacy. *Annual Review of Applied Linguistics, 12,* 31–48.

Gee, J. (2000). Discourse and sociocultural studies in reading. In. M. L. Kamil, P. B. Mosenthal, P. D. Pearson, & R. Barr (Eds.), *Handbook of reading research* (Vol. III, pp. 195–207). Mahwah, NJ: Erlbaum.

Genesee, F., Lindholm-Leary, K., Saunders, W., & Christian, D. (2005). English language learners in U. S. schools: An overview of research findings. *Journal of Education for Students Placed at Risk, 10*(4), 363–386.

Ginsburg, M. B., & Clift, R. T. (1990). The hidden curriculum of preservice teacher education. In W. R. Houston, M. Haberman, & G. Sikula, (Eds.), *Handbook of research on teacher education.* New York: Macmillan.

Giroux, H. (2009). Teacher education and democratic schooling. In A. Darder, M. P. Baltodano, & R. D. Torres (Eds.), *The critical pedagogy reader* (2nd ed., pp. 438–459). New York: Taylor & Francis.

Grosjean, F. (1998). Studying bilinguals: Methodological and conceptual issues. Mental control of the bilingual lexico-semantic system. *Bilingualism: Language and Cognition, 1,* 131–149.

Hancin-Bhatt, B., & Nagy, W. E. (1994). Lexical transfer and second language morphological development. *Applied Psycholinguistics, 15,* 289–310.

Hardin, V. B. (2001). Transfer and variation in cognition: Reading strategies of Latino fourth-grade students in a late-exit bilingual program. *Bilingual Research Journal, 25*(4), 539–561.

Heath, S. B. (1983). *Ways with words: Language, life, and work in communities and classrooms.* New York: Cambridge University Press.

Huerta, M. E. (2005). Biliteracy: Negotiating reading comprehension across two languages. Doctorial dissertation, University of Texas at San Antonio

Jiménez, R. T. (2000). Literacy and the identity development of Latina/o students. *American Educational Research Journal, 37*(4), 971–1000.

Jiménez, R. T. (2001). It's a difference that changes us: An alternative view of the language and literacy learning needs of Latina/o students. *The Reading Teacher, 54*(8), 736–742.

Jiménez, R. T. (2002). Fostering the literacy development of Latino students. *Focus on Exceptional Children, 34*(6), 1–12.

Jiménez, R. T., García, G. E., & Pearson, P. D. (1996). The reading strategies of Latina/o students who are successful English readers: Opportunities and obstacles. *Reading Research Quarterly, 31*(1), 90–112.

Kalmar, T. M. (2000). *Illegal alphabets and adult biliteracy: Latino migrants crossing the linguistic border.* Mahwah, NJ: Erlbaum.

Langer, J. A., Bartolomé, L., Vásquez, O., & Lucas, T. (1990). Meaning construction in school literacy tasks: A study of bilingual students. *American Educational Research Journal, 27*(3), 427–472.

Li, G. (2008). *Culturally contested literacies: American's "rainbow underclass" and urban schools.* New York: Routledge.

Lindholm-Leary, K. J. (2003). *Dual language education.* Tonawanda, NY: Multilingual Matters.

Mathes, P. G., Denton, C. A., Fletcher, J. M., Anthony, J. L., Francis, D., & Schatschneider, C. (2005). The effects of theoretically different instruction and student characteristics on the skills of struggling readers. *Reading Research Quarterly, 40*(2), 148–183.

McLaren, P. (2009). Critical pedagogy: A look at the major concepts. In A. Darder, M. P. Baltodano, & R. D. Torres (Eds.), *The critical pedagogy reader* (2nd ed., pp. 61–83). New York: Taylor & Francis.

Moll, L., Amanti, C., Neff, D., & Gonzalez, N. (1992). Funds of knowledge for teaching: Using a qualitative approach to connect homes and classrooms. *Theory into Practice, 31*(2), 132–141.

Moll, L. C., & Arnot-Hopffer, E. (2005). Sociocultural competence in teacher education. *Journal of Teacher Education, 56*(3), 242–247.

National Reading Panel. (2000). *Teaching children to read: An evidence assessment of the scientific research literature on reading and its implications for reading instruction.* Washington, DC: National Institute of Child Health and Human Development. Retrieved from: http://www.nationalreadingpanel.org/publications/summary.htm.

Oakhill, J., Garnham, A., & Reynolds, D. (2005). Immediate activation of stereotypical gender information. *Memory & Cognition, 33*(6), 972–983.

Pérez, B. (2004). *Becoming biliterate: A study of two-way bilingual immersion education.* Mahwah, NJ: Erlbaum.

Pérez, B., & Torres-Guzmán, M. E. (2002). *Learning in two worlds: An integrated Spanish/English biliteracy approach* (3rd ed.). Boston, MA: Allyn & Bacon.

Pérez, B. P., Flores, B. B., & Strecker, S. (2003). Biliteracy teacher education in the southwest. In N. H. Hornberger (Ed.), *The continua of biliteracy: An ecological framework for educational policy, research, and practice in multilingual settings* (pp. 207–231). Clevedon, UK: Multilingual Matters.

Perfetti, C. A., & Bell, L. (1991). Phonemic activation during the first 40 ms of word identification: Evidence from backward masking and priming. *Journal of Memory and Language, 30*(4), 473–485.

Proctor, C. P., Carlo, M., August, D., & Snow, C. (2005). Native Spanish-speaking children reading in English: Toward a model of comprehension. *Journal of Education Psychology, 97*(2), 246–256.

Purcell-Gates, V. (Ed.). (2007). *Cultural practices of literacy: Case studies of language, literacy, social practice, and power.* Mahwah, NJ: Erlbaum.

Ramírez, A. Y. (2003). Dismay and disappointment: Parental involvement of Latino immigrant parents. *The Urban Review, 35*(2), 93–110.

Rayner, K., & Pollatsek, A. (1989). *The psychology of reading.* Mahwah, NJ: Erlbaum.

Risko, V. J., Roller, C. M., Cummins, C., Bean, R. M., Block, C., Anders, P. L., & Flood, J. (2008). A critical analysis of research on reading teacher education. *Reading Research Quarterly, 43*(3), 252–288.

Scribner, S., & Cole, M. (1981). *The psychology of literacy.* Cambridge, MA: Harvard University Press.

Skilton-Sylvester, E. (2003). Legal discourse and decisions, teacher policymaking and the multilingual classroom: Constraining and supporting Khmer/English biliteracy in the United States. *International Journal of Bilingual Education and Bilingualism, 6*(3–4), 168–184.

Soto Huerta, M. E. (2010). Fourth grade biliteracy: Searching for instructional footholds. *Journal of Latinos and Education, 9*(3), 223–238.

Stanovich, K. (1986). Matthew effects in reading: Some consequences of individual differences in the acquisition of literacy. *Reading Research Quarterly, 21,* 360–407.

Sulzby, E., & Teale, W. (1991). Emergent literacy. In R. Barr, M. L. Kamil, P. Mosenthal, & P. D. Pearson (Eds.), *Handbook of reading research* (Vol. 2, pp. 727–757). New York: Longman.

Sunderman, G. L., Tracey, C. A., Kim, J., & Orfield, G. (2004). *Listening to teachers: Classroom realities and No Child Left Behind.* Cambridge, MA: The Civil Rights Project at Harvard University.

Valdés, G. (1996). *Con respeto: Bridging the differences between culturally diverse families and schools: An ethnographic portrait.* New York: Teachers College Press.

Vygotsky, L. S. (1986). *Thought and language.* Revised translation by A. Kozulin (Ed.). Boston: MIT Press.

Walpole, S., & McKenna, M. C. (2006). The role of informal reading inventories in assessing word recognition. *The Reading Teacher, 59*(6), 592–594.

Wong-Fillmore, L., & Snow, C. E. (2000). *What teachers need to know about language.* Washington, DC: Center for Applied Linguistics.

10 Bilingual/ESL Candidate Knowledge for Mathematics and Science Teaching

Sylvia Celédon-Pattichis and
Kimberly Gomez

Much of the work of science and mathematics classrooms revolves around communication (Ford & Peat, 1988; National Council for Teachers of Mathematics, 2000) of expectations, ideas, procedures, knowledge, outcomes, and next steps. Each form of communication works most usefully when teachers are clear about the form and type they expect to receive and when students know or understand the form and type of communication they should draw from, to communicate effectively with teachers about their ideas and understandings.

Torres-Guzman and Howe (2008) argue most teachers are not prepared to teach science to Bilingual Learners (BLs) and suggest that teachers value both the scientific discourse and the language and experiences that children use to interact in classrooms. According to Gutiérrez (2002), only recently have preparation programs offered multicultural courses but these rarely address language issues. Khisty and Chval (2002) found that teachers play a critical role in providing access to the mathematical discourse students need to appropriate the talk needed to communicate mathematical thinking. Clearly, preparation and professional development programs should offer explicit and scaffolded guidance about how to use language, culture, and ways of knowing to connect BLs to science, technology, engineering, and mathematics (STEM) disciplines.

Delpit (1988) argued that there are codes or rules for participating in classroom communication and other such contexts for talk, especially those in which one or more persons is in a more powerful position of knowledge and authority than the others. She alleges that these "codes or rules … relate to linguistic forms, communicative strategies, and presentation of self …" (Delpit, 1988, p. 86). She also stated that, "if you are not already a participant in the culture of power, being told explicitly the rules of that culture makes acquiring power easier" (Delpit, 1988, p. 86). In a similar vein, Villegas and Lucas (2002), in their framework for supporting linguistically and culturally diverse students, maintain that students need cultural and linguistic affirmation in their classroom context. In their view, this means that teachers provide a classroom context that recognizes and values the communication forms that students bring to the classroom and use language as a touch point for developing ways of talking and knowing in mathematics and science. For example, teachers invite students to participate in routines that engage the language of the discipline, while also making explicit the connections between the disciplinary talk and the everyday and home language.

In many mathematics and science classrooms, students are not experiencing culturally and linguistically affirming interactions, although their teachers would like to offer such contexts for learning (Curran, 2003). Teachers need support for engaging in mathematics and science teaching that moves beyond the narrow information delivery about the computation and procedures of mathematics and science; beyond the notion of texts, charts, graphs, and other representations as merely vehicles for content; and beyond classroom talk as merely opportunities for students to offer their answers to problems solved or procedures carried out. That is, teachers need to tightly couple mathematics and science learning to text and talk that support these subject areas. Experiencing and leveraging these moments as they arise in classroom instruction will help teachers recognize that text and talk about mathematics and science are essential to understanding, and particularly revealing of the ways that students are or are not learning to communicate in the forms of the discipline.

Delpit (1988) further reminds us that teachers need knowledge and skills that help students know that (1) they need to make sense of the language within the learning context; (2) they can get information with, and through that language; and (3) they can use the language for a purpose. The objective of this chapter is to illustrate classroom opportunities for such language use and to point to moments in which language can assist in the acquisition of mathematics and science knowledge. This chapter attempts to seek answers to the following critical questions:

1   How do teachers make communicative connections to students' community based "ways of knowing" during mathematics and science instruction?
2   How do teachers make explicit the connections between children's everyday ways of talking and canonical or form-based approaches of discussing mathematics and science in the classroom?
3   What are implications for teacher education?

Theoretical Influences

Several related theoretical strands influence our analytical approach to the work described in this chapter. These include sociocultural perspectives on teaching and learning, culturally responsive pedagogy, and language and literacy influences in mathematics and science learning.

Research and teaching informed by sociocultural approaches to mathematics and science centers on three related assumptions. First, the culture that many students experience in school in general, and specifically in mathematics and science, is often not consonant with the home culture (Aikenhead, 2001). Second, research and teaching with a sociocultural lens necessitates moving beyond an exclusive focus on the cognitive classroom environment and considers the social context of the learning environment. Third, and related to theoretical perspectives of language and literacy influences in mathematics and science learning (Lemke, 1990; Richardson-Bruna & Gomez, 2008), the content and form of the interactions that emerge in the social context should be considered. The language of argument supported by evidence and reasoning, the "objective" presentation of mathematics or science as "facts" rather than knowledge to be explored from multiple and differing perspectives can lead the learner to a bifurcated language and learning experience. Sociocultural approaches to teaching and learning (Vygotsky, 1978), reason that students need opportunities to see how their conceptual and linguistic home funds of knowledge and ways of knowing connect to classroom learning (González, Moll, & Amanti, 2005). Further, students need to see how this knowledge serves as bridges along a continuum of knowing (Strömdahl, 2003) from everyday to more canonical language in which ways of talking about, reasoning about, and approaching mathematics and science are leveraged by teachers and students according to context and need. Teachers and students benefit when students' linguistic resources are brought to bear on mathematics and science teaching and learning and connect students to scientific [and mathematical] ways of using language to engage in explorations and problem-solving. Next, we turn to explaining the methodology for the two studies.

Research Methodology

Data were drawn from multiple observations of two classrooms in urban school districts. Pseudonyms are used for places and participants. The first author spent over 18 months as a participant observer in a self-contained sixth to eighth grade mathematics classroom in Texas. The second author was a participant observer for three months in a sixth grade inquiry science classroom in a large Midwestern city, Westfield, and in the school conducting weekly observations for a year. The observation of the mathematics classroom was part of a larger study that involved an analysis of teachers' and students' language use to make meaning in an ESL/mathematics classroom (Celedón, 1998). The observation of the science classroom was part of a three-year study of sixth to eighth grade teachers' integration of literacy strategies into their science classroom teaching (Gomez & Madda, 2005). While the observations were part of different studies in separate regions of the country, they had similar aims, approaches, and populations. Celedón-Pattichis sought to identify ways in which a teacher leveraged language of her Spanish-speaking students to support mathematics teaching and learning. Gomez sought to understand how teachers, who participated in a literacy-infused (text and talk support) redesign of an animal behavior science curriculum enacted in their classrooms. We were deeply interested in understanding how teachers can help make content more accessible through explicit attention to language in their instruction.

Study Sites

The mathematics study was conducted in an urban public middle school located on the east side of Central, Texas. There were 1,175 students at Red Middle School. The school's ethnic distribution was 22% African American, 66.4% Latin@, 11.4% Anglo, and 0.2% Asian. Of the total population, 78.4% were low income, and 21.2% were BLs.

The science study was conducted in Regan Elementary (K-8, 1800 students) located in the inner city of a large metropolitan area. The school's K-8 population,

75% Latin@, 23% Polish, and 2% Black, reflected neighborhood changing demographics. Ninety-two percent of the student population was designated as low income and 41% BL. Within the district community, the school had a reputation for having teachers who were highly active in utilizing innovative curricula and participating in professional development activities.

Participants

The Teachers

Ms. Brown was selected as a participant because she taught mathematics to BLs. She had taught for almost five years, was certified to teach ESL and, in an interview, indicated that her teaching responsibilities were to teach both English and mathematics. In contrast to many teachers, Ms. Brown was an advocate for BLs. She moved students from the Advanced ESL/Mathematics classroom to regular or honors mathematics based on students' potential to perform in mathematics rather than on their English proficiency (Celedón-Pattichis, 2010).

Mr. Lewis sought participation in Gomez's study after learning about it through his principal. A child of Irish immigrants, Mr. Lewis professed a belief in the ability of all students to succeed in school in general and, specifically in science. He had taught for five years, expressed interest in improving the integration of literacy in science teaching and learning, and uniquely held an undergraduate degree in biology and a master's degree in reading education.

The Students

Ms. Brown's 90 minute block class had 22 middle-school Latin@ students (Mexican and Central American) identified as BL by their teacher and scores on the Language Assessment Battery. The students were in a self-contained ESL/mathematics class, which meant that 6th through 8th graders were taught in the same classroom. The students' English proficiency ranged from beginning to advanced levels.

Mr. Lewis' science classroom consisted of 30 sixth grade primary Spanish-speaking students. There were slightly more male students, 60–40 ratio, in the classroom and the students' ethnic group membership was 90% Latin@ (Mexican and Central American). The teacher identified students as BLs if they participated in up to three years of bilingual education as mandated by the district.

Students attended science three days a week including a 90-minute science block, twice per week, and one-day-a-week for 45 minutes of science instruction. All lessons were taught in English, and the students responded in English to the teacher's prompts, although they often spoke in Spanish to each other during group work.

Data Sources

We sought to understand and characterize teachers' and students' mathematics and science talk in the form of discourse scripts. We examined students' talk during a sixth to eighth grade mathematics classroom instruction and a sixth grade classroom science fair presentation. We contextualized the students' mathematics and science talk through teachers' interactions with the students during classroom teaching and learning contexts. We were participant observers in the classrooms two to three days a week during classroom instruction (Erlandson, Harris, Skipper, & Allen, 1993). During that time, students' and the teachers' talk were audio-recorded. We identified lessons that would best illustrate teachers' and students' math and science interactions based on three criteria: 1) community/school connections and/or use of the students' native language, 2) the lessons included reasoning/inquiry discussion or problem-solving, and (3) the audio-recordings were clear. This constituted our first broad level of analysis. In the data analysis section, which follows, we describe our specific analytic approach to the transcripts. In addition, we examined students' use of classroom learning materials and their interactions with peers and the teacher. The classroom data analyzed and reported here includes observational field notes and transcripts of the classroom presentation. The field note data were thematically analyzed. The classroom presentation transcripts were subjected to conversation analysis methods (Sacks, Schegloff, & Jefferson, 1974). To triangulate the data, we collected and analyzed classroom artifacts, such as teacher's records, textbooks, pictures, samples of individual student's work, handouts, and lesson plans, to support mathematics and science activities.

Data Analysis

The segments of talk highlighted are illustrative of the teacher-student interchange that often appears in the classrooms as teachers focused on encouraging students to explain their understandings. As described above, we selected audibly clear lessons for transcription in which there was evidence of talk that linked community/school connections and/or use of the students' native language and lessons, which included reasoning/inquiry discussion or problem-solving. Each segment of talk in the examples was first analyzed with respect to turn-taking and repair (Sacks et al., 1974). That is, we explored opportunities or obligations that students had to participate in an interchange with Mr. Lewis and Ms. Brown about the activity. The examples were also analyzed with respect to repair, in this case focused on the ways that teachers explained, extended, or advanced the students' thinking and offered corrections. Each segment of teacher and student talk (indicated by T and S respectively) was also analyzed. With respect to teacher talk, each segment was analyzed with evidence of teachers' use of canonical mathematics and science talk in interaction with the student and teacher connections to everyday meanings in language. With respect to student talk, we looked for evidence of students' use of procedural or heuristic mathematics and science terms, use of language that referred to artifacts displaying information (e.g., chart, axis), and use of everyday language to describe science phenomena that had a scientific or mathematics term and concept associated with it. In the following section, Ms. Brown and Mr. Lewis' interactions with their students during a discussion of percentages and fractions and weather changes, respectively, are the focus of this analysis.

Findings

Mathematics

In this section, we center on interactions between teacher-students to illustrate how teachers affirmed student everyday language to make sense of mathematics. We focus on how the teachers help make mathematics and science content more accessible to students. The teachers do this through explicitly clarifying homophones, words that sound alike but have different meanings and are spelled differently, and differences in everyday language and more formal content language, then making connections between the language students are most familiar with and mathematical concepts.

Mathematics and science discourse share several characteristics including, but not limited to 1) tendency to talk about phenomena as if it is constitutive with the phenomena itself (Gee, 1996); 2) related characteristic includes a tendency to nominalize (Unsworth, 1997); and 3) use of words that sound familiar in the primary or secondary language, but have different meaning and often have very specific meanings in mathematics and science. For example, words like linear and line again have similar sounds yet are spelled differently and have different meanings in usage. Linear refers to things created by lines. Lines are straight curves. The word line, however, also has many uses in English that could pose confusion for students. Teachers, who are cognizant of the role of language in content understanding and realize the need to help students gain access to content through language, are aware of instances when language confusion creates conceptual confusion.

In Example 1, Ms. Brown and students were solving a mathematics problem at the beginning of the year: Three-fourths of seventh grade students voted in the student council election. What percent of the seventh grade students did not vote?

EXAMPLE 1

1   T. We know how many voted, but we don't know how many did not. Right? So, let's go to step number two. I need a drawing, a table or some other picture of the information in the problem to help me understand…You're gonna make a model of the problem. That means you can draw a table. A table would be like what?

2   Ss. (pointing to a table in the classroom)

3   T. O.K.

4   S. *Mesa.* (Table)

5   T. *¿Qué es una mesa?* (What is a table?)

6   S. *Pa' comer.* (To eat)

7   T. So, this is a table to eat (pointing to the table in the classroom). In math, table doesn't mean this kind of table. It means a chart. It's like lists of things, and like that (pointing to a poster on the wall with a chart). That would be a table. It's almost the same thing as a chart. O.K. a graph. Very similar. So, what could we draw about the information we know? How could we show what we know?

In line 1 of the example, the teacher mentioned moving to step two which involved the students drawing a diagram, a table, or some other way to represent the given information. The teacher moved beyond following steps to ensure that everyone understood the mathematical meaning of the word "table." As shown in line 2, several students understood the everyday meaning of table, which they displayed by pointing to a table in the classroom. Ms. Brown replied with "O.K." in line 3, then a student switched to Spanish to confirm his understanding of the word. In lines 4–5, the teacher acknowledged the students' understanding of table and also used Spanish to ask what a table is used for, thus validating the student's home language. In line 6, one student thought a table was used to eat, which is the meaning associated with everyday language and context. In line 7, the teacher immediately affirmed the students' understanding by pointing at the same table students used and by expanding on the meaning of table in the context of the mathematics lesson by pointing to a chart that was on the wall and situating the discussion within the problem they were solving on percentages.

What is important in this teacher—student interaction is how the teacher supported students in communicating what they understood through their verbal and non-verbal language (Domínguez, 2005; Moschkovich, 2007). The teacher affirmed students' daily experiences with language and moved beyond the everyday context to make connections to the mathematical meaning (Khisty, 1995).

To begin a new unit on Bits and Pieces I of the Connected Mathematics Program, a standards-based curriculum, Ms. Brown wanted to establish where fractions were located on a number line to help students with number sense. She began by using 1 and 0 as benchmarks and having students find the location of those numbers on the number line first. She continued by asking students where a half and two-fifths would be located on the number line and by having students show the location of these fractions. Ms. Brown asked students if these fractions would be greater than 25 or 49 to check for number sense. After generalizing that a fraction whose denominator is greater than the numerator is located between 0 and 1, the teacher presented students with "what if ..." questions to ask about fractions where the denominator is less than the numerator (i.e., 24/8 and 25/8).

EXAMPLE 2

1   T. All fractions are between where?
2   T and Ss. Zero and one.
3   T. Any fraction you have is not a whole, O.K. *Bueno, hay una excepción. Si tienes una fracción ... si tienes una fracción* así (T writes 24/8.), *¿donde va?* (Well, there is an exception. If you have the fraction ... If you have the fraction like this (24/8), where is it [located]?
4   S. *Entre...* (In between ...)
5   Ss. Between the eight and the nine.
6   Ss. No, between zero and twenty-four.
7   Ss. Between the zero and the twenty-four.
8   T. What is this equal to?
9   S. Between three and the ...

10 T. This is equal to what?

11 S. Between three and six.

12 Ss. Three.

13 T. This is equal to three.

14 S. Oh, *sí porque ocho por tres son veinticuatro.* (Oh, yes, because eight times three is twenty-four.)

15 T. So, this goes at 3. This is 3. What if it was this? What if it was 25 over 8? (T writes 25/8.) That would be equal to three and what …

16 S. Five.

17 T. … So, twenty four eighths is three. So, twenty five eighths is three plus one left over, one eighth. So, three and one eighth would not go between zero and one. It would go between three and four. O.K., because you have three wholes, but you don't quite have four wholes. O.K., *entero.* (A whole)

18 S. *Como un pozo.* (Like a hole.) (Making the gesture of digging)

19 T. Oh, I don't mean hole like a hole. I mean whole like an *entero*, a whole with a "w." A whole with a "w" is not a hole without a "w." O.K. A hole without a "w" is that (pointing to what the student was showing). That's a hole. But a whole with a "w" *es un entero*, (It's a whole.) O.K. The whole, the whole thing. So, there are three wholes. (The teacher touches the number line so that students see where the three whole numbers are.)

In Example 2, Ms. Brown built up the concept of where fractions are located between 0 and 1 when the denominator is greater than the numerator. Then, in line 3 she presented students with a different case, where the denominator is greater than the numerator (i.e., 24/8). Between lines 4 and 14, the students were trying to figure out where to place 24/8 on the number line. Some students thought this fraction was between 8 and 9 or between 0 and 24 (lines 5–7). In line 14, one student used Spanish to make sense of why the fraction is actually a whole number. The teacher presented the case of 25/8 to see if students could make sense of the answer being between three and four wholes. In line 18, a student heard the use of the word whole and thought the teacher meant the homophone "hole." His gestures (Domínguez, 2005) conveyed his belief that when the teacher said "whole," she was referring to a hole in the ground. The homophone was a source of confusion that, in line 19, the teacher realized and then clarified the difference between the word hole and how a "whole" related to the mathematical meaning within the context of fractions, whole numbers, and mixed numbers.

These teacher–student interactions prompted the teacher to follow up with an activity that involved all students in creating a human number line to check for understanding of fractions. The teacher provided a fraction written on a card, and the students created a number line according to the order of the fraction they were given; students had to justify how they decided their placement in the number line (i.e., "I knew that 5/8 was more than half because 5 is more than 4, and 4 is half of 8"). She continued the discussion of fractions by referring to buying items that were 1/2 off the original price and making other connections to their personal experiences (field notes). Ms. Brown appeared to lead the students along a continuum of knowing (Strömdahl, 2003) about percentages and fractions. She also made the topic relevant to students by making connections to their personal, lived experiences and by extending students' understanding of everyday meaning of words (Khisty, 1995). A description of how this teacher's questioning patterns changed as she made the shift from a traditional curriculum to a standards-base curriculum is beyond the scope of this paper; however, Ms. Brown's experiences with implementing mathematics reform curriculum have been documented in Celedón-Pattichis (2010).

Science

In the first example, Mr. Lewis introduced the day's activity. The students had two sheets of paper on their desks. The first was a flat map of the world which was small enough to fit on their desks but large enough for the continents and many countries to be labeled. The second was a worksheet with seven questions.

EXAMPLE 1

1 T. … scientists have to explain why they did what they did … when you guys drew color maps or temperature maps … and you had to decide where the temperature ranges were and you had to have a reason why you put it there … And they're asking you why you may have drawn something on your map. They may ask you, did you draw the middle of the map red? They may ask you, how would you draw your map different if it wasn't drawn for the month of July? Remember, this was drawn for July?

2 S. Yeah, yea, yea, month of July fourth.

3 T. So, what if this was December, would this map be different?

4 S. Yes!

5 T. Why would it be different?

6 S. Because the weather changes each month.

7 T. Because we have a change of seasons, right? What's the temperature of [local city] going to be in December?

8 S. Like around 34.

9 T. What temperature range is that? What color would it be?

10 S. Blue

11 T. Blue

12 S. Green

13 T. So, think about it. The temperature in [local city] could be in the red range in the summer and the green range during the spring and fall, and in the winter it could be in the blue range. Do you think it could ever get down in the purple range?

14 S. No, it could.

15 T. It's possible. We've had some days where it has been 60 [degrees] below. How many of them have we had? A lot?

16 S. About three, three.

17 T. How many?

18 S. Three or five, a hundred!

19 T. We might have three or four in a year, right? Who said five hundred?

20   S. I said a hundred.
21   T. Only if you're living in Antarctica. There's only three hundred days in a year though.

In this example, Mr. Lewis tried to orient the students to the science task by reminding them that they had seen the worksheets before. In line 2, Mr. Lewis seemed to probe students' background knowledge by asking whether the map would be different if it reflected a December weather profile. In this way, Mr. Lewis seemed to try to tap into whether the students were aware of seasonal differences. Later, in line 13, Mr. Lewis sought to confirm and extend students' understandings by pushing them to consider the relationship between the colors on the range chart and the temperatures they represent. Moreover, he made a connection to their personal experiences, "Do you think it could ever get down to the purple range?" (line 13) and "We've had some days where it has been sixty below" (line 15). Throughout this initial segment of classroom talk, Mr. Lewis appeared to guide students along a continuum of knowing (Strömdahl, 2003) about temperature changes, seasonal changes, and graphic representations of those changes. He made connections to their personal lived experiences. He clarified responses and encouraged the students to engage in reasoning drawn from community (personal) experiences and the scientific knowledge that they were developing.

In the next segment, later in the same class period, Mr. Lewis began his review of students' responses to the questions on the worksheet.

EXAMPLE 2

1   T. O.K., let's try to answer number 3. We'll answer number two a little later. I'm going to skip to number three. What parts of the equator do you feel sure about? O.K., somebody mentioned the equator. How many of you feel sure about the equator?
2   S. I do.
3   T. O.K., where's my globe? Here's my globe. All right, shh. You guys are saying you feel sure about the equator, which is right here.
4   S. The center of the Earth.
5   T. O.K. How many feel sure about the equator?
6   S. Me.
7   T. All right, what other places do you feel sure about?
8   S. Antarctica
9   T. How many of you others feel sure about Antarctica? O.K., what's another spot?
10   [Students are talking to each other. There is a lot of noise in the room.]
11   T. Greenland. Tell me something about Greenland. I don't know that much about Greenland.
12   S. It's cold.
13   T. Ah, yeah, it's near the North Pole. Does everybody feel sure about that? And the what?
14   S. Ice caps.

15 T. The ice caps, tell me about the ice caps.
16 S. It's colder.
17 T. So where are they located? [Noise in the classroom]
18 T. So we know it's got to be cold air. So, we're sure about the middle, sure about the top. How about these places in between, like Westfield?
19 S. It's going to be blue.
20 T. It's going to be blue, is it going to be blue all the time?
21 S. No! Once in a while it gets green, once in a while it gets blue.
22 T. Yea why?
23 S. Because the weather changes in the seasons.
24 T. Because we have seasons.

In this segment, what stands out is Mr. Lewis' repeated effort to draw all students into the discussion and aim for group consensus. Group effort, rather than individual collaboration and effort, is a characteristic of many Latin@ and Native American children's home and community experiences (Aikenhead, 2001). In lines 1, 3, 5, 13, and 18, Mr. Lewis referenced the group and asked students, "We're sure ..." "You guys are saying," "How many of you ...?"

In the final segment of the class, Mr. Lewis discussed the climate of Africa with the students. He asked probing questions that encouraged students to reason from the representation and their background knowledge.

EXAMPLE 3

1 T. What color would you color that? Red. How many of you were not sure about Africa?
2 S. I'm very sure.
3 T. You're very sure? O.K. You help them out. Africa, like in Egypt is very hot. It has sand. What about the rest of Africa?
4 S. Some parts are like green, dry, and have waters.
5 T. How can you explain the differences?
6 S. The differences?
7 T. You're telling me there's different temperatures?
8 S. Yeah, it depends on the ...
9 T. O.K., why?
10 S. Because Africa, the bottom part is close to Antarctica, a couple of thousand miles. And the coldness of Antarctica can go to South Africa. And the heatness of the equator above Africa ...

In this final segment, Mr. Lewis clarified and extended a student's use of evidence by introducing the word differences into the students' explanation. In the first few lines (1–4) Mr. Lewis and the student considered the continent of Africa. The student (in line 4) explained that the climate and terrain of Africa varies. In line 5, Mr. Lewis asked for an explanation—essentially asking for supporting evidence for a claim through detailed comparison. When, in line 6, the student asked, "The differences?" giving the impression that he either does not understand the term differences as applied to the discussion or perhaps that he hasn't thought through the comparisons, Mr. Lewis clarified his question by replying in line 7, "you're telling me there's [sic] different temperatures?" This clarification led to (in line 10) the student's quite complex explanation of the range of temperatures and terrains on the continent.

What seems clear, from the analysis of the three science classroom segments, is that Mr. Lewis showed evidence of using language to embrace students' ideas, to encourage them to work as a group to consider evidence, extend, and clarify understandings in science (Sherer et al., 2008). The findings here do not offer a simple formula for affirming students' language and culture in mathematics and science classrooms. However, they do provide specific cultural examples of the moment-to-moment ways that teacher candidates and teachers can invite students into the language of mathematics and science classrooms.

Transforming Teacher Preparation

We have discussed the importance of affirming students' culture and language. We have provided examples of how teachers make connections to advance students' thinking in mathematics and science to their community-valued ways of learning. It is critical that candidates and teachers are prepared to notice cultural and linguistic nuances in the classroom and recognize that students need to speak comfortably and fluently in the languages of mathematics and science, their home language, and English. Candidates and teachers need to understand how to use and move between these languages explicitly. They must understand, pedagogically, how a lack of skill in using and moving between languages (STEM, home, and English) can impact student understanding. Lastly, teachers must have the tools to support this use and movement.

What might be the nature and goals of such tools? First, candidates, especially in mathematics and science, rarely receive training that integrates pedagogy, practice, cultural, and linguistic contexts. They do not emerge from preparation programs with a pedagogical content knowledge about how to fully and seamlessly couple cultural and linguistic characteristics of BLs with what and how they teach. This tight and seamless coupling requires teachers to take a metacognitive perspective of BLs as cultural and linguistic beings. Uncovering their "ways with words" (Heath, 1983) and "ways with the world" would include classroom whole group and small group discussions that provide spaces, during instruction, for students and teachers to make connections to background knowledge, to linguistic cognates, to myths, stories, jokes (Richardson-Bruna, 2008) and to misconceptions (see Chapter 9). Second, and related to the first point, candidates must understand how to integrate the knowledge gained during these discussions with approaches to teaching subject matter. Third, in keeping with Torres-Guzman's and Howe's (2008) call for greater awareness of the role of language in teaching, candidates and teachers must have tools to build linguistic connections between the first language, STEM disciplinary language, and academic English more broadly defined (see Chapter 7). This can be as simple as being explicit about Spanish-English cognates, English-STEM linguistic connections, or as complex as building word walls or concept maps for students that illustrate through text analysis or analysis of discussion with respect to the structures through which claims are made, evidence is offered, and groups develop ideas.

We envision preparation for candidates to include interdisciplinary work among teacher educators. There are few scholars in the nation whose areas of expertise include bilingual/ESL and mathematic/science education. Bringing together experts in mathematics, science, bilingual/ESL, and language, literacy, and sociocultural studies so that content for preparation courses is greatly needed. An example of an effort is the Center for the Mathematics Education of Latina/os (CEMELA) (http://cemela.math.arizona.edu) where experts in mathematics, mathematics education, and language, literacy, and sociocultural studies join to improve the mathematics education of low-income Latin@ students. One of its goals is to prepare teachers with integrated knowledge of language, culture, and mathematics. However, candidate secondary preparation deserves more attention.

Rodríguez and Kitchen (2005) inform teacher educators how to prepare mathematics and science candidates for diverse classrooms. Issues addressing the needs of culturally and linguistically diverse students should be pervasive in preparation programs. Typically, most programs include one course especially designed for culturally and linguistically diverse students (Gutiérrez, 2002; see Chapter 6). We are calling for a curriculum focused on the schooling needs of diverse students, especially BLs.

Research Directions

There is a paucity of research in mathematics and science with BLs, particularly at middle to high school level (Gomez & Madda, 2005; Gutiérrez, 2002). Future studies should pay more attention to high school settings with significant numbers of BLs enrolled in science and mathematics. Research has begun in this STEM area (Gomez et al., 2010; Richardson-Bruna, 2008; Sherer et al., 2008), but there remains much to be done.

Research must inform candidate development and professional development. We know little about the secondary level regarding:

- Exemplary candidate preparation for BLs in mathematics and science.
- Teaching practices that promote advancement of culturally and linguistically diverse students in mathematics and science.
- Role parents and other community stakeholders play in advancing student knowledge of mathematics and science.

Through qualitative research, we can begin unraveling this needed knowledge. Unequivocally, there is much we need to learn and the need has never been greater.

References

Aikenhead, G. S. (2001). Integrating western and Aboriginal sciences: Cross-cultural science teaching. *Research in Science Education, 31*(3), 337–355.

Celedón, S. (1998). *An analysis of a teacher's and students' language use to make meaning in an ESL/mathematics classroom.* Unpublished doctoral dissertation. The University of Texas, Austin.

Celedón-Pattichis, S. (2010). Implementing reform curriculum: Voicing the experiences of an ESL/mathematics teacher. *Middle Grades Research Journal, 5*(4).

Curran, M. E. (2003). Linguistic diversity and classroom management. *Theory Into Practice, 42*(4), 334–340.

Delpit, L. D. (1988). The silenced dialogue: Power and pedagogy in educating other people's children. *Harvard Educational Review, 58,* 280–298.

Domínguez, H. (2005). Bilingual students' articulation and gesticulation of mathematical knowledge during problem solving. *Bilingual Research Journal, 29*(2), 269–289.

Erlandson, D. A., Harris, E. L., Skipper, B. L., & Allen, S. D. (1993). *Doing naturalistic inquiry: A guide to methods.* Newbury Park, CA: Sage.

Ford, A., & Peat, F. D. (1988). The role of language in science. *Foundations of Physics, 18*(12), 1233–1242.

Gee, J. P. (1996). *Social linguistics and literacies: Ideology in discourses* (2nd ed.). London: Taylor & Francis.

Gomez, K., & Madda, C. (2005). Vocabulary instruction for ELL Latino students in the middle school science classroom. *Voices in the Middle, 13*(1), 42–47.

Gomez, K., Sherer, J., Herman, P., Gomez, L., Zywica, J. D., & Williams, A. (2010). Supporting meaningful science learning: Reading and writing science. In A. Rodríguez (Ed.), *Science education as a pathway to teaching language literacy.* (pp. 93–112) Rotterdam, Netherlands: SENSE.

González, N. E., Moll, L., & Amanti, C. (Eds.). (2005). *Funds of knowledge: Theorizing practices in households, communities, and classrooms.* New York: Erlbaum.

Gutiérrez, R. (2002). Beyond essentialism: The complexity of language in teaching mathematics to Latina/o students. *American Educational Research Journal, 39*(4), 1047–1088.

Heath, S. B. (1983). *Ways with words: Language, life, and work in communities and classrooms.* New York: Cambridge University Press.

Khisty, L. L. (1995). Making inequality: Issues of language and meanings in mathematics teaching with Hispanic students. In W. G. Secada, E. Fennema, & L. B. Adajian (Eds.), *New directions for equity in mathematics education* (pp. 279–297). New York: Cambridge University Press.

Khisty, L. L., & Chval, K. (2002). Pedagogic discourse and equity in mathematics: When teachers talk matters. *Mathematics Education Research Journal, 14,* 154–168.

Lemke, J. L. (1990). *Talking science: Language, learning, and values.* Norwood, NJ: Ablex.

Moschkovich, J. (2007). Learning mathematics in two languages. *Educational Studies in Mathematics, 64*(2), 8–13.

National Council of Teachers of Mathematics. (2000). *Principles and standards for school mathematics.* Reston, VA: NCTM.

Richardson-Bruna, K., & Gómez, K. (Eds.). (2008). *The work of language in multicultural classrooms: Talking science, writing science.* New York: Routledge.

Rodríguez, A., & Kitchen, R. (2005). *Preparing mathematics and science teachers for diverse classrooms: Promising strategies for transformative pedagogy.* Mahwah, NJ: Erlbaum.

Sacks, H., Schegloff, E. A., & Jefferson, G. (1974). A simplest systematics for the organization of turn-taking for conversation. *Language, 50,* 696–735.

Sherer, J., Gomez, K., Herman, P., Gomez, L., White, J., & Williams, A. (2008). Literacy infusion in a high school environmental science curriculum. In K. Richardson-Bruna & K. Gómez (Eds.), *The work of language in multicultural classrooms: Talking science, writing science* (pp. 93–114). New York: Routledge.

Strömdahl, H. (2003). Modeling conceptual attainment of physical quantities. http://www1.phys.uu.m/esera2003/programme/pd%5C158Spdf

Torres-Guzman, M., & Howe, E. (2008). Experimenting in teams and tongues: Team teaching in a bilingual science education course. In K. Richardson-Bruna & K. Gomez (Eds.), *The work of language in multicultural classrooms: Talking science, writing science* (pp. 317–339). New York: Routledge.

Unsworth, L. (1997). "Sound" explanations in school sciences: A functional linguistic perspective on effective apprenticing texts. *Linguistics and Education, 9*(2), 199–226.

Villegas, A. M., & Lucas, T. (2002). Preparing culturally responsive teachers: Rethinking the curriculum. *Journal of Teacher Education, 53*(1), 20–32.

Vygotsky, L. S. (1978). *Mind in society: The development of the higher psychological processes.* London: Harvard University Press.

11 Meaningful Assessment in Linguistically Diverse Classrooms

Guillermo Solano-Flores and Lucinda Soltero-González

We live in an era of accountability in which assessment plays a key role. Results on the performance of students in mandated large-scale assessments are the main source of information on which schools are funded or sanctioned and decisions made concerning students' promotion or retention (Linn, 2003). These accountability trends are especially challenging for teachers and schools who serve Bilingual Learners (BLs). Schools with BL enrollment are required to meet adequate-yearly-progress (AYP) criteria on English proficiency, in addition to content knowledge. These criteria may be unfair because the validity of AYP reporting is threatened by factors that are not properly considered in testing policy. For example, classifications of students as limited English proficient (LEP) are inconsistent due to limitations of tests used to measure English proficiency. Also, the linguistic complexity of tests used to assess content knowledge may affect their validity for BLs. Finally, BLs who attain certain level of English proficiency move out from the LEP category, which limits schools' opportunity to improve AYP English proficiency indicators for LEPs (Abedi, 2004).

Challenges stemming from increased testing and accountability policies add to the formidable challenges inherent in teaching heterogeneous linguistic groups, who typically attend low-income schools with high teacher turnover rates. Due to increased pressure on teachers and schools, probably never before in history have teachers, especially those who teach BLs, needed to be more knowledgeable on testing issues as they do in these times.

Regrettably, teacher education programs and research concerning the BLs do not seem to have changed in recent years in ways that address these increased demands. The number of assessment courses that future bilingual education teachers are required to take, if these courses are required at all, has not changed. An unfortunate consequence of this gap in preparation and research trends is a serious disconnect among assessment classroom practices, state/national large-scale assessment practice, and policy. Ironically, while BLs, their teachers, and schools are probably the most vulnerable to the limitations of assessment systems, they may be the last to benefit from current research on assessment.

As teacher educators, we often feel astonished that many teachers seem to view assessment as a school, district, or state requirement, rather than as an activity to inform their teaching. Several factors may contribute to that view. One, the kind of information on student performance on large-scale assessment and the timing when this information is available to schools does not help teachers' practice. Another factor may be that, because assessment is associated with the special pressure that accountability trends put on schools, especially those with high enrollments of BLs, teachers may perceive assessments solely as instruments for sanctioning and control, not as potential resources for enriching their teaching activities.

In this chapter, we provide future and beginning teachers of BLs with reasonings on assessment that we believe are critical to supporting BLs' learning and survival in an era of testing and accountability. We address Shepard's (2000) view that a revolution in classroom assessment must take place so that assessment supports a social-constructivist model of teaching and learning. Deep transformation needs to happen regarding how assessment is viewed and used in classrooms.

To make assessment benefit teachers and BLs, teachers need to become active participants in the process of assessment and critical users. We also attempt to make the case that, for transformation to happen, assessment has to be meaningful to teachers and students. Providing information on assessment resources, techniques, or diagnostic instruments is beyond the scope of this chapter. Rather, we attempt to explain the reasonings behind assessment and show that it is a meaningful, constructive classroom activity.

Our chapter is organized in three sections. First, we discuss main issues in BLs' assessment. We discuss the notions of reliability and validity and their relation with fairness in testing and refer the reader to Kopriva (2008) for a detailed review of issues and recent advances in BLs large-scale testing.

The second section discusses formative assessment, the kind intended to promote learning, rather than simply appraise it. In spite that formative assessment has been a prominent area of research in the last years, little of this research has been conducted with BLs or in the context of bilingual education. Becoming familiar with the basic reasoning underlying effective formative assessment is especially critical for teachers of BLs, who need to take advantage of all resources available to provide appropriate, differentiated instruction.

The third section submits the notion that if assessment is to effectively inform teaching to benefit BLs, teachers should appropriate assessment as a meaningful part of their teaching activities in a community of practice (Lave & Wenger, 1991). Increased participation of teachers in large-scale testing programs or in research projects involving assessment should contribute to both improved assessment practices and significant professional development.

We use assessment to refer to both the act of appraising students' knowledge or skills and an instrument used with that purpose. We use "assessment" and "test" as synonyms; and, in most cases also use "item" and "task" as synonyms.

Basic Ideas and Challenges in BL Assessment

Reasoning about Assessment

In examining the soundness of assessments and assessment practices, two aspects are usually discussed, fairness and the so-called technical properties of assessment instruments, reliability and validity. These two aspects should be thought of as separate but intimately related.

Given the scope of this chapter, we do not provide formal definitions of reliability and validity. However, we can say that reliability has to do with decisions made about the relative standing of a given student in relation to other students on the competency measured. Reliability can be thought of as the degree of consistency of observations (Kane, 1982). These observations can consist of items. For example, a multiple-choice test is considered to be reliable if the scores computed are based on any two halves of the items that it comprises (used as though they were separate tests) tend to give similar rank orderings of the students tested (Crocker & Algina, 1986).

Observations can also consist of scoring decisions made by raters, as is the case of constructed-response tasks (e.g., essays, hands-on tasks, open-ended items), whose scoring involves human judgment. Reliability for this task takes the form of consistency in the scoring of several raters. The scoring is considered to be reliable if the scores computed are based on the scores given by different raters give similar rank orderings of the students tested.

We can say that validity has to do with the kinds of generalizations that can be made about the students' competencies and knowledge based on test scores (Shavelson & Webb, 2009). Efforts to examine validity are essentially oriented to determine the extent to which students' test performance can be attributed to the extent to which they possess the competencies and knowledge, not for other reasons (Messick, 1989).

A test can be thought of as a sample of tasks from a knowledge domain (e.g., the domain of 4th grade science knowledge). If the content of the items in the test is not representative of that knowledge domain, then the generalizations about the student's competencies in that knowledge domain will not be appropriate (Shavelson & Webb, 1991). There is evidence that different types of tasks (e.g., multiple-choice, open-ended, hands-on tasks, computer simulations) tap into different forms of knowledge (Ruiz-Primo & Shavelson, 1996). See Figures 11.1–11.3, which show different types of tasks for assessing knowledge of the topic, Physics of Soap Bubbles (Solano-Flores, 2000). While multiple-choice items are more appropriate for assessing factual knowledge, hands-on tasks are more suitable for assessing critical thinking, problem-solving, and inquiry skills.

As a part of the process of assessment development, the tasks that compose an assessment are tried out with samples of students from the target population to make sure that it is sensitive to student differences in the knowledge of the topic assessed. For example, assessment developers need to be sure that not everybody responds correctly or incorrectly to a given item.

Also as part of the process of assessment development, ideally, some students participate individually in what are called cognitive labs (Ericson & Simon, 1993). In these cognitive labs, students are asked to think aloud as they solve the problems posed by the items or to report how they solved the problems right after they responded to the items. They also may be asked questions about the ways in which they interpret the problem, or the reasons why they responded to the items in the ways they did. Based on data from these cognitive labs, assessment developers can infer the students' cognitive activity elicited by the items (Baxter & Glaser, 1998).

Information obtained from cognitive labs allows assessment developers to ensure that the knowledge and reasonings used by the students to respond to

Which of the following is the most important factor involved in the formation of a bubble?

a) gravity

b) viscosity

c) surface tension

d) density

Figure 11.1 The Physics of Soap Bubbles: Multiple-Choice Item

In the lines below, tell a friend how to do an experiment to find out which of three soapy solutions makes the bubbles that last the longest time. Make sure you describe materials and equipment.

_____

_____

_____

_____

_____

Figure 11.2 The Physics of Soap Bubbles: Open-ended Task

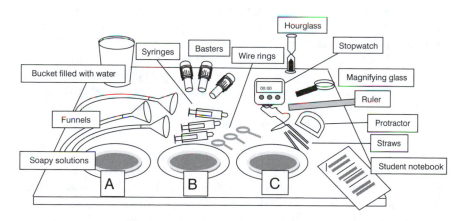

Figure 11.3 The Physics of Soap Bubbles: Hands-on Task. The student is asked to find out which of three soapy solutions makes the bubbles with the longest and the shortest duration. The problem can be solved in multiple ways, using different pieces of equipment which vary as to their effectiveness for manipulating, controlling, or measuring variables. For example, bubbles of the same size for the three solutions can be made using the funnels in combination with the bucket filled with water; the stopwatch is better for measuring bubble duration than the hourglass; the protractor is irrelevant to solving the problem. Three pieces of each equipment for manipulating variables are provided to make it possible for students to avoid contamination across soapy solutions.

the items are relevant to the construct an item is intended to measure (DeBarger, Ayala, Minstrell, Kraus, & Stanford, 2009). Cognitive labs may reveal that some students arrive at correct answers to an item using knowledge, reasonings, and strategies that do not have much to do with the construct; or, some students who use knowledge, reasonings, and strategies that are relevant to the construct, may still arrive at incorrect answers because they are misled by certain characteristics of the items (Ruiz-Primo, Shavelson, Li, & Schultz, 2001).

Bilingual Learners in Large-Scale Testing

Despite the increased reliance on high-stake testing to comply with accountability policies, substantial training in assessment is still lacking in teacher preparation and professional development programs. Assessment training is necessary to provide teacher candidates with the knowledge and skills needed to properly administer and interpret mandated assessments as well as develop and interpret classroom assessments (Cizek, 2010). Equally important is to prepare teacher candidates to become critical users of assessment, which includes being informed about research findings as well as shortcomings identified with current assessment practices for BLs.

BLs are largely excluded from the development process of high-stake testing (Abedi, Hofstetter, & Lord, 2004). From what we do know from research, most current high-stake assessments fail to produce dependable measures of BLs (Solano-Flores, 2006, 2008). Therefore, training in assessment should support teachers in identifying factors that may affect student outcomes, such as linguistic and cultural bias as well as technical aspects of tests such as reliability, validity, utility, and feasibility. (For a detailed description of technical quality of formative assessment for BLs, see Abedi, 2010.) Assessments with a complex linguistic structure (i.e., unfamiliar vocabulary, complex grammatical structures and discourse style), and cultural bias can negatively affect BLs' performance (Abedi, 2010; Solano-Flores & Nelson-Barber, 2000; Solano-Flores & Trumbull, 2003), provide questionable measures of student achievement, and misguide instructional decisions. Also, unfortunately, approaches to testing BLs with blanket approaches such as testing in their native language, are limited in their effectiveness because they fail to address that BL populations are constituted by tremendously heterogeneous linguistic groups (Solano-Flores, 2006, 2009; Solano-Flores & Li, 2006). It is crucial that candidates and teachers are knowledgeable about these aspects of assessment because the high-stake test results are used to make important decisions about schools, teachers, and students (e.g., grade promotion or retention, placement in special education and ESL programs, and ELL re-classification criteria).

It is also important that teachers resist a pervasive assumption in current assessment practices: the homogenization of BLs. BLs are a diverse population that includes a wide variety of countries of origin, cultural and socio-economic backgrounds, prior school experiences, as well as levels of language and literacy competence in English and in their home language (see Chapter 1 and 16). Teachers need to consider these differences to avoid making false assumptions about their students' backgrounds, knowledge, and abilities. If teachers understand the variability among BLs, it is more likely that they will employ appropriate assessment tools to obtain valuable information to inform instruction.

While some of the problematic aspects of assessment mentioned above pertain to mandated-assessment and teachers may feel that they do not have control over it, they should feel empowered to create a more robust classroom assessment system. In the following section we introduce formative assessment, present some key characteristics, and discuss their importance in promoting student learning.

Basic Principles of Formative Assessment

Formative Assessment for Bilingual Learners

Because of current trends on the use of testing to comply with accountability policies, teachers in schools with high BL enrollments may perceive assessments merely as instruments for sanctioning and control, and may overlook their potential for improving instruction. Clearly, a change in culture with regards to the use of assessment at the classroom level must occur for it to have an impact on student learning.

We begin our discussion with the distinction between summative and formative assessment. Summative assessment focuses on providing information on students' learning typically at the end of formal instruction (Abedi, 2010). This type of assessment, especially annual district tests and mandated large-scale assessments, is often the most visible and valued form of assessment. However, a single, summative assessment is not sufficient to capture students' needs and progress throughout the learning process.

In contrast, formative assessment includes all the information teachers can gather during an instructional term to monitor student progress in relation to established learning goals (Abedi, 2010; Heritage, Kim, & Vendlinski, 2008). This assessment helps teachers adapt teaching and learning so that all students learn (Furtak, 2009). Examples include assignments with scoring rubrics (e.g., projects, portfolios, group work with peer feedback), observations, teacher-student dialogues, homework, and self-assessment among others. Traditionally, formative assessment collects information that supports teachers' instructional plans. A more recent usage of the term formative assessment emphasizes its value in promoting students' active engagement in and ownership of the learning process, student self-assessment, and self-direction (Cizek, 2010).

Appropriate, differentiated instruction is fundamental for BLs, and formative assessment has the potential to provide specific, valuable information to enable meaningful instruction. Yet, formative assessment for BLs must take into account important issues affecting its development, use, and interpretation. In what follows, we present features of formative assessment that are essential when working with BLs.

Characteristics of Effective Formative Assessment for BLs

Effective instruction starts with good assessment. It is through ongoing assessment that teachers are able to identify students' strengths and needs. Designing an effective formative assessment system is a challenge for any school and can be especially complex in schools serving BLs needing differentiated instruction (Klingner, Soltero-González, & Lesaux, 2010).

Several characteristics should be considered when designing, using, and interpreting formative assessment for BLs. This assessment: is ongoing; provides non-evaluative, concrete, and timely feedback; enables differentiated instruction; includes multiple measures and modes of response; and, considers the multidimensional nature of second-language acquisition. We concur that "not all of the characteristics must be present for an assessment to be considered formative; each characteristic has been identified for its potential to maximize the achievement, development, and instructional benefits of this type of assessment" (Cizek, 2010, p. 7). While this list of formative assessment characteristics draws from existing work in formative assessment in general (Andrade, 2000; Black & William, 1998; Cizek, 2010; Ruiz-Primo, Furtak, Ayala, Yin, & Shavelson, 2010; Sadler, 1989; Shepard, 2006) and assessment of BLs (Abedi, 2010; Solano-Flores & Trumbull, 2003), it highlights essential aspects in the assessment of BLs.

We propose key characteristics of formative assessment to guide teachers in the designing of tools to capture daily teacher–student interactions, information about student understanding, and identify areas for improvement. This information should help teachers plan appropriate instruction.

- *Is ongoing:*
  It takes place while it is still possible to modify instruction. Rather than being detached from classroom interactions, formative assessment is embedded in daily instructional activities. It requires a disposition to observe students' levels of engagement, participation, and expression of understandings during learning activities with the purpose of using this information to guide instruction.
- *Provides non-evaluative, concrete, and timely feedback:*
  Rather than assigning a grade or judging student performance, its purpose is to understand students' learning, identify strengths and areas for improvement, provide timely and specific feedback related to the learning goals, and engage the students in active learning (Cizek, 2010). Corrective feedback is especially helpful for BLs who may need explicit instruction and opportunities to develop and expand their second-language proficiency, such as academic vocabulary, sentence structures related to specific language functions, and the text features of specific disciplines. The non-evaluative nature of formative assessment promotes a classroom environment that helps decrease BLs' affective filter enabling them to take risks without fear of making mistakes due to their developing English language abilities.
- *Enables appropriate, differentiated instruction:*
  This type of assessment allows teachers to capture specific information about individual students that is necessary to differentiate instruction according to students' needs. For example, it can make apparent misconceptions or confusions created by words with multiple meanings. If teachers notice these misconceptions during the course of instruction, they can modify their instruction to best meet students' needs.

- *Includes multiple measures and modes of response:*
  There is no single best assessment to use with BLs; therefore, utilizing multiple measures and interpreting their results in appropriate ways promotes student success. Different assessments are designed to capture distinct knowledge and abilities. Students' responses to different assessments might vary depending on the assessment format, their background knowledge and familiarity with the topic or skill of interest, and the interaction between language and topic. For instance, some BLs might show better comprehension of a topic that they have experienced at home when they use their home language and a story-telling format rather than using a written English recall. Teachers should encourage students to use all their linguistic resources, both English and their home language, to demonstrate their learning and full potential.
- *Considers the multidimensional nature of second-language acquisition:*
  Second-language acquisition is an uneven process (Bialystok, 1991). BLs' relative proficiency in the different language domains, listening, speaking, reading, and writing, might vary depending on factors such as language and literacy proficiency, background knowledge, interests, and classroom instruction. It is also common for BLs to show varying ability levels across language components, including syntactic and pragmatic knowledge as well as morphological, semantic, and phonological skills (Solano-Flores, 2006). For example, some BLs may have relatively strong vocabulary knowledge on a specific topic but may struggle with the syntactic structure when expressing their knowledge about that topic. When teachers understand varying levels of English proficiency and the complexities of second-language acquisition, they are in a better position to design quality formative assessment tools to support student learning.

Formative assessment that adequately identifies the strengths and needs of individual students may facilitate equal and adequate opportunities to learn. Furthermore, effective formative assessment practices have the potential to promote learning and achievement (Black & William, 1998; Ruiz-Primo & Furtak, 2007), motivation (Ruiz-Primo et al., 2010), and self-direction (Cizek, 2010). It is a promising tool with intrinsic pedagogical value for improving the quality of instruction for BLs. The results of formative assessment can be used to inform instructional decisions about what to teach, how and when to teach it, to which students, and why to use different languages and learning strategies.

Appropriating Assessment Practice Through Assessment Development

Classroom assessment

If used properly, assessment is a powerful tool to probe student understanding and inform teaching. Careful examination of students' responses beyond grading them as correct or incorrect allows teachers to develop a better understanding of students' reasonings and the role that language plays in their interpretation of items and the ways in which they respond to them. The use of multiple forms of assessment, from multiple-choice to hands-on tasks, allows examination of different forms of knowledge.

While the reasonings about assessment described in the first section are from the development of tasks for large-scale assessments, they can be transferred to the classroom. To make this happen, assessment needs to be seen from a constructivist perspective. Teachers need to appropriate assessment as a cultural practice.

As Table 11.1 shows, a constructivist perspective in assessment focuses not only on the product of solving a problem—the student's response—but also on the process that leads to a given solution, knowledge, strategies, and reasonings used by the student. This approach informs teaching based on a clear understanding of the specific aspects of content, skills, and learning strategies that need to be worked out with students.

A constructivist approach also promotes the development of tasks with intrinsic pedagogical value. Compare the items in Figures 11.4 and 11.5, which show respectively two tasks assessing different aspects of the knowledge of the circle. The multiple-choice item (Figure 11.4) is similar to the majority of the items included in large-scale tests. It assesses factual knowledge necessary to calculate the perimeter of a circle. To respond, students need to know a formula or at least recognize it among the four options given in the item. The open-ended task, Plates and String (Figure 11.5) is seen less frequently in large-scale tests. To respond, students need to have or develop an understanding of what perimeter and diameter mean. Moreover, arriving at a correct solution helps students make sense of the fact that π is a constant.

Few would challenge the assertion that those who perform well on Plates and String are also likely respond correctly to the multiple-choice item, while those who respond correctly to the multiple-choice item may not necessarily perform well on Plates and String. Indeed, when the first author administered Plates and String to teachers and other professionals, many had difficulty coming up with the correct solution, since textbooks do not necessarily promote the kind of thinking assessed by Plates and String. Indeed, since Plates and String is simultaneously

Table 11.1 Instruction and Assessment From a Constructivist Perspective

	Instruction	Assessment
Students	Students are regarded as active, not passive learners	Tests ask students to think critically, in addition to recalling or recognizing information
Problem solution	Students are encouraged to actively find solutions to problems	Students are asked to propose and justify solutions
Knowledge	Knowledge is assumed to be imprecise but perfectible	Tasks admit to a variety of responses with varying degrees of correctness
Learning	Learning is promoted through meaningful activities	Taking the test has an intrinsic learning experience
Student performance	Making mistakes is viewed as part of the process of learning	Both the process (actions taken) and the product (solution) in problem solving are considered in scoring student performance

The formula for calculating the perimeter of a circle is

a) π × d

b) π × r²

c) π × d / 2

d) (π × r²) / 3

Figure 11.4 Perimeter Of a Circle: Multiple-choice Item

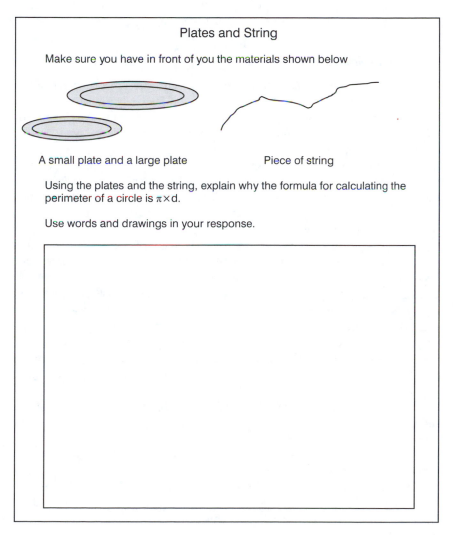

Plates and String

Make sure you have in front of you the materials shown below

A small plate and a large plate   Piece of string

Using the plates and the string, explain why the formula for calculating the perimeter of a circle is π×d.

Use words and drawings in your response.

Figure 11.5 Perimeter Of a Circle: Open-ended Task.

difficult and engaging, it can be used as a simple, low cost assessment activity to promote higher-order thinking.

Our discussion on constructed response tasks is not intended to imply that multiple-choice items should not be used. However, there is evidence that different types of tasks (e.g., multiple-choice, open-ended, hands-on tasks, computer simulations) tap into different forms of knowledge (Martinez, 1999) and pose different sets of linguistic demands to students. Thus, an important strategy for sound classroom assessment with BLs consists of using multiple forms of assessment in combination. The use of multiple forms of assessment promotes learning in multiple ways and gives BLs opportunities to demonstrate learning through tasks using different sets of linguistic demands.

Assessment development

It is unfortunate that teachers have many experiences to share as users of tests developed by others (e.g., standardized tests or commercially available diagnostic tests); however, they have few stories about experiences as test developers. The absence of assessment development as a part of their professional activities may pose a serious limitation to the enrichment of their practice. We contend that, by developing engaging, challenging assessments for classroom use, teachers can improve their teaching. This notion is consistent with the observation that the process of assessment development allows teachers to think critically about curriculum and enables them to identify areas of improvement in the curriculum they teach (Shavelson, 1995).

To make that happen, teachers need to view their own assessments as long-term projects. Figure 11.6 shows a model for teachers to develop their own assessment tasks iteratively. An initial version is developed by the teacher, then reviewed by colleagues, who provide comments and feedback. The teacher revises the task, conducts cognitive labs with a few students, and then uses it in their teaching. After using the task and examining the results from the cognitive interview, the teacher prepares another version, which is tried out again with a new set of students.

The cognitive labs conducted with the purpose of evaluating the validity of tests requires the use of interview protocols that, for reasons of space, cannot be included here. We refer the readers to Ericson and Simon (1993) for a detailed description of the methodology. Teachers cannot necessarily be expected to have the time to conduct cognitive labs with the same level of detail as in research (Hamilton, Nussbaum, & Snow, 1997; Ruiz-Primo, Shavelson, Li, & Schultz, 2001). However, they can perform the actions listed in Table 11.2, which provides a guide for classroom cognitive interviews.

This cycle of review and revision shown in Figure 11.6 can take place every school year. After a few school years with iterations, the tasks developed can become highly effective instructional tools sensitive to the characteristics and linguistic needs of BLs.

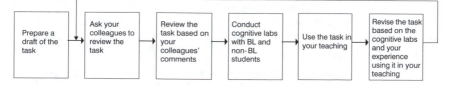

Figure 11.6 Continuous, Iterative Process of Assessment Development

Table 11.2 Conducting Cognitive Interviews in the Classroom

Training

Explain to students that you want to know how they understand the item and respond to it. Tell them that you will need to share their thoughts—to think aloud as they are engaged in solving the problem posed by the item.

Provide practice problems. For example: How many light bulbs are there in your house? or How would you tell a friend how you tie up your shoe laces?

As students try to respond to each question, prompt them with comments such as, "Remember to think aloud" and "Keep thinking aloud."

Read aloud

Ask students to read the item aloud. Take note of the words that they read incorrectly or that they have a hard time reading or any other difficulty that may influence how they interpret the item.

Concurrent think-aloud

Once students read the item aloud, have them solve the problem posed by it. Make sure the student talks all the time. If student are silent, remind them to think aloud with comments such as, "Please make sure to think aloud" and "Keep thinking aloud."

Retrospective think-aloud

Once students complete their response, ask them to tell you their thinking as they were completing their response. You can provide a direction such as: "Now, I would like you to tell me all what you were thinking when you were solving the problem."

General questions

Ask questions that may help you find ways to improve the item. For example:

1. Did you have any problem understanding the item?

2. What do you think this item is about? What is it asking you to do?

3. What changes would you make in this item to make sure that everybody can understand it properly?

Do not correct or help the student during the cognitive interview, so that you can have a good understanding of their thinking.

Including BLs in the process of assessment development

Including BLs in the process of assessment development cannot be emphasized enough. Inclusion should take place even if teachers are not bilingual, or if the level of students' English proficiency is low. A common mistake made in the process of assessment development in large-scale testing is to assume that not much information relevant to refining assessments can be obtained from trying them out with BLs or conducting cognitive interviews with them because they cannot communicate in English or because tests are not administered in the BLs' native language. Another error is to assume that including BLs in the process of assessment development is appropriate only in the context of bilingual education programs or when the teachers of these students are bilingual. However, while it may take several years for BLs to develop academic language in English, relatively soon in their process of development of a second-language, they develop the communicative competencies needed to effectively communicate in English (Cummins, 2003; Hakuta, 2001). There is evidence that BLs have multiple patterns of language use when they are asked to think aloud as they take test items. Many have the minimum level of proficiency in English needed to communicate with interviewers in English about the ways in which they understand test items and to explain the reasonings they use to respond to them (Prosser & Solano-Flores, 2010).

Only by including BLs in the process of assessment development do teachers have opportunity to identify the linguistic challenges that items pose to BLs. Many of those linguistic challenges are difficult to anticipate. See the item shown in Figure 11.7. The idiomatic expression, "have to do," is interpreted by a BL as "need to do," which leads to the intended response, "Shadows don't have to do anything. The earth just moves." While it is not possible to determine whether the student would have been able to give a correct answer had the question been phrased differently, it is clear that lack of familiarity with the idiomatic expression can mislead BLs in their interpretation of the question.

Professional development through assessment development

The need for collaborative work cannot be emphasized enough as critical to effective assessment development. This collaborative work ensures high quality in the assessments developed and constitutes an excellent opportunity for professional development. We have evidence that even skilled bilingual education teachers become more sophisticated in their reasonings about language when they have the opportunity to develop assessments for BLs in collaboration with other teachers.

What do shadows have to do with the movement of the earth?

Shadow don't have to do anyting.
The eart just mubs.

Figure 11.7 Open-ended Item On Earth Science and The Answer from a BL

This evidence comes from a project in which bilingual teachers in a school district with a high enrollment of BLs (Spanish/English) were charged with developing concurrently mathematics in two language versions, English and Spanish, as an alternative approach to test translation, with the intent to promote more equitable testing (Solano-Flores, Trumbull, & Nelson-Barber, 2002). Project staff facilitated a series of item development sessions in which teachers developed the items iteratively—following a process similar to that shown in Figure 11.6— and interactively—any modification made on one language version needed to be negotiated with the other language version, to ensure item content and linguistic equivalence.

An analysis of the transcriptions of the development sessions revealed that, as teachers refined the items, they became more sophisticated in their reasonings about the linguistic and cultural factors that were relevant to testing their BLs. In their first discussions, they focused on content and the structure of the exercises and addressed concerns about BLs' literacy levels, adequacy of item illustrations, and familiarity of the students with everyday life terms (e.g., tissue paper and *papel de China*). One of the issues had to do with the appropriateness of technical terminology in both Spanish and English; and, more specifically, the appropriateness of using the metric system in mathematics items. Should decimal metric system units be used in the exercises in Spanish? If the English system units were kept in the Spanish version, should English or Spanish abbreviations be used?

As the discussion went on, deeper levels of analysis were reached in which the sociocultural context was addressed. Should the items be contextualized according to the students' background (e.g., using kilograms and grams, which are units used in Latin American countries) or according to their everyday lives (e.g., using pounds and ounces, which are part of everyday life experiences in the US)? Later, teachers abandoned the use of simplistic assumptions about cultural groups and went beyond thinking about the BLs as a homogeneous cultural group. Now, their discussions considered the lives of their BLs in the context in which they taught.

An even deeper level of analysis was reached when teachers identified discursive structure as a factor that could potentially affect content equivalence across items. The concern was that real content equivalence across language versions of the same item might not be attained unless serious consideration was given to the fact that languages vary as to the frequency of certain discursive structures. Thus, different discursive structures like those shown in Figure 11.8, might not work in the same way for BLs even if they were to be tested only in English and the two versions of the same item had about the same wording.

As with other issues raised by teachers who participated in the project on concurrent assessment development project, the issue of discursive structure could not be resolved. Research is yet to be done to determine how sensitive BLs' performance is to variations in discursive structure and other linguistic features. However, the main lesson from this experience is that, when bilingual teachers collaboratively refine the linguistic features of items with their BLs in mind, they reach unprecedented levels of sophistication in their discussions about language and the characteristics of their students. Assessment development is a meaningful context for professional development.

Look at the table below:

(Table with information on
the cost of several materials)

Based on the prices shown in the table, find out how much money your
class needs to build a bird feeder.

Use the space below to give your answer. You can use words and drawings.

Find out how much money your class needs to build a bird feeder.

Use the prices shown in the table below:

(Table with information on
the cost of several materials)

Use the space below to give your answer. You can use words and drawings.

Figure 11.8 An Open-ended Item with Two Discursive Structures

Final Comments

Our goal in this chapter has been to support bilingual teachers and teachers
of BLs to become critical assessment users and to support them to appropriate
assessment as a meaningful component of their professional activity. Underlying
our discussion is the notion that, if assessment is to work to benefit BLs, teachers
need to develop a culture of assessment that promotes collegial work and the
exchange of ideas about learning, cognition, and second-language acquisition
around assessment activities. In this culture of assessment, teachers need
to become critical assessment users and developers of their own classroom
assessment.

The development of this culture of assessment cannot happen overnight. We hope that we have taken a successful step—to make bilingual teachers and teachers of bilingual students view assessment as a tool for teaching, rather than an activity dictated by someone external to the classroom.

References

Abedi, J. (2004). The No Child Left Behind Act and English language learners: Assessment and accountability issues. *Educational Researcher, 33*(1), 4–14.

Abedi, J. (2010). Research and recommendations for formative assessment with ELLs. In H. L. Andrade & G. J. Cizek (Eds.), *Handbook of formative assessment* (pp. 181–197). New York: Routledge.

Abedi, J., Hofstetter, C., & Lord, C. (2004). Assessment accommodations for English language learners: Implications for policy-based empirical research. *Review of Educational Research, 74*(1), 1–28.

Andrade, H. L. (2000). Using rubrics to promote thinking and learning. *Educational Leadership, 57*(5), 13–18.

Baxter, G. P., & Glaser, R. (1998). Investigating the cognitive complexity of science assessments. *Educational Measurement: Issues and Practice, 17*(3), 37–45.

Bialystok, E. (Ed.). (1991). *Language processing in bilingual children*. New York: Cambridge University Press.

Black, P., & William, D. (1998). Assessment and classroom learning. *Assessment in Education, 5*(1), 7–74.

Cizek, G. J. (2010). An introduction to formative assessment. In H. L. Andrade & G. J. Cizek (Eds.), *Handbook of formative assessment* (pp. 3–17). New York: Routledge.

Crocker, L., & Algina, J. (1986). *Introduction to classical and modern test theory*. Fort Worth, TX: Harcourt Brace.

Cummins, J. (2003). BICS and CALP: Origins and rationale for the distinction. In C. B. Paulston & G. R. Tucker (Eds.), *Sociolinguistics: The essential readings* (pp. 322–328). Malden, MA: Blackwell.

DeBarger, A. H., Ayala, C., Minstrell, J. A., Kraus, P., & Stanford, T. (2009). *Facet-based progressions of student understanding in chemistry* (Chemistry Facets Technical Report 1). Menlo Park, CA: SRI International.

Ericson, K. A., & Simon, H. A. (1993). *Protocol analysis: Verbal reports as data.* (rev ed.). Cambridge, MA: MIT Press.

Furtak, E. M. (2009). *Formative assessment for secondary science teachers*. Thousand Oaks, CA; Corwin.

Hakuta, K. (2001). *How long does it take English learners to attain proficiency?* University of California Linguistic Minority Research Institute. Policy Reports. Santa Barbara: Linguistic Minority Research Institute. Retrieved from http://repositories.cdlib.org/lmri/pr/hakuta.

Hamilton, L. S., Nussbaum, E. M., & Snow, R. E. (1997). Interview procedures for validating science assessments. *Applied Measurement in Education, 10,* 181–200.

Heritage, M., Kim, J., & Vendlinski, T. (2008, March). *From evidence to action: A seamless process in formative assessment?* Paper presented at the annual meeting of the American Educational Research Association, New York.

Kane, M. T. (1982). A sampling model of validity. *Applied Psychological Measurement, 6,* 125–160.

Klingner, J., Soltero-González, L., & Lesaux, N. (2010). RTI for English-language learners. In M. Y. Lipson & K. K. Wixson (Eds.), *Successful approaches to RTI: Collaborative practices for improving K-12 literacy*. Newark, DE: International Reading Association.

Kopriva. R. J. (Ed.). (2008). *Improving testing for English language learners.* New York: Routledge.

Lave, J., & Wenger, E. (1991). *Situated learning: Legitimate peripheral participation.* Cambridge, MA: Cambridge University Press.

Linn, R. (2003). Accountability: Responsibility and reasonable expectations. *Educational Researcher, 32*(7), 3–13.

Martinez, M. E. (1999). Cognition and the question of test item format. *Educational Psychologist, 34*(4), 207–218.

Messick, S. (1989). Validity. In R. L. Linn (Ed.), *Educational measurement,* (3rd ed., pp. 13–103). Washington, DC: American Council on Education & National Council on Measurement in Education.

Prosser, R. R., & Solano-Flores, G. (2010). *Including English language learners in the process of test development: A study on instrument linguistic adaptation for cognitive validity.* Paper presented at the Annual Conference of the National Council of Measurement in Education, Denver, Colorado, April 29–May 3.

Ruiz-Primo, M. A., & Furtak, E. M. (2007). Exploring teachers' informal formative assessment practices and students' understanding in the context of scientific inquiry. *Journal of Research in Science Teaching, 44*(1), 57–84.

Ruiz-Primo, M. A., & Shavelson, R. J. (1996). Rhetoric and reality in science performance assessments: An update. *Journal of Research in Science Teaching, 33*(10), 1045–1063.

Ruiz-Primo, M. A., Shavelson, R. J., Li, M., & Schultz, S. E., (2001). On the validity of cognitive interpretations of scores from alternative concept-mapping techniques. *Educational Assessment, 7*(2), 99–141.

Ruiz-Primo, M. A., Furtak, E. M., Ayala, C., Yin, Y., & Shavelson, R. J. (2010). Formative assessment, motivation and science learning. In H. L. Andrade & G. J. Cizek (Eds.), *Handbook of formative assessment* (pp. 139–158). New York: Routledge.

Sadler, D. R. (1989). Formative assessment in the design of instructional assessments. *Instructional Science, 18,* 119–144.

Shavelson, R. J. (1995). On the romance of science curriculum and assessment reform in the United States. In D. K. Sharpes & A. L. Leino (Eds.), *The dynamic concept of curriculum: Invited papers to honour the memory of Paul Hellgren.* (Research Bulletin 90). Helsinki: University of Helsinki, Department of Education, 57–76.

Shavelson, R. J., & Webb, N. M. (1991). *Generalizability theory: A primer.* Newbury Park, CA: Sage.

Shavelson, R. J., & Webb, N. M. (2009). Generalizability theory and its contribution to the discussion of the generalizability of research findings. In K. Erickan & W. M. Roth (Eds.), *Generalizing from educational research* (pp. 13–32). New York: Routledge.

Shepard, L. A. (2000). The role of assessment in a learning culture. *Educational Researcher, 29*(7), 4–14.

Shepard, L. (2006). Classroom assessment. In R. Brennan (Ed.), *Educational measurement* (4th ed., pp. 624–646). Westport, CT: Praeger.

Solano-Flores, G. (2000). Teaching and assessing science process skills in physics: The "Bubbles" task. *Science Activities, 37*(1), 31–37.

Solano-Flores, G. (2006). Language, dialect, and register: Sociolinguistics and the estimation of measurement error in the testing of English language learners. *Teachers College Record, 108*(11), 2354–2379.

Solano-Flores, G. (2008). Who is given tests in what language, by whom, when, and where? The need for probabilistic views of language in the testing of English language learners. *Educational Researcher, 37*(4), 189–199.

Solano-Flores, G. (2009). The testing of English language learners as a scholastic process: Population misspecification, measurement error, and overgeneralization. In K. Erickan & W. M. Roth (Eds.), *Generalizing from educational research*. New York: Routledge.

Solano-Flores, G., & Li, M. (2006). The use of generalizability (G) theory in the testing of linguistic minorities. *Educational Measurement: Issues and Practice 25*(1), 13–22.

Solano-Flores, G., & Nelson-Barber, S. (2000, April). *Cultural validity of assessments and assessment development procedures*. Paper presented at the annual meeting of the American Educational Research Association, New Orleans, LA.

Solano-Flores, G., & Trumbull, E. (2003). Examining language in context: The need for new research and practice paradigms in the testing of English-language learners. *Educational Researcher, 32*(2), 3–13.

Solano-Flores, G., Trumbull, E., & Nelson-Barber, S. (2002). Concurrent development of dual language assessments: An alternative to translating tests for linguistic minorities. *International Journal of Testing, 2*(2), 107–129.

12 *Preparando Maestros*

ESL Candidate/Teacher Preparation

Francisco Rios and Marcela van Olphen

Can ESL teacher candidates complete programs without basic foundational knowledge related to Bilingual Learners (BLs)? What is the role of preparation programs in assuring that all candidates are prepared to meet the social, academic, and language needs of BLs? These questions are significant considering that numbers of BLs continue to increase substantially (see Chapter 1).

The preparation of candidates to work productively with BLs is critical given that many current teachers were not adequately prepared to address the cultural and linguistic differences evident in most US classrooms. Two-thirds of all BLs enrolled in English-only classes are quickly mainstreamed into traditional content classes (Hopstock & Stephenson, 2003). While over 40% of all US teachers reported having BLs in their classrooms, only 12.5% of those teachers had at least eight hours of professional training around language diversity within a three-year period (National Center for Education Statistics, [NCES], 2002).

Candidate preparation in ESL is important even when BLs are classified as English proficient, since these students are still learning English (Evans, Arnot-Hopffer & Jurich, 2005). Additionally, indicators of English proficiency are often minimal and may not include levels of ability in academic English. Also, while BLs may become proficient linguistically, ESL candidates need to acquire cultural competency skills to avoid misunderstandings, lower expectations, deficit thinking, and attitudes dismissing cultural and linguistic capital.

In this chapter, we detail central concepts related to the preparation of ESL candidates for BLs. We begin with a brief overview of our guiding principles organized around four central topics: (a) identity, (b) ideology, (c) instruction and curriculum, and (d) institutional policies and supports. We detail the preparation of ESL candidates for BLs and end with recommendations for future research.

Guiding Principles

Drawing from current research and the intersections among language acquisition, development and maintenance, policy, and teacher preparation, the four topics share underlying principles grounded in the beliefs that second language acquisition is a developmental process that fosters maintenance and development of the primary language (Cummins, 1981; Krashen, 1983). We emphasize that while the focus is on English language development, we believe that English development is a necessary but insufficient component of the education of BLs. It is necessary because English is a language of power and privilege central to opening doors of opportunity to almost all residents of the nation. It is insufficient because the language development of BLs includes the maintenance of bilingualism in its own right and as a human right (Ruiz, 1988). Thus, any preparation for ESL must assure that candidates place high value on BLs' primary language development. Candidates should be prepared to either implement primary instruction when they share the same language as the student or when they do not share the same language, provide primary language support through reading materials in the primary language, peer-tutoring, allowing students to use the primary language in the classroom and school, and providing translations to critical materials in the primary language. Other principles include:

[handwritten margin note: Accommodations an ESL Teacher should make]

- Candidates must be prepared to value and pursue a robust involvement among schools, students, and their families (Cummins, 2001; Moll, 1992; Moll, Tapia, & Whitmore, 1993).
- Candidates need a clear understanding of language acquisition theories and how to translate them to practice (Pavlenko & Lantolf, 2000; Wong-Fillmore & Snow, 2000).
- Commitment to continued professional development throughout their career (Eun & Heining-Boynton, 2007; Knight & Wiseman, 2005).
- Candidates must recognize the deep connection between language and cultural diversity (Faltis, 2008).
- Teaching and learning are a political, moral, and human endeavor that requires candidates to develop ideological clarity (Cochran-Smith, 2004).

Issues in ESL Candidate Preparation

Identity

Much of teacher preparation involves the development of a professional identity (see Chapter 3), centering on helping candidates develop a sense of self as teacher and refining that identity throughout their career. Thus, preparation of candidates includes assisting them being a teacher of BLs in their identity cluster.

People hold many identities and these identities shift, are relational, and contextual (West & Olson, 1999). We acknowledge that discussions of linguistic or cultural identity include multiple aspects of identity, such as race, class, gender, and their intersection with student identities. Consider, for example, how BLs' identities coalesce around what it means to be an English speaker, in terms of level of fluency.

As suggested, an interdependent relationship exists between identity and language learning (Pavlenko & Lantolf, 2000). Cummins (2001) explored this relationship between the teacher/student identities and language learning/teaching. Morgan (2004) asserts that these identities, which he refers to as image texts, are being "co-created, its authorship belonging to both teacher and students. Thus, an image-text must be discovered contingently and relationally if it is to be utilized" (p. 174). Importantly, Cummins (2001) reminds us that these identities are situated in larger power dynamics. That is, teacher and student identities are situated within institutional and national discourses and are not simply an issue of psychological development.

These identities are not exclusively psychological. Rather they tangibly and concretely impact the ways candidates approach curriculum and instruction. Morgan (2004) describes the connection between psychological and behavioral aspects as a performance of identities. Teacher identity is unlike any other teaching resource since generally, its application cannot be predicted. Teachers can either support or subvert the stereotypes of the orthodox identities associated with being a teacher and being a teacher of BLs.

Simon (1995) advanced the connection between identity and practice by suggesting that teacher identity is pedagogy. This idea of teacher identity as a tangible resource supports and extends Cummins' (2001) notions of the continual interaction of identity development and language learning. In Morgan's (2004) study, "even at the suprasegmental, phonological level, identity negotiation was taking place and seemed to be occurring throughout L2 instruction" (p. 183).

Other factors influencing identity include the candidate level of proficiency with both the target language and student home language, confidence and efficacy, quality of preparation program, degree of school level support, degree of cultural knowledge, and ability to continually improve classroom instruction (Bayliss & Vignola, 2007). These issues are especially salient for candidates who are non-native speakers of English thrust into teaching English. Reves and Medgyes (1994), who studied such ESL teachers, assert "a constant realization of their limitations in the use of English may lead to a poorer self-image, which may further deteriorate language performance, and in turn may lead to a cumulatively stronger feeling of inferiority" (p. 364). This sense of inferiority might lead an ESL teacher to focus more on grammatical rather than communicative approaches to teaching (Bayliss & Vignola, 2007). Coursework in the preparation of candidates working with BLs must engage the nexus of identity and language, consider identity development, and in learning ways to monitor social, linguistic, and academic interactions with student identity development as new speakers of English.

Ideology

Fairclough (1992, p. 4) describes a hegemonic ideology as "an implicit philosophy, which governs practice and is often a taken-for-granted assumption linked to common sense, contributing to sustaining existing power relations and dominant discourses." He notes connections among ideology, power, and language. Cochran-Smith and Fries (2004) explain how competing ideologies are evident in assumptions about teaching and, by extension, teacher education. For them, the broad ideological question is whether teachers are technicians or professionals. Those who view teaching as technical believe that the only knowledge of value is subject-specific and teachers can follow pedagogical scripts. Those who advocate for understanding the role of teachers as thoughtful, reflective, principled, creative, and responsive professionals committed to serving the needs of children assert a strong need for teacher education. We assert that the prevailing national ideology about schooling and teaching has a strong influence on candidate ideology (see Chapter 4 and 6). For example, Skilton-Sylvester (2003) found a seamless ideological web operating in US multilingual classrooms. Assumptions about learning English and about BLs included: a widespread, prevailing language-as-problem orientation with learning English as the solution; an emphasis on subtractive bilingualism in schooling policy; questioning immigrant and refugee rights to maintaining native languages; and, a belief that other languages are useful only if they serve an instructional function.

While Nolan (2001) points out that theories and ideologies are evident in the curriculum choices we make, there is a direct relationship between candidate ideology and their theories of practice. Tsang (2004) asserts that what candidates think and believe shapes the way they understand teaching and the priorities they give to different dimensions of work. In his study, candidate ideology was informed by their beliefs in the ideal teaching-learning model as well as by their understanding of the process of language acquisition. While some knowledge was positive and inspired candidates to test their understandings, others served as biases making candidates resistant to alternative thoughts and actions.

The dominant ideological question for candidates working with BLs includes challenging deficit oriented thinking, which is difficult given the language, such as limited English proficient and non-English proficient, used in the field. The name change in the Department of Education's Office of Bilingual Education and Minority Language Affairs (OBEMLA) to the Office of English Language Acquisition (OELA) promotes a deficit and hegemonic ideological position. Recent policy geared to the near myopic focus on developing English and reinforcing traditional US culture results in movement away from multiculturalism and bilingualism. This is reinforced structurally by standards, standardized exams, segregation of BLs, and integration without support for specialized language needs.

Instruction and Curriculum

Curriculum, defined as "a series of activities in which students engage with subject matter" (Thornton, 2010), is a tool educators use to influence classroom instruction and student learning. Curriculum content is organized in ways that highlight some aspects of the subject matter and disregard others. Different types of curricular designs denote what is recognized as academically important and, therefore influence what students learn (Thornton, 2010). Candidates need to recognize that as teachers, they are the curricular and instructional gatekeepers. Teachers decide how classrooms are organized, which instructional activities students will perform, and which learning strategies students will acquire.

ESL candidates, who are aware of the academic and linguistic needs of BLs and are skilled to take advantage of the cultural and linguistic capital students bring into the classroom, have potential to make instructional decisions that promote cultural and linguistic pluralism. These candidates understand that students bring vibrant home languages and cultures. Moll, Amanti, Neff, and González (1992) maintained that "this relationship can become the basis for the exchange of knowledge about family or school matters, reducing the insularity of classrooms, and contributing to the academic content and lessons" (p. 139). This approach allows culture and language to become an integral informing principle when designing curriculum and planning instruction. Téllez (2002) identifies the challenges of including deep cultural knowledge in the curriculum. He warns about the risks associated with the types of cultural knowledge taught by candidates during student teaching who lack cultural understandings. For ESL candidates, a helpful illustration of how this would apply in instruction is the model lesson taught by Ivonne Blank, a kindergarten teacher on Earth Day (Cruz & Thornton, 2008). Ms. Blank taught an integrated lesson during which students learned about the environment, recycling, geography, and art. She adapted instruction to meet the needs of Roberto, a Puerto Rican non-English speaking student, as well to challenge the other students. Her use of comprehensible input, visuals, student cultural knowledge, and reinforcement of the importance of working together and helping each other promote student learning. Ms. Blank's lesson planning and instructional decisions were based on the assumptions that Roberto was a valued member of the group and that his contributions were important not only for himself but also for the whole class. Using her student knowledge and home cultures was an integral part of the instructional activities as well as the classroom organization. Although a Spanish native speaker, Ms. Blank relied on her English for Speakers of Other Languages (ESOL) strategies to communicate with Roberto. If needed, she spoke Spanish to him, but she was pointing to objects as she spoke, using cognates, paraphrasing, and providing him with opportunities to express his thoughts via art and praising him and the class continuously. Her goal was for Roberto to learn English while maintaining his native language. Her instruction was carefully planned, executed, and most importantly, predicated on the belief that Roberto would learn English and that he was a valued member of their classroom.

Language learning strategies are another important component of instruction and curriculum. Candidates should be taught how these strategies can be carefully identified and planned in consonance with instructional objectives. For instance, the strategies teachers present to BLs to learn social studies may be closely related to those for reading instruction but may differ from those taught to learn algebra or chemistry. Swan (2008) suggests that the use of strategies should be a principled process and warns that training students in those techniques should not be a substitute for language teaching. Griffiths (2007), who studied the intersections of teacher and learner views as they pertain to learning strategies, found a 71% match between the types of learning strategies that teachers place high and those strategies most frequently used by BLs. She also found an upward trend in terms of teacher awareness of the importance of language learning strategies as part of teaching and learning languages. This awareness involves engaging BLs in their own understanding of why these strategies are important.

Teacher candidates of BLs who establish classroom management practices drawing from what they know about their students' cultural backgrounds tend to be more successful than those whose classroom policies are not rooted in these values. Because of the interplay between classroom management and classroom organization, it is vital that candidates understand that BLs need explicit cultural knowledge to be able to function in U.S. educational settings. Candidates should not judge student behaviors without a basic knowledge of student cultural backgrounds. For instance, whether a student makes eye contact with a teacher often causes cultural misunderstandings leading to classroom management concerns. While some children know the importance of making eye contact with teachers or other adults, for other children such direct eye contact is a sign of disrespect and they believe doing so would be perceived as challenging authority.

Helping ESL candidates develop the skills and intellectual capacity to systematically learn about their students has productive outcomes. As candidates become involved in studying and learning more about their specific students, classroom, and practices, they become intellectually stimulated. Gibbons (2008) noted that teachers, teaching in linguistically and culturally diverse classrooms, strengthened the curriculum as a result of involvement in action research projects. This collaborative process promoted an environment of sustained contributions between teachers and students and created an affective dimension in the classroom where students felt valued. Action research projects provide opportunities for students and teachers to discuss instruction, curriculum, and classroom policies. Candidates, willing to learn about student perspectives, share responsibilities and plant seeds of democratic education.

In sum, ESL candidates need to understand that as teachers they will hold the keys to instruction and curriculum. Despite national, state, district, and school policies, once the classroom door is closed, it is up to teachers to use the wealth of the social capital and funds of knowledge that BLs bring to the classroom. And, therein rests the responsibility of instilling the knowledge, skills, and professional dispositions in programs that advocate for educational equity and democratic societies.

Institutional Policies and Supports

ESL candidates need to learn how policies at the federal, state, district, and institutional level impact classrooms. These structures make tangible an implicit, ideological orientation. They shape a particular kind of teacher identity based on the roles teachers assume (Evans, Arnot-Hopffer, & Jurich, 2005).

Federal policies, such as No Child Left Behind (NCLB), and the standards movement more broadly impact the schooling of BLs. For example, Meyer (2005) pointed out that in its overzealous focus on English, NCLB could signify "no child left bilingual." More specifically, federal policies in the first years of the 21st century tend to discount student linguistic and cultural resources, codify a Eurocentric knowledge and language base, and widen the very academic gaps the policies purport to close (Valenzuela, 2004; see Chapter 15). District policies mirroring this federal stance promote English as the Only Language (EOL). According to Salazar (2008), the underlying assumption is that academic success relies exclusively on English competency. Salazar (2008) illustrated how language limitations generate cultural limitations and minimize expressive possibilities, since students cannot fully share salient aspects of their culture if they do not have command of English.

Varghese and Jenkins (2005) observed that beyond the broad ideological orientation and related policies, many specific federal government rules are either unclear, non-existent, or both. In states with low numbers of BLs, districts decide how to structure specialized language programs. Policy decisions generally rest on the number of BLs within the district, whether the population is transient/stable, their status in the community, available district support and resources, languages spoken, and number of teachers with specialized language endorsements.

ESL candidate role as advocates for BLs may be consequential. To illustrate, Varghese and Jenkins (2005) found that the teacher roles impacted the nature, quality, and development of ESL programs. The teachers in the study reported feeling disempowered, without access to resources, and not recognized as full professionals. Many of these teachers developed a strong opposition to their marginalization including developing family literacy programs, creating their own literature, offering inservice training, and mentoring school staff. Varghese and Jenkins (2005) maintained that it is important for candidates to advocate for systemic change:

> The presence of an active advocate with either the power to effect change (e.g., a curriculum coordinator) or a teacher/tutor with persuasive, yet non-threatening interaction skills can be a powerful catalyst for change. These should be sought out, courted and actively promoted as change agents
>
> (p. 94)

Candidates also need to understand how district language policies impact how they approach schooling for BLs. Salazar's (2008) study showed that district and school policies affected teacher approaches to curriculum, instruction, language use, and social relations with students and caregivers. The district language policies, with a focus on an English-only ideology and a surface approach to cultural diversity influenced, but did not always determine, teacher instructional approach in the classroom. However, these policies sent a message to both students and teachers about what was valued and what practices should be implemented.

For Salazar (2008), it was not just explicit policies but also the practices and ideologies permeating practice. Teachers mirror district orientations by failing to include students in the co-construction of curriculum and parent involvement in the teaching-learning process. Teachers not only heard and read the explicit message about language but incorporated implicit messages about decision-making. Surprisingly, the teachers in her study did not appear to be aware of how their pedagogy and practices were influenced by broader district and federal policies.

Questions regarding state credential requirements are also problematic. In Florida, a bill was proposed to minimize coursework addressing language diversity from 300 to 60 training hours (Zehr, 2008). This decrease contradicts current recommendations around the knowledge base and skills needed for teachers of BLs (Salazar, 2008; Wong-Fillmore & Snow, 2000). A positive trend requires all teachers to have some level of competency in working with BLs (Zehr, 2008). For example, in California and Virginia, all candidates must receive ESL training. Evans, Arnot-Hopffer and Jurich (2005) explain:

> More helpful are certification requirements that are explicit about prerequisite understandings of language, second language acquisition, the histories of the major cultural groups in the State, and strategies for teaching ELL students. Such requirements must also be substantively apparent in state teacher testing

programs. Neither standards nor test items can capture (or force) the personal and professional development which may be required for first, altering one's assumptions about teaching and second, preparing oneself to teach children of other language and cultural backgrounds. In the current context of standards and accountability, however, these issues cannot be absent from the explicit expectations states announce and require for their teachers.

(p. 86)

ESL teacher preparation must include helping candidates to develop an advocacy oriented stance in relation to public policy including challenging policies and institutional structures, understanding how they might be able to influence these processes, and creating spaces within their own classrooms related to improving the education of culturally and linguistically diverse students (Salazar, 2008; see Chapter 15). In short, ESL is still marginalized within universities and schools. We need to identify candidates who are willing to be change agents, action researchers, and professional development specialists (Salazar, 2008). As Salazar (2008) described:

> Furthermore, educators must advocate for an inclusive vision of ESL at a federal, state, and district level. Moreover, a new vision for ESL must move beyond a myopic view of the acquisition of English alone to include an emphasis on valuing, acknowledging, and building and extending students' cultural, linguistic, and familial resources to improve teaching and learning. This vision must support heritage language development in official and unofficial spaces of school.
>
> (p. 353)

Research Directions

Overall, we assert that ESL candidate preparation for BLs is understudied and under theorized. Thus, we end with a few central questions and issues requiring further research in the preparation of ESL candidates and general education candidates seeking ESL endorsements.

- Examine the ways different models prepare candidates with pedagogical content knowledge as well as the professional and personal dispositions to serve the needs of BLs.
- Identify and study which preparation experiences foster productive orientations resulting in higher achievement outcomes for BLs.
- Document the relevance of particular knowledge and skills candidates use when engaged in fieldwork and student teaching.

References

Bayliss, D., & Vignola, M. J. (2007). Training non-native second language teachers: The case of Anglophone FSL teacher candidates. *Canadian Modern Language Review, 63*(3), 371–398.

Cochran-Smith, M. (2004). *Walking the road: Race, diversity, and social justice in teacher education*. New York: Teachers College Press.

Cochran-Smith, M., & Fries, K. (2004). Sticks, stones, and ideology. In M. Cochran-Smith, (Eds.), *Walking the road: Race, diversity, and social justice in teacher education* (pp. 120–139). New York: Teachers College Press.

Cruz, B., & Thornton, S. J. (2008). Social studies for all: ESOL strategies for the elementary classroom. *Social Studies and the Young Learner, 21*(2), 11–16.

Cummins, J. (1981). The role of primary language development in promoting educational success for language minority students. In California State Department of Education (Ed.), *Schooling and language minority students: A theoretical framework* (pp. 3–49). Los Angeles: California State University; Evaluation, Dissemination and Assessment Center.

Cummins, J. (2001). *Negotiating identities: Education for empowerment in a diverse society* (2nd ed). Ontario, CA: California Association of Bilingual Education.

Eun, B., & Heining-Boynton, A. L. (2007). Impact of an English-as-a-Second-Language professional development program. *Journal of Educational Research, 101*(1), 36–48.

Evans, C., Arnot-Hopffer, E., & Jurich, D. (2005). Making ends meet: Bringing bilingual education and mainstream students together in preservice teacher education. *Equity & Excellence in Education, 38*(1), 75–88.

Fairclough, N. (1992). *Discourse and social change*. Cambridge, UK: Polity Press.

Faltis, C. (2008). Editorial. *Multicultural Perspectives, 10*(4), 183.

Gibbons, P. (2008). "It was taught good and I learned a lot": Intellectual practices and ESL learners in the middle years. *Australian Journal of Language and Literacy, 31*(2), 155–173.

Griffiths, C. (2007). Language learning strategies: Students' and teachers' perceptions. *ELT Journal, 61*(2), 91–99.

Hopstock, P. J., & Stephenson, T. G. (2003). *Descriptive study of services to LEP students and LEP students with disabilities*. Washington, DC: Office of English Language Acquisition.

Knight, S. L., & Wiseman, D. L. (2005). Lessons learned from a research synthesis on the effects of teachers' professional development on culturally diverse students. In K. Téllez & H. C. Waxman (Eds.), *Preparing quality educators for English language learners: Policies and practices* (pp. 71–98). Mahwah, NJ: Erlbaum.

Krashen, S. (1983). *The natural approach: Language acquisition in the classroom*. New York: Pergamon Press, Inc.

Meyer, L. (2005). *No child left bilingual? An analysis of U. S. educational policy and its impacts on English language learners and their school programs, parents and communities*. Portsmouth, NH: Heinemann.

Moll, L. C. (1992). Bilingual classroom studies and community analysis: Some recent trends. *Educational Researcher, 21*(2), 20–24.

Moll, L. C., Amanti, C., Neff, D., & Gonzalez, N. (1992). Funds of knowledge for teaching: Using a qualitative approach to connect homes and classrooms. *Theory into Practice, 31*(2), 132–141.

Moll, L. C., Tapia, J., & Whitmore, K. (1993). Living knowledge: The social distribution of cultural resources for thinking. In G. Salomon (Ed.), *Distributed cognitions: Psychological and educational considerations* (pp. 139–163). New York: Cambridge University Press.

Morgan, B. (2004). Teacher identity as pedagogy: Towards a field-internal conceptualization in bilingual and second language education. *International Journal of Bilingual Education & Bilingualism, 7*(2/3), 172–188.

National Center for Education Statistics (NCES), (2002). *Schools and staffing survey, 1999–2000*. Washington, DC: National Center for Education Statistics. Retrieved from http://nces.ed.gov/pubsearch/pubsinfo.asp?pubid=2002313

Nolan, R. E. (2001). The power of theory in the administration of ESL programs. *Adult Basic Education, 11*(1), 3–17.

Pavlenko, A., & Lantolf, J. P. (2000). Second language learning as participation and the (re) construction of selves. In J. P. Lantolf (Ed.), *Sociocultural theory and second language learning* (pp. 155–177). New York: Oxford University Press.

Reves, T., & Medgyes, P. (1994). The non-native speaking EFL/ESL teacher's self-image: An international survey. *System, 22,* 353–367.

Ruiz, R. (1988). Orientations in language planning. In S. McKay & S. Wong (Eds.), *Language diversity: Problem or resource?* (pp. 3–25). Cambridge, MA: Newbury House.

Salazar, M. (2008). English or nothing: The impact of rigid language policies on the inclusion of humanizing practices in a high school ESL program. *Equity & Excellence in Education, 41*(3), 341–356.

Simon, R. I. (1995). Face to face with alterity: Postmodern Jewish identity and the eros of pedagogy. In J. Gallop (Ed.), *Pedagogy: The question of impersonation* (pp. 90–105). Bloomington, IN: University of Indiana Press.

Skilton-Sylvester, E. (2003). Legal discourse and decisions, teacher policymaking and the multilingual classroom: Constraining and supporting Khmer/English biliteracy in the United States. In A. Creese & P. Martin (Eds.), *Multilingual classroom ecologies: Inter-relationships, interactions and ideologies* (pp. 8–24). Clevedon, UK: Multilingual Matters.

Swan, M. (2008). Talking sense about learning strategies. *RELC Journal, 39*(2), 262–273.

Téllez, K. (2002). Multicultural education as subtext. *Multicultural Perspectives, 4*(2), 21-26.

Thornton, S. J. (2010). Curriculum design. In C. Kridel (Ed.), *Encyclopedia of Curriculum Studies.* Thousand Oaks, CA: Sage.

Tsang, W. K. (2004). Teachers' personal practical knowledge and interactive decisions. *Language Teaching Research, 8*(2), 163–198.

Valenzuela, A. (2004). *Leaving children behind: How "Texas-style" accountability fails Latino youth.* Albany, NY: State University of New York Press.

Varghese, M., & Jenkins, S. (2005). Challenges for ESL teacher professionalization in the US: A case study. *Intercultural Education, 16*(1), 85–95.

West, T., & Olson, G. A. (1999). Critical negotiation(s): Transformative action in cultural studies and border pedagogy. *The Review of Education/Pedagogy/Cultural Studies, 21*(2), 149–163.

Wong-Fillmore, L., & Snow, C. E. (2000). *What teachers need to know about language.* Washington, DC: Center for Applied Linguistics.

Zehr, M. A. (2008). Florida bill would ease ESL-training mandate. *Education Week, 27*(32).

13 Transformative Teacher Education for Gifted Students in Bilingual/ESL Programs

Virginia González and
Mariella Espinoza-Herold

Currently BLs are underrepresented in gifted programs and achievement gaps are increasing between high-performing lower socioeconomic (SES) students and their peers from higher economic groups. According to the US Department of Education (2004/2006), the national percentage of all public school students identified as gifted and talented was 6.7%, with 7.9% for White students, 4.3% for Latin@s, 5.2% for American Indian/Alaskan Natives, 3.5% for African Americans, and 11.7% for Asian/Pacific Islanders.

The availability of gifted education programs varies dramatically between and within states. Public schools serving lower SES students often face funding shortages and difficulties hiring qualified teachers. Preparation programs need to address the training of highly qualified teachers who are prepared to identify and teach gifted bilingual children. These BLs may have academic language skills below mainstream standards; however, they show potential for high levels in areas such as, non-verbal cognitive and metacognitive, and first-language conceptual and metalinguistic skills (Gonzalez, 2009; Gonzalez, Brusca-Vega, & Yawkey, 1997). Going beyond traditional definitions of giftedness, Gonzalez, Bauerle, and Clark (2007) differentiated linguistic and cultural dimensions of giftedness. Using non-traditional assessment, they were able to identify verbal and non-verbal cultural aspects of giftedness. Research findings using statistical and other analytical methods demonstrate that the cultural and linguistic validity of identification and assessment instruments, and adequate teacher training in the unique characteristics of BLs are the most important school variables affecting their representation in gifted programs (Clark & Gonzalez, 2000). Factors to consider in teacher preparation include knowledge of various definitions of giftedness, alternative assessments to determine giftedness, and differentiation of curriculum (Gonzalez, Bauerle, & Clark, 2007).

This chapter presents a research-based teacher curriculum model for infusing change into gifted bilingual/ESL programs. We propose that for teacher candidates to be highly qualified and effective with gifted BLs, pedagogical praxis should drive BLs' identification, assessment, and instruction. Pedagogical praxis relies on research-based pedagogy through continual reflection and systematic documentation of practice. Pedagogical praxis involving the teacher as an action researcher with a community of learners results in research-based practice that stimulates optimal social adaptation and academic achievement for gifted BLs.

This approach enables candidates to learn knowledge and skills associated with progressive, pluralistic ideologies, which will change in practice. Candidates can learn to exercise flexible and adaptive responses to gifted BLs.

In the first section, we discuss pedagogical praxis as a process of change in teacher preparation programs. Infusing change is a challenging task involving the systematic application of research-based knowledge to the school curriculum, while stimulating reflection on how school cultures and candidates' attitudes, values, and beliefs affect BLs' learning and academic achievement (see Chapter 4). An effective way to change teacher beliefs and pedagogical praxis is to stimulate reflections about their practice of teaching and its effect on student learning. Changes in teacher beliefs and teaching practices about what constitutes giftedness can also be achieved through critical thinking and examination of how culture and language influence gifted BLs' learning and developmental processes.

The second section introduces four key components of pedagogical praxis framed by social-cognitive theory: reflective practice and critical thinking, action research, skills, and research-based knowledge. These are required to help candidates develop commitment and advocacy, intercultural sensitivity and competency, and ability to build partnerships with bilingual families and communities.

Infusing Change through Pedagogical Praxis

Pedagogical praxis is used to describe a systematic educational practice, in which teachers collaborate with researchers, and together engage in action research and active reflection. In this collaborative pedagogical praxis, teachers are mentored by researchers to reflect on their practices and document effective instructional and assessment strategies to increase gifted BLs' academic achievement and cognitive development.

Pedagogical praxis is action, involving primarily a search for truth, as well as a commitment to human well-being and respect for others; hence, it bears a strong connection to social justice and involves wise and prudent practical judgment (Carr & Kemmis, 1986). Pedagogical praxis involving school/university faculty and administrators, and bilingual communities must be generative, educative, and liberating. It must include trust and interactive connectedness between teachers and BLs. Pedagogical praxis serves as the guiding element and generator of processes of change and adaptability. Whether teachers come from majority or ethnic minority groups, pedagogical praxis enables them to recognize and negotiate the intricacies of social power relationships and ever-changing range of cultural identities of diverse gifted students. Pedagogical praxis moves the profession away from traditional assimilation ideologies about teaching and learning and introduces progressive and pluralistic ideologies that support multicultural and bilingual identities in diverse students. Most importantly, teacher quality is associated with high expectations, positive attitudes, rapport, empathy, commitment, and advocacy for meeting the educational needs of gifted BLs.

In preparation programs, infusing change must develop candidates' academic knowledge about teaching and learning, while simultaneously focusing on their attitudes, commitment, and advocacy towards BLs; increasing leadership skills; and gaining multicultural and multilingual experiences through immersion in diverse settings. The experiences candidates are exposed to in programs can have an immense impact on their pedagogical praxis with gifted BLs. The transformative program we propose promotes the integration of social-cognitive theory, progressive, pluralistic ideologies, intercultural sensitivity, and cultural/linguistic competency.

Transformative Teacher Preparation for Gifted BLs

This proposed curriculum model focuses on the preparation of candidates for gifted BLs. It has four dimensions: reflective practice, action research, skills, and content knowledge based on research in bilingual/ESL education. We maintain that generalist teacher candidates can develop a personal connection or rapport with gifted BLs by connecting to their family history which most likely includes immigrant ancestors who struggled to adapt to a new society, language, and culture. It is also important for candidates to recognize that being bilingual and bicultural can impact BLs' cognitive and metacognitive abilities, which, as initially determined by Clark (1981), can result in giftedness. We also recommend the development of reflective practice and critical thinking skills using mentors and role models, extended field practice opportunities, and immersion in cultural and linguistic communities. These opportunities and experiences can infuse change and growth in candidates' attitudes, social values, beliefs, multicultural knowledge, and global worldview, as well as their pedagogical praxis with gifted BLs.

Pedagogical praxis also can effect change in candidate ideology (see Chapters 4 and 6) from assimilation and remedial perspectives to progressive and pluralistic ideologies that value multicultural and bilingual identities in diverse students as educational enrichments. Pedagogical praxis as an action research teaching practice helps teachers to systematically apply research-based knowledge to the school curriculum and to document records of best practice. The proposed program also integrates the development of new skills and research-based knowledge in candidates that enables them to develop and apply new pedagogical praxis for better serving gifted BLs. Most importantly, teacher quality and effectiveness is associated with high expectations, positive attitudes, rapport, empathy, and commitment to meet the needs of BLs.

Reflective Practice

Reflective practice involves critical thinking about progressive and pluralistic ideologies, equity, and social justice. It allows candidates to: (1) recognize and negotiate social power relationships and acknowledge the ever changing cultural identities of BLs; and (2) develop positive attitudes, social values, and beliefs for improving their commitment, advocacy, intercultural sensitivity, and competency. We endorse the Ethnic Educator Approach (Gonzalez, 2001, 2009; Gonzalez et al., 1997; Gonzalez, Yawkey, & Minaya-Rowe, 2006), which helps candidates develop a personal connection between the diversity factors in their family history with those of a bilingual student population.

Scholars agree that merely addressing teacher-content knowledge and teacher quality is not sufficient (Darling-Hammond, 2006). Instead, we need to look at the composition of the teaching force, which does not reflect the diversity of the student population (Ladson-Billings, 1999), since most teachers are White, female, monolingual from middle-class backgrounds (Zumbault & Craig, 2005).

However, we must realize that many generalist candidates are descendants of immigrants who came to the US in waves from the mid-1800s to the mid-1900s. Most can identify non-English speaking ancestors that immigrated from eastern and southern Europe, who shared similar economic characteristics with today's immigrants (Gonzalez, 2001; Gonzalez et al., 2006). Exploration of personal family history of immigration helps candidates re-discover familial immigrant experience; and, this common experience can support rapport, advocacy, and commitment to BLs (Gonzalez et al., 1997, 2006; Gonzalez, 2001, 2009). Programs must provide generalist candidates with opportunity to develop empathy and broadening their lens about BLs' potential in various settings, enabling them to meet the schooling needs of large numbers of BLs in schools (see Chapter 1).

Although, our teaching force does not reflect the linguistic, ethnic and racial background of the K-12 student population nor do they identify with students' communities; we argue that most teachers can learn about commonalities through family histories. For example, they may learn about an innovation developed out of necessity or for survival of harsh, demanding living conditions during different historical periods. Transformative programs can use this sense of identification with BLs to develop greater levels of cultural and linguistic competency. The inherently cultural nature of learning and knowing (Sheets, 2009) supports the importance of connecting teaching and learning processes to diverse students' prior cultural experiences.

Action Research

This research-based teaching practice allows candidates to systematically apply research-based knowledge to school curriculum and to document records of practice; thus, linking assessment to instruction. Pedagogical praxis through action engages candidates in a collaborative mentorship with practitioners and researchers. For example, candidates can research about communities' views and definitions of giftedness; they can also examine home practices that can enhance giftedness in bilingual children.

This approach can challenge candidates to think comprehensibly about what the new "intercultural teacher of the 21st century" looks like (Partnership for 21st Century Skills, 2007). We propose that candidates who have developed intercultural sensitivity and competency can apply action research for responding to the specific educational needs of gifted BLs.

Skills

Pedagogical praxis through the development of leadership skills and advocacy positions advances candidate potential to implement change; provides extensive experience and field practice with BLs in sociocultural communities through mentoring, apprenticeship of observation, and dialogic praxis-exposure to real-life social problems; increases proficiency in native pedagogy involving first language and native culture; and, encourages learning a second language and educational technology.

In the last decade, we have set high expectations about the types of professional development learning communities candidates and teachers should help create, yet we have not engaged them in vibrant learning communities that model and support transformative learning opportunities (Gutierrez, 2000). For example, as a society, we want candidates to help BLs become informed, well-prepared individuals for an increasingly globalized and diverse reality. Yet, we seem to support reforms that effectively dismantle bilingual education programs and devalue bilingual/bicultural teachers and diverse communities in the US.

In the past 25 years, we have seen a growing interest in preparing candidates to meet the schooling needs of BLs, many who are at-risk of underachievement. Likewise, educational reform movements have urged researchers to address issues of teacher quality (Darling-Hammond, 2006) and to meet the needs of gifted BLs (Castellano, 2002). Nieto (2000) proposes that teachers should become multilingual and multicultural themselves, so that by learning students' realities, teachers can develop meaningful relationships. The model that we propose calls for skill development to achieve intercultural competency levels. We suggest immersing candidates and teachers in structured intercultural competency training aimed at providing an extensive contact between and across culturally diverse groups. These experiences can include home visits and home-stays in the US and abroad, as part of the core curriculum. Cultural immersion provides opportunity to learn a second language, so they can experience similar social adaptation and language learning difficulties as their diverse students.

Because the model that we propose for the preparation of candidates for gifted BLs is based on social-cognitive theory, experience is an essential element to stimulate thinking and reflection processes that lead to growth and change. Darling-Hammond (2006) refers to extended experience in field practice as an "apprenticeship of observation," which allows candidates to identify a problem in the community and then collaborate to solve it. Therefore, candidates should be provided with continuous guided, mentored opportunities to engage in dialogic praxis in order to: (1) experience directly the real-life dynamics of BLs; (2) reflect and question deficit notions about BLs' learning potential; and (3) develop positive attitudes, advocacy, and commitment to better serve BLs.

We need to develop substantial leadership skills among candidates, teachers, and administrators in districts and university faculty, especially those involved in the preparation and professional development of teachers. Leadership skills can be developed in conjunction with understandings of policy, utilization of reflective practice, and action research. Effective leaders learn to assess the socio-cultural reality of the schools and communities they serve, which when duly acknowledged, can serve as a strategic point of departure for school reform efforts and research-driven preparation of teachers. An understanding of the complex interaction of cultural and linguistic diversity with poverty becomes critical to develop research-based teacher preparation programs to better serve diverse students.

Educational technologies, such as online virtual observations and forum discussions can be complemented with commentaries and readings from various experts on social-cognitive and gifted theories. Classroom based observation videotapes can become part of a vicarious apprenticeship with role models and mentors. These expert teachers are examples of situated learning and the application of social-cognitive theory in school-based settings for BLs and communities. However, each teacher needs to find a balance between experts facilitating discussion forums and their own version and thoughtful changes in their pedagogical praxis. Multimedia formats can provide tools for documenting real-life scenarios of teaching and learning, including: videotapes of gifted BLs and parent interviews; virtual observations of family environments; actual products such as curriculums, lesson plans, instructional materials, and assessment tools; samples of teacher journals and reflections; and analysis of real-life gifted cases. Multimedia formats can provide a very open-ended and rich learning environment for teachers to engage in discussion forums with colleagues and experts that can stimulate and support changes in pedagogical praxis for BLs. Through group discussions, candidates engage in the analysis of the applications of cognitive theories through virtual classroom-based observations and multimedia case studies.

Research-Based Content Knowledge

Candidates need research-based content knowledge about gifted bilingual/ESL education, second-language learning and development, multicultural knowledge, and how low SES may affect learning and academic achievement. Pedagogical praxis applies research-based knowledge about theories, models, and strategies in gifted education to improve opportunities for BLs' learning and development.

Candidates need to develop a better understanding of the complex sociocultural mediating factors such as language, culture, and poverty to understand how the home culture and language affect, both externally and internally, BLs' attitudes and school performance. Examples of internal factors include individual differences in learning and cultural thinking styles, aptitudes, maturational levels, interests, and intrinsic motivation. External factors also influence BLs' development such as parents' language proficiency, education and literacy levels, parent's adaptation to the mainstream culture, number of siblings, and birth order. Where giftedness is concerned, an understanding of the cultural and social factors becomes of critical importance to insure that BLs have access to the best possible programs.

BLs and lower SES students need to have equal access to social capital in order to develop academic and social competence associated with gains in socioeconomic power. That is the core value of a democratic society for every child. This is the social justice principle underlying true democracy that affirms social policy supporting affirmative development. We have a moral responsibility to develop cognitive, linguistic, and cultural capacity in BLs, which will in turn increase the numbers of BLs in advanced, gifted programs where they have been previously underrepresented.

True access for developing competencies for gifted BLs means a departure from a school culture that focuses on remediation over accelerated learning and an enriched curriculum that engages students in high efficacy, high-expectations, and high performance learning communities. Accelerated learning for gifted BLs means emphasis on the development of academic competence through critical thinking and also means providing enriched learning experiences to develop scholastic aptitude, with a focus on these : (1) academic/cognitive competence, the socialization of general intellectual ability to problem solve and apply knowledge across content areas using critical thinking skills, (2) social competence, the general intellectual ability to apply knowledge to solve real-life problems that can be developed and internalized through mediated learning within diverse socio-cultural contexts, and (3) bilingual bicultural competence, the ability to operate cognitively within differing cultural and linguistic arenas. These competencies are developed through mediated learning within particular socio-cultural learning contexts.

Conclusion

This chapter proposes that for candidates to be highly qualified and effective with gifted BLs, pedagogical praxis should serve as the dynamic heart and drive identification, assessment, and instructional activities. While many of the suggestions provided could be used to serve all BLs, it is important to consider the specific needs of gifted BLs. Today's learners need to become critical thinkers, problem-solvers, effective communicators, and innovators. Above all, they need to acquire new literacy skills and knowledge about the world beyond our nation. Thus, it is incumbent upon all of us to truly comprehend the widening scale of skills and knowledge that candidates need to meet the needs of all learners, but also gifted BLs, in an increasingly globalized and technology-driven society.

Improving BLs' achievement and opportunities depends on how we prepare candidates. Teachers in a rapidly-evolving multicultural world must have the reflective and critical thinking dispositions, and research-knowledge and skills to connect with BLs. Rather than simply addressing the large number of learning standards and an irrelevant school curriculum that has changed little in the past 50 years, transformative programs must infuse change in attitudes, social values, and beliefs; and inspire candidates to become advocates for gifted BLs and their families.

References

Carr, W., & Kemmis, S. (1986). *Becoming critical: Education, knowledge, and action research.* London: Falmer Press.

Castellano, J. A. (2002). Researching new horizons: Gifted and talented education for culturally and linguistically diverse students. In J. A. Castellano & E. Díaz (Eds.), *Gifted education programs: Connections to English language learners* (pp. 117–132). Boston: Allyn & Bacon.

Clark, E. R. (1981). *Determination of giftedness in lower socio-economic Mexican-American students.* Unpublished Dissertation. The University of Texas at Austin.

Clark, E. R., & Gonzalez, V. (2000). Voices and *voces:* Cultural and linguistic dimensions of giftedness. Reprinted in *ANNUAL EDITIONS: Educational Psychology 2000/2001.* 5, 80–85.

Darling-Hammond, L. (2006). Constructing 21st-century teacher education. *Journal of Teacher Education, 57*(3), 300–314.

Gonzalez, V. (2001). Immigration: Education's story past, present, and future. *College Board Review, 193*, 24–31.

Gonzalez, V. (2009). *Young learners, diverse children: Celebrating diversity in early childhood education.* Thousand Oaks, CA: Corwin Press.

Gonzalez, V., Brusca-Vega, R., & Yawkey, T. D. (1997). *Assessment and instruction of CLD students with or at-risk of learning problems.* Boston: Allyn & Bacon.

Gonzalez, V., Yawkey, T. D., & Minaya-Rowe, L. (2006). *ESL teaching and learning: Pre-K-12th grade classroom applications for students' academic achievement & development.* Boston: Allyn & Bacon.

Gonzalez, V., Bauerle, Clark, E. R. (2007). Cultural and linguistic giftedness in Hispanic kindergartners: Analyzing the validity of alternative and standardized assessments. In Virginia Gonzalez, Ed. *Academic achievement: An alternative research and educational minority and mainstream children's development and view.* Lanham, MD: University Press of America.

Gutiérrez, K. (2000). Teaching & learning in the 21st century. *English Education, 32*(4), 290–298.

Ladson-Billings, G. (1999). Preparing teachers for diverse student populations: A critical race theory perspective. *Review of Research in Education, 24*(1), 211–247.

Nieto, S. (2000). Placing equity front and center: Some thoughts on transforming teacher education for a new century. *Journal of Teacher Education, 51*(3), 180–187.

Partnership for 21st Century Skills. (2007). Teaching & learning for the 21st century: Report of the AZ summit for 21st century skills. Retrieved from http://www.coe.arizona.edu/includes/tinymce/jscripts/tiny_mce/plugins/filemanager/files/documents/general/Arizona%20Summit.pdf

Sheets, R. H. (2009). What is diversity pedagogy theory? *Multicultural Education, 16*(3), 11–17.

US Department of Education (2004/2006). Gifted and talented education statistics. Office of Civil Rights.

Zumbault, K., & Craig, E. (2005). Teachers' characteristics: Research on the demographic profile. In M. Cochran-Smith & K. Zeichner (Eds.), *Studying teacher education: The report of the AERA panel on research and teacher education* (pp. 111–156). Mahwah, NJ: AERA/Erlbaum.

14 It's My Responsibility!

Teacher of Bilingual Learners in an English-Immersion Context

Courtney Clayton and María Estela Brisk

While generalist teachers are increasingly faced with teaching Bilingual Learners (BLs), most are unprepared; yet, it is critical to understand the preparation needed for this student population. Research is abundant regarding the qualities and behaviors of exemplary teachers in general education settings (Allington & Johnston, 2000; Snow, Barnes, Chandler et al., 1991); however, there is limited research of effective teachers for BLs (García, 1991; Tikunoff, 1983). This chapter presents a case study of an exemplary generalist teacher of BLs in an English-immersion classroom.

Theoretical Framework

Exemplary Teachers

According to the scholarship, successful teachers of BLs have positive efficacy, articulate their instructional philosophies, routinely seek opportunities to enhance their knowledge, and have high student expectations (García, 1991; Gersten, 1996; Tikunoff, 1983). These highly dedicated teachers work hard, are involved with school and district-wide initiatives, and care deeply for their students (García, 1991). They consider being bilingual and bicultural enriches students' lives. When teaching in English, effective bilingual education teachers accept native language responses while encouraging English acquisition (García, 1991; Tikunoff, 1983). These teachers organize the curriculum into thematic units and provide BLs opportunities for active learning and collaboration (García, 1991).

Studies on effective practices for BLs with monolingual teachers revealed that they emphasized the importance of teaching English along with content (Brisk, 2006; Gersten & Baker, 2000; Facella et al., 2005). Successful practices cited in these studies included the importance of using the native language and culture; establishing clear goals for the lessons, communicating clearly when giving directions, specifying tasks, obtaining and maintaining student interest through pacing instruction, monitoring student progress, and providing immediate feedback. Teachers used strategies such as visual cues, gestures, and comprehension aids such as graphic organizers and semantic maps (Chamot & O'Malley, 1996; Echevarria et al., 2000).

August and Hakuta (1998) and Lucas, Donato and Henze (1990) identified the following attributes of effective English-only classrooms: (a) supportive school-wide climate with strong school leadership, (b) learning environments tailored to local goals and resources, (c) use of native language and culture in instruction, (d) balanced curriculum incorporates higher-order thinking skills, (e) multiple opportunities for student-directed activities, (f) systematic student assessment, (g) staff development, and (h) home and parent involvement. Much can be learned from studying exemplary teachers that have direct implications in preparing generalists who will have BLs in their classrooms.

Case Study Methodology

Liz, the teacher discussed in this chapter, was part of a qualitative case study examining four exemplary teachers in English immersion, bilingual contexts (Clayton, 2008). We examined how pedagogical strategies were influenced by the teaching context and challenges faced. Data sources included interviews, observations, focus group, lesson plans, photographs of teaching materials, and BL's writing samples. This case study was grounded directly in the teaching practices of exemplary generalist teachers of BLs in terms of background, knowledge, and practices, and how these practices were mediated by the teaching-learning contexts (Clayton, 2008).

An Exemplary Mainstream Teacher

Liz, who is White, grew up in a middle-class northeastern town and has taught for 12 years. Currently, she is a third-grade teacher with a MA in education, teaches in a working-class suburban school district, with a 5.9% second-language learners population, in a major US city.

Liz was nominated by the school principal as being an exemplary teacher of bilingual students. The main criteria the teacher needed to be considered an exemplary teacher of BLs were: (a) a minimum of three to five years teaching experience, (b) observable bilingual student progress on the school's measures of achievement including both standardized and holistic assessments, and (c) nomination from principal and/or administration as being particularly effective at working with bilingual students.

The principal was asked to describe behaviors that distinguished Liz from others in her ability to work effectively with BLs. He wrote:

> [Liz] is a sterling example of an educator who actively seeks ideas from colleagues, professional development programs, and personal research. She has confidence ... that ...is strengthened through her constant self-reflection. [Liz] recognizes instructional activities that successfully promote student learning. She shares those successes with her colleagues. She is also able to recognize when things are not working or could be more successful. In those cases, [Liz] seeks ideas and suggestions. [Liz's] classes have presented her with significant challenges—some years more than others. She accepts her students and moves forward—each child of equal importance. [Liz] then works diligently to meet the needs of her students—she does not see this as above and beyond normal duties, she sees it as an integral part of her professional responsibilities.

These characteristics were evident in the researchers' classroom observations and extensive interviews with Liz. There were four main areas that affected Liz's ability to effectively work with BLs:

Experience

Liz felt that her experience was an important factor: "I think the more confident I am as I acquire new strategies as a teacher, obviously the more I feel I can work with [BLs]." Liz felt that experience had given her a sense of responsibility for BLs' success. She felt that the responsibility resided in the classroom teacher and not merely in the ESL support staff. Liz's teaching experience helped her support students, involve parents, understand BLs' grammatical mistakes, and anticipate content area difficulties.

Traveling

Liz realized that English-speaking classrooms could be frightening for new students; and, in that regard, she felt traveling abroad had helped her develop empathy towards the difficult experiences her students might have. She said: "I learned from traveling abroad just how scary it can be not to understand [language] … and … the difficulties that can arise."

Learning a Second Language

Learning Spanish in high school and college helped her become aware of grammatical mistakes BLs might make when learning English. She explained: "Because I took Spanish in school, I can correct … [Luis's] errors that much easier. I can almost see where he's coming from … sometimes I can tell the word he's trying to write."

Professional Development

Liz felt that the two-day ESL workshop on teaching BLs was useful. She said: *"Ideally it would be great for all teachers to receive formal ESL training."*

Dispositions

Liz exhibited the following main dispositions when teaching:

1 sensitivity—awareness of BLs' needs and emotions;
2 kindness—being warmhearted and considerate with words and actions during lessons, such as allowing students to communicate their understanding of what they know versus what they still need to learn;
3 encouragement—actively encouraging students through positive expressions of support, such as "wow" and "keep it going";
4 positive attitudes—Liz never saw teaching BLs as a burden; rather, she saw it as an opportunity to improve her teaching with different techniques with students' needs in mind; and

5humor—she demonstrated the importance of using humor, even at the expense of looking pretty silly, if it helped her BLs feel more relaxed in the classroom.

Teaching Strategies

Liz used a variety of effective research-based strategies to work with BLs in her preparation, planning, and teaching:

1   themes and units as a foundation to access content;
2   student language and previous school experiences as a critical element in the teaching-learning process;
3   conceptual areas of difficulty were anticipated resulting in scaffolded learning through activities, materials, and active student participation through breaking down concepts, repeating, and/or clarifying directions;
4   visual tools, such as posters, videos, drawings, artwork, and books, to connect concepts with language;
5   questioning techniques to check for understanding and continuously monitoring;
6   prompting and coaching to guide learners and to provide access to content; and
7   repetition of key phrases to build vocabulary.

It was evident that Liz's strategies were effective for BLs; the students' writing samples demonstrated significant progress throughout the year. While Liz was successful with BLs, she expressed challenges working in the ESL program. She saw a disconnection between what the BLs were learning and the ESL curriculum. She found it frustrating not to know the student's first language because she could not discern if the student was struggling due to not understanding English or whether the student had a learning disability. Liz also felt the pressure that standardized testing placed on teachers and students since BLs were required to take the math portion even if they had just arrived not speaking English.

This case study illustrates the successes and challenges faced by a generalist teacher working with BLs. Liz's experiences can resonate with teachers around the country working with BLs. In Liz's words: "as a teacher, you just have to keep trying whatever avenue you can to help bilingual students understand and succeed … it is ultimately my responsibility."

Transforming Teacher Preparation

This case study highlights effective practices for BLs in English-immersion settings. These findings have direct implications for teacher preparation in the following areas:

- *Student Background*: Candidates need to understand the importance of BL's backgrounds in the teaching-learning process.
- *Second language Acquisition*: Candidates may benefit from courses in second language acquisition.

- *Learning a Second Language/Being Bicultural*: Learning a second language and experiencing cultures different from one's own can positively influence teaching effectiveness when working with BLs.
- *Dispositions*: Specific dispositions such as sensitivity, kindness, humor, encouragement when working with BLs can be encouraged and developed in candidates.
- *Methods Coursework*: Courses need to focus on content as well as the language demands placed on BLs. Understanding the vocabulary in content such as math where words can have multiple meanings for BLs is important.
- *Learning a Second language:* Candidates should be encouraged to learn a second language to understand the challenges in learning a second language.
- Incorporating BLs' Native Language: Teachers and candidates working in English-immersion contexts need to learn how to use students' native language for instructional purposes.

Research Directions

There are several research areas needing to be explored:

- Examining the impact of monolingual candidates mentored experiences in using students' first language.
- Investigating the role dispositions play in candidates' working effectively with BLs.
- Locating and studying the instructional strategies used by effective monolingual teachers of BLs.

References

Allington, R. L., & Johnston, P. H. (2000). *What do we know about effective fourth grade teachers and their classrooms?* Washington, DC: Office of Educational Research and Improvement.

August, D., & Hakuta, K. (Eds.). (1998). *Educating language-minority children*. Washington, DC: National Academy Press.

Brisk, M. E. (2006). *Bilingual education: From compensatory to quality schooling* (2nd ed.). Mahwah, NJ: Erlbaum.

Chamot, A. U., & O'Malley, J. M. (1996). The cognitive academic language learning approach: A model for linguistically diverse classrooms. *The Elementary School Journal, 96*(3), 259–273.

Clayton, C. (2008). *Whatever it takes: Exemplary teachers of English language learners.* Ph.D. dissertation, Boston College, United States—Massachusetts. Retrieved from Dissertations & Theses: Full Text database. (Publication No. AAT 3331433).

Echevarria, J., Vogt, M., & Short, D. J. (2000). *Making content comprehensible for English language learners: The SIOP model*. Boston: Allyn & Bacon.

Facella, M. A., Rampino, K. M., & Shea, E. K. (2005). Effective teaching strategies for English language learners. *Bilingual Research Journal, 29*(1), 209–221.

García, E. (1991). Effective instruction for language minority students: The teacher. *Journal of Education, 173*(2), 130–141.

Gersten, R. (1996). Literacy instruction for language-minority students: The transition years. *The Elementary School Journal, 96*(3), 227–244.

Gersten, R., & Baker, S. (2000). What we know about effective instructional practices for English-language learners. *Exceptional Children, 66*(4), 454–475.

Lucas, T., Donato, R., & Henze, R. (1990). Promoting the success of Latino language minority students: An exploratory study of six high schools. *Harvard Educational Review, 60*(3), 315–340.

Snow, C., Barnes, W., Chandler, J., Goodman, I. F., & Hemphill, L. (1991). *Unfulfilled expectations: Home and school influences on literacy.* Cambridge, MA: Harvard University Press.

Tikunoff, W. J. (1983). *Compatibility of the SBIF features with other research on instruction for LEP students* (Research/Technical No. SBIF-83-R.9/10). San Francisco: Far West Lab for Educational Research and Development.

Part IV

Concientización

To be what I want to be, the way I want be and in the space that I want to be in.
To shatter the quiet with my thoughts, my actions, … and my presence.
To be responsible for my culture, my history, my [community], and for all
    that I honor.
To learn the world for what it has to share and for what I still need to learn. …
To be like the *huiples* that I wear, for they make me strong and ever-evolving.
This is what I want to do. This is what I want to be. This is what I will be …
Ellen Riojas Clark. (2009). Latina Arte Roars Exhibit.
San Antonio, TX: Blue Star Gallery.

15 Subtractive Legislative Policy

The Plight of Texas Bilingual Learners

Claudia Cervantes-Soon and
Angela Valenzuela

Based on documentary analyses and observations pertinent to the 2009 eighty-first Regular Session of the Texas State Legislature, this study explores the impact of 2008 Supreme Court decision on the *U.S.A., et al. v. the State of Texas* litigation on the development of policies related to the schooling of bilingual learners (BLs) together with implications for bilingual teacher preparation. Our examination suggests that a subtractive policy context prevails. It is one that perpetuates a systematic neglect and invisibility of BLs (Valenzuela, 1999). This subtractive policy context implicitly frames BLs as "other people's children," and helps explain the widespread phenomenon of subtractive schooling in classrooms (McNeil & Valenzuela, 2001; Valenzuela, 1999, 2004).

With insight from conversations with teachers, bilingual teacher education faculty, bilingual/ESL candidates, and our own experiences as teacher educators, the chapter discusses the need for preparation programs to deliberately prepare all candidates to provide high-quality education to BLs, the majority of who are immigrant youth. While this is an obvious emphasis in bilingual and ESL preparation programs, it is imperative that preparation extends to include mainstream and secondary-level candidates. This chapter conveys the need for practitioners and policy makers to consider the political and historical contexts where candidates and BLs are situated. Specifically, we suggest that programs facilitate candidates' political awareness and agency to counter subtractive policies.

Background

BLs have increasingly taken center stage in education research and policy agendas. This attention comes at a time when hostility toward immigration is intensified in a deeply troubled economy. BLs represent the fastest-growing segment of the school-aged population (National Clearinghouse for English Language Acquisition, 2006; Valenzuela et al., 2006; see Chapter 1), their achievement and educational opportunities are not to be taken lightly. This population has seen a dramatic increase in the past decade, spilling over into states where non-English speakers are a new phenomenon. That the majority of BLs are Spanish speakers adds significance when one considers that this designation correlates with poverty and educational attainment relative to other immigrants or language minority populations (see Chapter 1). While conventional wisdom suggests that the large majority of these youth are immigrants (Capps et al., 2005), the great majority (84%) are either US born or immigrant children who do not return to their country of origin (Fry & Gonzalez, 2008). For most, this country is their only home. It behooves us to consider both the cost of not educating them but also the productive role that policy can play in their social and economic betterment despite our present, punitive framework (Valenzuela, 2004).

The passage of the No Child Left Behind Act (NCLB) of 2001 into law reversed a decade of language policy advancements toward increased acceptance of multilingualism and multiculturalism. In 2002, Congress replaced bilingual education with an English-only bill (San Miguel, 2004). While some argue that Title III brought BLs "out of the shadows" by demanding an increase in accountability and adequate yearly progress, in the case of Texas, this has neither been a transparent process, nor has it resulted in higher levels of academic achievement for BLs.

The Case of Texas

Although pejorative, the official term for English language learners in Texas is "limited English proficient," (LEP). While all LEPs are BLs, not all BLs are categorized as LEPs. With an enrollment of 775,432 students identified as Limited English Proficient (LEP) in the 2007–2008 school year (Texas Education Agency, 2009), Texas has the second largest BL population in the country and Latin@s are the largest ethnic group within the LEP population, accounting for almost 93% of the total. As opposed to California, Arizona, Massachusetts, and Colorado, Texas law continues to support, at least in theory, bilingual education and special language programs. This has nonetheless been a contested terrain.

Despite a long history of struggle for civil rights for BLs, the state has yet to offer quality schooling. In July 2008, the late US District Judge William Wayne Justice issued a court order against Texas asserting that the state violated the rights of BLs under the Equal Educational Opportunities Act. This case warrants attention as the most comprehensive legal decision concerning the civil rights of BLs in the last 25 years. In a context of growing hostility against bilingual education and immigration and increased accountability pressures, the actions (or inactions) taken to address the ruling offer important implications for preparation programs.

According to a recent report by the Schott Foundation for Public Education (2009), Texas ranks 43rd among all 50 states in students' opportunity to learn the state's curriculum as measured by a high-quality, early childhood education, highly effective teachers, well-funded instructional materials, and a college preparatory curriculum. Moreover, Latin@ students in Texas rank at the very bottom relative to all other non-Latino sub-groups. Consequently, according to national-level data, Latin@s are at near bottom. Though this analysis failed to further disaggregate by LEP status in either Texas or the rest of the country, this group consistently registers among the lowest levels of test scores that in turn signal a systematic lack of access to adequate resources, quality teachers, and schools (Blanton, 2004; Darling-Hammond, 2004; Ruiz de Velasco et al., 2000; Valenzuela, 1999, 2004).

Attributing poor academic performance solely to students' linguistic differences, and sociocultural and economic backgrounds has concealed some of the most determining factors for student achievement, including adequate identification, assessment and placement; adequate academic English instruction; a rigorous content-area curriculum; adequate implementation of research-based programs; and instruction by qualified teachers in both English as a second language (ESL) and subject-area methodologies and content, respectively (Gándara & Contreras, 2009).

In light of these challenges, candidates cannot afford to receive a preparation that limits their role to the four walls of the classroom or to mere instructional toolkits. Failing to acknowledge teachers' potential as change agents and the subtractive outcomes of policies permeating preparation programs and classrooms perpetuates the cycle of silence and invisibility of BLs and teachers. Court directives and legislative mandates together with effective leadership, a research-based understanding of bilingual education, and the exertion of political power are necessary if constructive change is to occur—at least, theoretically.

Bilingual Learners and Texas Law

Bilingual, ESL, and special language programs are intended to "ensure equal educational opportunity to every student" (Texas Education Code §29.051). Under Texas law, school districts with 20 or more LEPs in the same grade level must offer bilingual education in the elementary grades; bilingual education, ESL, or other transitional language instruction in middle school; and ESL in high-school. In practice, bilingual education is implemented at the elementary grades with the primary goal of transitioning BLs into English-only instruction, and typically within a three-year time frame. ESL instruction is implemented for all non-special education LEPs with parent approval in grades 7–12 and in the elementary grades when bilingual education is not feasible. In the 2007–2008 school year, the Texas Education Agency (TEA) reported an enrollment of 93% of LEPs in a bilingual education or special language program, with 7% of LEPs' parents getting denied services. Texas law also orders standards for bilingual and ESL program content and instructional methods, facilities and class sizes, and bilingual and ESL teacher certification (Texas Education Code §29.055, §20.057, §20.061).

Regarding preparation programs, Texas is among the fourteen states that do not require that all teachers have training or expertise in working with BLs, according to a policy assessment conducted by the National Clearinghouse of English Language Acquisition (2008). While some federal and state grants have been available for loan forgiveness or scholarships to recruit prospective teachers to bilingual and ESL preparation programs, candidates tend to concentrate in the elementary grades.

Among the functions listed under Texas law, TEA is to "administer and monitor compliance with education programs required by federal or state law" and "conduct research, analysis, and reporting to improve teaching and learning" (Texas Education Code §7.021 (b)(1)(2)). According to Chapter 29 of the Texas Education Code, the agency must also monitor and evaluate several aspects of the bilingual education and special language programs by establishing a performance-based, monitoring system (PBMS) in lieu of on-site inspections. This monitoring system compares such academic excellence indicators as dropout, graduation, and passing rates on the current state standardized test—the Texas Assessment of Knowledge and Skills (TAKS). Furthermore, the code requires TEA to monitor programs in content and design, program coverage, identification procedures, staffing, learning materials, testing materials, reclassification of students, and school-based, language proficiency assessment committees (LPACs), which are responsible for the initial student classification. TEA has authority to apply sanctions when districts fail to meet expectations.

The PBMS monitors activities based on student performance data. Rather than holding schools accountable for the processes, program structures, and inputs provided to teachers and students, current law only focuses on the outputs. This *ex post facto* type of monitoring too often results in interventions addressing symptoms rather than systemic inequities (Valencia et al., 2001). At least for the layperson, the state's exclusive focus on student test outcomes may easily lead to an incorrect, reductive notion that the system is fine and the onus of school failure is on students, their language, and culture (Valenzuela, 2004). Our present system masks data (Vasquez Heilig & Darling-Hammond, 2008; McNeil, Coppola, Radigan, & Vasquez Heilig, 2008), and foments prejudice when BLs get constructed as deficient or unteachable.

The Urgent Call: Bilingual Learners at the Secondary Level

ESL instruction is typically utilized as the only source of support for BLs at the secondary level. Too often, however, this approach results in a subtractive process both for students and teachers (Valenzuela, 1999). While secondary students' native language fluency may be relatively secure at this point to prevent language loss, schooling may still negatively impact their self-confidence, including their ethnic, cultural and linguistic pride, and thus, their ability to access and master rigorous academic content. Moreover, because of the stigma that is often associated with ESL as a remedial program, BLs are often perceived as less cognitively and academically capable, and are consequently expected to perform at lower levels (Gándara & Contreras, 2009).

Because BL youth have the highest dropout and lowest completion rates, quality oversight and accountability for the progress of this subgroup is critical (Valenzuela, Fuller, & Vasquez Heilig, 2006; also see Vasquez Heilig & Darling-Hammond, 2008; McNeil et al., 2008). Yet, a problem that merits attention is a prevailing inadequacy of program structure for BLs that considers the diversity within this student population (Ruiz de Velasco et al., 2000). Valdés (2001) refers to "ESL lifers" stuck in an "ESL ghetto" to illustrate this problem of systemic negligence. Far too many remain in ESL courses for several years with no signs of improvement. Mainly, she attributes this problem to a lack of structure and thoughtful planning and implementation, low expectations, watered-down curricula, and poor instructional methods. BLs at different levels of linguistic and academic proficiency are often lumped together in overcrowded classrooms, with inadequate materials, and without clearly defined goals tailored to students' individual needs.

Unfortunately, ESL programs often serve the dual role of placing students in lower academic tracks (Valenzuela, 1999; Valdés, 2001; Callahan et al., 2009).

Many BLs in ESL programs rarely have an opportunity to take college preparatory courses or advanced content-area curricula. Generally ESL classrooms, viewed as remedial, are used to "dump" students with disciplinary issues and those judged as underperforming (Valdés, 2001).

Recently, during an informal conversation, an ESL teacher from an underperforming Texas high school talked about the consequences of using ESL classrooms as a disciplinary "dumping ground" for regular, non-BL students with behavioral problems. She complained that she had to stop student fights in the classroom, and on one occasion—after unsuccessfully trying to get help from the administrators—she had to step out of the classroom to call 911 for help. "I see state and district policies that deliberately oppress and marginalize my students," she said. "My ELLs want to learn and they're smart kids, but it is impossible to do it in that context" (ESL Teacher, Personal Communication, 2009).

In many cases, ESL teachers receive little support or professional development, so it is not surprising to find one ESL teacher for an entire high school, serving over 300 LEP students. ESL teachers often overwhelmed and isolated work at the margins of the school community. They are considered the only ones responsible for supporting BL linguistic and academic performance, while holding a lower status among colleagues.

Struggle in the Courts

In February, 2006, the League of United Latin American Citizens (LULAC) and the American GI Forum filed a lawsuit against Texas stating that the TEA had abandoned monitoring, enforcing, and supervising school districts to ensure compliance with Texas bilingual education law, and that it had failed to provide equal educational opportunity to LEP students above the elementary level. Some of the evidence they provided included high dropout and retention rates, low graduation rates, and an alarming achievement gap between LEPs and non-LEPs.

The plaintiffs argued that Texas' monitoring system is seriously flawed. First, it masks data by under-identifying LEPs by measuring LEP academic achievement against arbitrary and unequal standards derived from non-LEP youth. Second, it combines data across multiple grade levels, hiding the gravity of the dropout rates in certain grade levels. Finally, by aggregating district-wide data that hide information on specific campuses, the extent of the crisis gets obscured. This blurry data display may lead educators and community members to believe that the gravity of the achievement gap is not as severe or that solving the problem is a mystery, for it involves addressing unidentifiable factors or problems within the students that are out of the educational system's control.

The 2008 US v. Texas Court Ruling

On July 2008, the Court concluded that the perpetual stagnation of secondary BLs in Texas and the State's failure to provide the necessary resources and programs to ensure the closing of the gap between LEP and non-LEP students did not satisfy the requirements of the Equal Educational Opportunity Act (1974). This federal law states the following:

No State shall deny equal educational opportunity to an individual on account of his or her race, color, sex, or national origin, by (f) the failure by an educational agency to take appropriate action to overcome language barriers that impede equal participation by its students in its instructional programs.

(U.S. Code, § 1703)

While the Court recognized some success for students in the state's K-6 bilingual education programs, secondary LEPs had a dismal history of widespread school failure. By failing to overcome language barriers, the state violated the main goal of equal educational opportunity expressed in this federal statue.

William Wayne Justice, a federal judge, ordered that in order to fulfill the requirements of the EEOA, TEA must submit a monitoring plan that addresses the failures of the Texas monitoring system and proposed a new language program for secondary LEPs by January 31, 2009. Without a doubt, this was the most comprehensive legal decision concerning the civil rights of BLs in the last 25 years.

A month later, the state filed a Notice of Appeal and asked the court to temporarily relieve the state of Texas from meeting the January 31, 2009 deadline to fix the monitoring system and secondary ESL program on the grounds of a lack of funding and resources. The Court denied the State's appeal in December 2009, stressing that any alleged administrative inconveniences to the State were not a sufficient reason to continue to neglect the immediate and more urgent educational interests of BLs.

The Fifth US Circuit Court of Appeals, which has the authority to override the previous ruling, then granted the TEA's request for a stay, pending oral arguments, on June 2, 2009. This pushback by the Fifth Circuit had important consequences, not the least of which is the TEA's confidence that they would win on appeal. It further delineated the parameters within which change must occur while slowing down the process, and lowering the possibilities of passing any legislation aiming to improve the education of BLs.

The Eighty-First Texas Legislative Session: Turning Good Intentions into Law

Regardless of the Fifth Circuit Court of Appeals' decision, Senator Judith Zaffirini (D-Laredo) and Senator Leticia Van de Putte (D-San Antonio) recognized the urgency to address Judge Justice's requests and filed two pieces of legislation in January 2009, during the eighty-first legislative session. Both of these bills were the result of extensive work and collaboration between the Senators' staff, the Mexican American Legal Defense and Educational Fund (MALDEF), and the Intercultural Development Research Association (IDRA), with input from BL advocacy groups such as the Texas Association for Bilingual Education (TABE), Multicultural Education, Training, and Advocacy (META), and the Effective Network for the Advancement of Bilingual Education (ENABLE), among others. We also actively collaborated in these efforts as part of the research activities for the Texas Center for Education Policy (TCEP), a university-wide policy center housed at the University of Texas at Austin. Throughout this process, questions of how much could be addressed, how much should be mandated, how comprehensive bills could be, remained debatable. This was indeed a historical moment.

Not only were recent reports on changing demographics compelling, together with alarming data that the court case provided, but Judge Justice's ruling opened a door that had been shut for decades. This was a singular opportunity to address the long-neglected issues facing BLs. Was this not a prudent moment for the advocacy community to take advantage of this momentum and propose comprehensive, research-based policies that attempt to completely revamp both the accountability and secondary-level BL programs? Unfortunately, as the narrative that follows suggests, not every legislator, policy maker, or educational organization understood or cared to understand this sense of urgency.

Despite this apparent lack of sufficient political will or muscle for passing great mandates and comprehensive policies regarding language minority students, the conventional piecemeal strategy toward systemic change was disregarded. With risks to their political capital on the line, Senators Van de Putte and Zaffirini, their staff, advocacy groups, and research entities involved working on drafting legislation to create as much change as possible to address the court ruling and effectuate positive change for BLs.

Senator Van de Putte's Senate Bill 2002: A New Secondary-Level ELL Program

To upgrade, if not significantly alter, the status of ESL programs, Senator Van de Putte focused on program quality outlining requirements for a research-based ELL program. The bill covered several components including: 1) the identification of BLs by language proficiency levels in English and the primary language and background about prior schooling experiences; 2) assessment in the two languages; 3) rigorous content area curriculum delivered through sheltered instruction; 4) ESL and sheltered instruction aligned with the various levels of English language; 5) the inclusion of parents in program development; and 6) the establishment of supplementary programs. However, there were two most significant aspects of this bill that merit attention.

First, the comprehensive nature of this bill deliberately aimed to redefine secondary-level, ELL programs by eliminating the notion that ESL classes were the one and only key component of ESL. Utilizing ESL as the only tool to support BLs at the secondary level is problematic because students spend far more time in subject-area courses in which typically no accommodations are made. Moreover, the need for BLs to acquire English vocabulary and syntax should be consistent with the goal of making them college ready.

Second, teacher and leadership quality were the central features of this bill. SB 2002 proposed that teachers serving BLs, including those in the content areas, and administrators should be adequately prepared by completing six semester-credit hours of higher education coursework in ESL methodology or equivalent professional development in sheltered instruction in the subject areas by the end of their second year in the classroom. Once trained, they would continue to receive support through 12 additional clock hours of professional development each year on ELL instruction. Without a specification of the funding sources on the bill, these professional development requirements turned out to be the most controversial. Hence, the responsibility was to be assumed mainly by teacher preparation programs.

Co-authored by Senator Zaffirini and carried in the House by Representative Jessica Farrar, Senator Van de Putte filed the bill on March 12, 2009. On March 31, 2009, the bill was heard before the Texas Senate Committee on Education. When Senator Van de Putte laid out the bill, several groups testified in favor, but others also objected to what they deemed to be a large, unfunded mandate, especially in terms of professional development. The opposition came mainly from teacher groups who rejected any mandates for professional development, especially when the bill cast the net too widely. They tended to prefer a previously laid out bill authored by Senator Shapiro, which proposed professional development in the form of ESL academies. This bill provided a stipend to participating teachers and it was later amended to make the training voluntary for teachers in acceptably performing schools. It became mandatory, however, for teachers in underperforming schools whose annual evaluation indicated a need for support. With no more granted hearings, the bill died in the Senate's Education Committee, alongside Senator Shapiro's bill on ESL Academies.

SB 2002 Discussion: Revamping Program Quality

Granted, professional development should take into account teachers' difficult roles, respect their autonomy, and fairly compensate for additional time and work. But neither should we sacrifice the most underserved children in the process. Assigning preparation solely to teacher education programs without providing current teachers with the opportunity to receive any support, fails to address the problems where most BLs are currently found. Needless to say, as policy makers turn to institutions of higher education for preparing teachers to work with BLs, there will be new challenges including the coursework required for traditional and alternative certification programs. Furthermore, preparation programs will have to design exemplary secondary preparation programs and professional development for teachers in the field (see Chapter 2).

With political will, all of these challenges can be addressed. The bill never made it out of committee. The resistance of teacher groups against the professional development mandate was enough to end the entire conversation. On the one hand, we were left to wonder whether our legislative bodies really saw BLs either as "ours," or as "other people's children" who we may consider only if time, resources, and potential political benefit permits. Would we have the same response if the education of middle-class White students were on the line? On the other hand, if we had such a large population of BLs, why were there such few advocates? Where were our bilingual and ESL teachers? Why had it been so difficult to organize in such a historical moment?

During the hearing, Senator Dan Patrick kept questioning why we must offer bilingual education or any kind of accommodation for Spanish-speaking BLs and why taxpayers should be held responsible for teaching English to US born BLs. He deemed it illogical that schools should do this. In his view, as American children, they should naturally be raised as English speakers by their parents. Otherwise, we must question how American they really are and whether they deserve any investment. Senator Patrick's opinion and concerns demonstrated the subtractive policy context within which these policies were proposed. It is a policy context embedded in a naïve consciousness of white privilege that naturalizes the English language as the American common denominator (Freire, 1970). In other words, if parents want their children to become English-speaking Americans, they must pay for it. Senator Patrick could not have been more explicit: Until then, these are not our children; these are "other people's children."

Senator Zaffirini's Senate Bill 548: A New Monitoring and Accountability Measure

As educational standards increase and the achievement gap between LEPs and non-LEPs continues to grow, the policies and practices used with LEPs require further scrutiny. In January 2009, Senator Zaffirini filed SB 548, a comprehensive school accountability measure for bilingual education, ESL, and other special language programs. The bill offered guidelines that directed TEA to monitor and evaluate the effectiveness of bilingual education and ESL programs. This monitoring measure addressed Judge Justice's concern with the accountability system by requiring an analysis of specific data points disaggregated by school district or open-enrollment charters and school campuses.

In contrast to the PBMS system that merely compared LEP achievement to all-students' achievement rates, data points included: rate of waivers and exceptions made by districts, rate of parental denial of bilingual education services, retention rate among LEP and non-LEP students, achievement gap between LEP and non-LEP students, and other significant differences existing between LEP and non-LEPs. To address the masking of underachievement and underperforming campuses and districts at various levels, another improvement to the current system was the disaggregation of student data by elementary, middle, and high school levels, as well as by campus.

Based on TEA's evaluation of district's programs, the bill required districts to examine assessment procedures and ESL programs to identify areas for improvement and establish goals addressing weaknesses. It also required TEA to conduct on-site monitoring by evaluators certified in bilingual education or ESL and provide corrective action when necessary. Finally, the bill required districts to report additional data for students exiting bilingual education, ESL, or special language programs until the student graduated or exited school, facilitating both the acquisition of longitudinal data and research and the tracking of students after exit.

Senator Zaffirini's staff worked extensively with apparently supportive staff from TEA despite some objections to the bill. The original bill underwent some modifications to satisfy TEA's objections and requests, including: 1) the evaluation of data at the district level for campuses with fewer than 30 students enrolled in bilingual education or ESL programs; 2) limiting the data that districts must report to TEA as triggers for non-compliance, focusing specifically on the achievement gap in student performance, retention rates, and graduation rates; 3) feasibility concerns, meaning that only the lead monitor be required certification in ESL; and

4) the designation of TEA to take appropriate corrective action if the district failed to meet one or more annual improvement goals for two consecutive school years.

Besides offering more transparent accountability, the bill offered the ability to assess school processes through on-site monitoring, such as the quality of instruction, program implementation, teacher credentials, professional development, and materials. Assessing not only student outputs, but school inputs, as well, would place the responsibility of educating all students on the school system.

SB 548 Discussion: Gatekeepers and Empty Words

SB 548 advanced further than SB 2002, but not far enough to become law. Several obstacles stood in the way. First, Senator Zaffirini was taken off the Senate Education Committee that addresses K-12 policy and placed on the Senate's Higher Education Committee at the beginning of the session, minimizing her power on this bill from the start. Thus, the bill did not get a first hearing until later in the session. Despite this late start, SB 548 began to move rather quickly. It received apparent approval and support from most stakeholders and committee members, even TEA appeared cooperative. Within a week, the modified version was unanimously passed. But once in the Public Education Committee in the House of Representatives, the bill failed to get a hearing.

As the legislative session drew closer to the end, troubled times required desperate measures. The only viable way to move the bill along would be to amend it into House Bill 4091, which had already passed in the House. HB 4091 proposed a voluntary reading intervention program for secondary BLs. However, because HB 4091 was a "vendor bill," this caused controversy and limited its political power both as a vehicle for SB 548 and as a bill itself. Ultimately, HB 4091 died in the House of Representatives.

How could such an apparently popular bill get caught up in a snare of internal politics? Its ultimate fate was a collateral effect of the Chairs of both the Senate and the House committees prioritizing the passage of HB 3, a large bill on state accountability. At the heart of HB 3 was an agenda to track youth in a way that would stratify students further by race and class. Consequently, the bill became a major lightening rod and focal point for the entire legislative session in a way that detracted attention from other equally significant bills like those carried by Senators Van de Putte and Zaffirini.

Perhaps because SB 548 paid "too much attention" to BLs, even as HB3 flatly ignored them; it became impossible to tag it onto HB 3 despite eleventh-hour attempts. Or perhaps because rather than blaming the child, SB 548 held schools, districts, and TEA accountable for how they administer programs to BLs. Throughout the process, the empty rhetoric of good intentions to address these students' needs was exposed. During one of the public hearings for HB 3, Senator Shapiro stated,

> Despite the progress, there are still disparities in our racial and economic disadvantaged students but we're working towards making progress. As we continue to focus on these subgroups, we will continue to make progress. We

should design a system that focuses on advancing all students and not one that makes schools look good by masking who those students are and the problems that we have.

(March 17, 2009; Senate Committee on Education, Public Hearing)

Similar statements addressing the quality of education for BLs abounded in all of the hearings for SB 548, SB 2002, and others. Yet, when it was time for Senator Shapiro to demonstrate that commitment, she refused to do so. After SB 548 died, BL advocates asked both Representative Eissler and Senator Shapiro to include its provisions as an amendment to their accountability bill, HB 3. While Representative Eissler was supportive of this request, Senator Shapiro considered it to be "out of bounds" and denied the request. At the end, the weaker political power of minority advocacy groups combined with the state's own lack of urgency toward BLs and empty rhetoric resulted in total inaction.

Transforming Teacher Preparation

Valenzuela (1999) examines the ways in which American schools enact assimilationist practices that hinder US-Mexican youth from building their own social and cultural capital, while denying them opportunities for academic success. The complacency, lack of political will, or deliberate neglect took its toll during Texas' eighty-first legislative session, demonstrating a similar subtractive process. Rather than possessing knowledge, resources, and capabilities that should be identified and developed, BLs are constantly constructed based solely on their English language skills, and are thus perceived in a pejorative manner and as a burden to the state and to the schools.

This subtractive policy context undermines and destroys BL's prospects for academic and social mobility. Students not only lose their native language, pride in their culture, and self-confidence, they also rarely acquire the tools needed to graduate and pursue a college degree. As determined by statute, English proficiency remains limited to functional skills. The policies we have in place lead BLs to speak English just well enough to survive, but nowhere near what they need to be: fully-vested, biliterate individuals poised with twenty-first century literacy skills that allow them to be competent actors in today's increasingly interconnected, multilingual, global economy. Tragically, many of these students' linguistic competencies never reach a level that allows them to master academic content, much less to use discourse in powerful ways. To add insult to injury, BLs so framed are not only perceived as mentally incompetent, they are also silenced, unable to attend college, and relegated to the permanent margins of a society marked by reduced, if exclusionary, access to the good life. In this policy context, BL youth and their advocates are constructed as second-class citizens (Valenzuela & Brewer, 2010). At best, they are invisible to the law; at worst, they are oppressed by it.

Clearly, both legislators' and advocates' struggle for sound ELL policy was about creating a research-based, culturally- and linguistically-affirming "new commonsense" in Texas policy and education. Yet, policies that provide access to rigorous curricula and qualified teachers are forced to linger in a cloud of rhetoric, and then crumble in the face of neglect. What intrigues at the end of the legislative debate is the kind of instruction that goes beyond even our best-conceived proposals in order to effectuate the positive outcomes we seek.

In light of changing demographics, the greatest challenge at the secondary level is for programs to prepare all candidates with knowledge of Second Language Acquisition (SLA), as well as ESL, sheltered instruction, and bilingual pedagogy. This includes candidates specializing in ESL, content area specialists, and teachers. Sometimes, content-area teachers may not see a need for professional development; however, meeting the academic and linguistic demands for secondary students is consequential. While this may seem reasonable, this is not always possible considering that universities are embedded in their politics and subtractive policy frameworks often determine program delivery. It requires substantial collaboration among faculty and a high degree of advocacy from bilingual and ESL teacher educators to assume responsibility.

During meetings with BL advocates, David Hinojosa, MALDEF staff attorney, repeatedly questioned the effectiveness of conventional professional development. He had seen multiple teacher workshops on ESL strategies with disappointing results. While he was referring to professional development, his observations lent insight into preparation programs following the same pattern. There is no doubt that teacher educators need to develop foundational principles for linguistically responsive teaching (Lucas, Villegas, & Freedson-Gonzalez, 2008). Preparation must go beyond instructional methods to develop strong teacher agency (see Chapter 2).

Research Directions

Future research is needed to demystify the development of teacher advocacy in the context of teacher preparation programs. For example, examining how candidates' field experiences foster political awareness and influence the development of advocacy. Research can focus on the ways preparation curricula influences quality education for BLs. Studies can compare traditional bilingual education programs with alternative certification programs. Scholarship can evaluate the usefulness of multiple pedagogical approaches with explicit goals to develop critical knowledge, political agency, and self-reflexivity in candidates.

Research can address professional development and the role of teacher educators in these initiatives. For example, this may include the use of technology, distance learning, teacher coaching, action research, and mentorship. To develop the next generation of scholars, graduate students can be matched with experts; and as such, can contribute to the discussion. Collaborative research efforts can bring down walls and create new forms of scholarship that weaves academic, pedagogical, and political identities with the potential to improve the schooling experiences of BLs.

References

Blanton, C. K. (2004). *The strange career of bilingual education in Texas, 1836–1981.* College Station, TX: Texas A&M University Press.

Callahan, R. M., Wilkinson, L., Muller, C., & Frisco, M. (2009). ESL placement and schools: Effects on immigrant achievement. *Educational Policy, 23*(2), 355–384.

Capps, R., Fix, M., Murray, J., Passel, J. S., & Herwantoro, S. (2005). *The new demography of America's schools: Immigration and the No Child Left Behind Act.* Washington, DC: The Urban Institute.

Darling-Hammond, L. (2004). Inequality and the right to learn: Access to qualified teachers in California's public schools. *Teachers College Record, 106*(10), 1936–1966.

Freire, P. (1970). *Pedagogy of the oppressed.* New York: Continuum.

Fry, R., & Gonzalez, F. (2008). *One-in-five and growing fast: A profile of Hispanic public school students.* Pew Hispanic Center. Retrieved from http://pewhispanic.org/reports/report.php?ReportID=92

Gándara, P., & Contreras, F. (2009). *The Latino education crisis: The consequences of failed social policies.* Cambridge, MA: Harvard University Press.

Lucas, T., Villegas, A. M., & Freedson-Gonzalez, M. (2008). Linguistically responsive teacher education: Preparing classroom teachers to teach English language learners. *Journal of Teacher Education, 59*(4), 361–373.

McNeil, L. M., & Valenzuela, A. (2001). The harmful impact of the TAAS system of testing in Texas: Beneath the accountability rhetoric. In M. Kornhaber & G. Orfield (Eds), *Raising standards or raising barriers? Inequality and high stakes testing in public education* (pp. 127–150). New York: Century Foundation.

McNeil, L. M., Coppola, E., Radigan, J., & Vasquez Heilig, J. (2008). Avoidable losses: High-stakes accountability and the dropout crisis. *Education Policy Analysis Archives, 16*(3). Retrieved from http://epaa.asu.edu/epaa/v16n3/

National Clearinghouse of English Language Acquisition. (2006). *The growing numbers of limited English proficient students 1995/96—2005/06.* Washington, DC: NCELA. Retrieved from http://www.ncela.gwu.edu/files/uploads/4/GrowingLEP_0506.pdf

National Clearinghouse of English Language Acquisition. (2008). State requirements for pre-service teachers of ELLs. *Educating English language learners: Building teacher capacity.* (3) Washington, DC: NCELA. Retrieved from http://www.ncela.gwu.edu/files/uploads/3/EducatingELLsBuildingTeacherCapacityVol1.pdf.

Ruiz de Velasco, J., Fix, M. E., & Clewell, B. C. (2000). Overlooked and underserved: Immigrant students in U.S. secondary schools. *The Urban Institute.* Retrieved from http://www.urban.org/url.cfm?ID=310022.

San Miguel, G. (2004). *Contested policy: The rise and fall of federal bilingual education in the United States 1960–2001.* Denton, TX: University of North Texas Press.

Texas Education Agency. (2009). *Enrollment in Texas Public Schools, 2007–08.* Retrieved from http://ritter.tea.state.tx.us/research/pdfs/enrollment_2007–08.pdf.

Schott Foundation for Public Education. (2009). Lost opportunity: A 50-state report on the opportunity to learn in America. Texas State Data and Analysis. Retrieved from http://www.otlstatereport.org/states/texas

Valdés, G. (2001). *Learning and not learning English: Latino students in American schools.* New York: Teachers College Press.

Valencia, R., Valenzuela, A., Sloan, K., & Foley, D. (2001). Let's treat the cause, not the symptoms: Equity and accountability in Texas revisited, *Phi Delta Kappan,* December, 318–321, 326.

Valenzuela, A. (1999). *Subtractive schooling: U.S.-Mexican youth and the politics of caring.* Albany, NY: SUNY.

Valenzuela, A. (Ed.). (2004). *Leaving children behind: How "Texas-style" accountability fails Latino youth.* New York: SUNY.

Valenzuela, A., & Brewer, C. (2010). Submerged in neoliberal utopia: Disruption, community dislocation and subtractive citizenship. In R. Van Heertum, C. Torres, & L. Olmos (Eds.), *Educating the global citizen: Globalization, educational reform, and the politics of equity and inclusion.* Oak Park, IL: Bentham Science Publishers.

Valenzuela, A., Fuller, E. J., & Vasquez Heilig, J. (2006). The disappearance of high school English language learners from Texas high schools. *Williams Review, 1,* 170–200.

Vasquez Heilig, J., & Darling-Hammond, L. (2008). Accountability Texas-style: The progress and learning of urban minority students in a high-stakes testing context. *Educational Evaluation and Policy Analysis, 30*(2), 75–110.

16 *Trabajando y Comunicando con Nuestras Comunidades Indígenas Inmigrantes*

Margarita Machado-Casas and
Barbara Flores

Despite the growing diversity of Latin@ indigenous immigrants in the US, the Latin@ population is often considered to be homogeneous. Perplexingly, schools and educational programs aimed at educating Bilingual Learners (BLs) often do not consider the language diversity and versatility of its students, as this vignette illustrates:

> The teacher called us because we were still speaking to our children in Spanish and in our [indigenous] language and they were not doing well [in school]. "She noted that all the Mexican kids were not doing well but our children seem to be doing worse because we speak to our kids in our [indigenous] language. She told me I had to stop! That we needed to stop teaching our kids that [our indigenous language] if we wanted them to pass. The teacher told me that if we did not stop, we were going to be the reason they failed. That she is really trying but we are not helping. She asked; why can't you just speak to them in Spanish? I think the teacher is wrong and does not know that we can't stop. It is our [first] language, and we also use Spanish [daily], and now, also English…and in other words we learn from other indigenous people. Our kids will know all the languages! All of them we use!" *"Sí todas las maneras de hablar las necesitan."*

Even bilingual educators can lack interest and knowledge about US Indigenous Latin@ Immigrants (ILI) that can lead them to make incorrect assumptions about these children and their families.

Using a sociocultural theoretical framework, this chapter contributes to the seminal body of research on Latin@ families and their experiences in US schools by adding the often-ignored experiences of ILIs. We examine the lives and experiences of ILI families with school-age children and look at the ways they use multiple languages to enact everyday social practices. We believe this research can serve teacher preparation programs to: 1) educate teacher candidates of the realities of ILI families and their experiences with US schools; 2) understand the ways in which indigenous families deliberately transmit multilingual knowledge to their children; and 3) provide candidates with knowledge about these families to impact current schooling practices that fail to differentially position ILIs and their experiences. This chapter explores the following questions:

1   How can teacher candidates learn about the everyday social practices enacted by ILIs in the US?
2   Why are the experiences of ILIs within US schools important for the education of teacher candidates?
3   What can teachers learn from these experiences in order to transform the pervasive deficit ideology regarding the linguistic and cultural diversity of working class ILI in US communities?

The next sections will address these critical questions by looking at the theoretical frameworks and historical accounts of multilingual/multicultural ILI families in the US.

Theoretical Framework

Indigenous Latin@ Immigrant Multilingual Families and Communities

Typically, when one thinks of US Latin@ immigrants, one thinks of Spanish-speaking immigrants that come from urban cities in Latin America. Yet, recent research tells us that immigrant communities, particularly in the US, have been predominantly rural in origin and indigenous (Flores, Hernández-León, & Massey, 2004; Machado-Casas, 2009; Stephen, 2007). According to Rivera-Salgado (1999), "the incorporation of large numbers of indigenous peoples in the US-bound Mexican migratory flow illustrates just how dramatically migration patterns are changing" (p. 1440). With the influx in migratory patterns from urban to rural areas, we are finding more and more communities that are multicultural, multilingual, and not bound solely by Spanish as their first language.

Other researchers who have studied migration shifts report that Mixtec, Nahuas, Purepechas, Triques, and Otomí indigenous communities are among the largest groups migrating to the US (Anderson, 1997; Stephen, 2007; Zabin, Kearny, García, Runsten, & Nagengast, 1993). According to Fox and Rivera-Salgado (2004), "some Mexican indigenous peoples have many decades of experience with migration to the United States, dating back to the Bracero Program (1942–1964). In the early years, Mexican natives were migrating to areas such as California and Texas where there has been a long-standing history of migration from Mexico" (p. 2). Another trend noted is that the indigenous immigrant population historically settled in large cities in Mexico and the US (Fox & Rivera-Salgado, 2004). That trend is rapidly shifting and newly arrived immigrants are entering states that have not had a long standing history of Latin American immigrants such as, North Carolina, Georgia, Iowa, and Nebraska among others (Passel & Suro, 2005; Machado-Casas, 2006).

Indígenas no Latin@s: Sociolinguistic Patterns

For many immigrants, identity is not necessarily tied to a nation-state, but instead to an indigenous community or group. When referring to their identity, many ILIs identify with the region where they lived or with their particular indigenous community. This way of identifying is contradictory to the way others see them in the US—as Spanish-speaking Latin@s. Machado-Casas (2009), uses the term "los ocultos" when referring to the ways in which indigenous communities are often treated in the US. "The term oculto means hidden—something or someone that is behind or under something, not seen, or ignored" (p. 84). She posits that because they live under the discourse of Latin@, it ignores indigenous people's ethnic and linguistic diversity, it,

> serves as another form of continued oppression, marginalization, and colonization of indigenous communities. Although the use of the term Latin@ is a more inclusive term than Hispanic—its definition is supposed to include peoples of indigenous and African descent—one needs to be careful not to generalize the characteristics of those who are considered Latinos and its implications on people's lives.
>
> (p. 84)

Therefore, the term Indigenous Latin@ Immigrants (ILIs) will be used throughout this chapter, "if not, we again will *ocultarlos* (make them invisible)" (p. 85). This is particularly important for educators who work with indigenous families who often assume that most immigrant families and students are monolingual, monocultural, and share the same social practices and experiences. Many educators who work with multilingual ILI children and their families see the use of other languages as a deficit and an impediment for social and academic advancement (Machado-Casas, 2009).

Latin@ Home Education and Schooling

Latin@, Latin@ immigrant, and ILI families' past educational experiences have a direct affect on their experience with educational settings in the US. It affects their experiences with education that values the cultural practices of the Whitestream (Grande, 2000) mainstream group. Second, ILI families live under supposed expectations (Machado-Casas, 2006, 2009) that schools have about family involvement that does not value cultural experiences or family webs of social relationships or social capital, including cultural knowledge (Trueba, 2004) within Latin@ communities.

An extensive body of research has explored the Latin@ families' involvement in US schools (Delgago-Gaitan, 2004; Machado-Casas, 2006, 2009; Moll & Greenberg, 1990; Riojas-Cortez & Flores, 2009). Other studies indicate that schools see newly arrived Latin@ families as unaware of school expectations and as a hindrance to their children's education (Suarez-Orozco, 1988; Valdez, 1996). Because of their vulnerability as newly arrived immigrants, Latin@ families are the first to be blamed for their children's educational failure due to their language, cultural beliefs, and traditions because they go against the assumptions made about parental involvement in US schools.

Schools stereotype Latin@ families as unsupportive, not caring about their children's education, because they are not seen coming to the schools to find out what is going on (Flores, Cousin, & Díaz, 1991). These stereotypes become more poignant when referring to ILI communities with distinct cultural and linguistic practices as notions about what caring families look and act like are transformed into school expectations (Machado-Casas, 2006, 2009). These expectations of parental involvement limit understanding the lives of Latin@s, Latin@ immigrants, and ILI's in the US.

Latin@ families have strong cultural values such as *familialísmo, confianza, respeto,* and *dignidad* (Valdés, 1996; Valenzuela, 1999). These values are additive (Murillo, 2002) and an asset to children's education though not understood by US educators. These cultural values frame parents' expectations of schools and teachers, as well as their experiences within the school setting. There has been an array of research on the socialization and home cultural beliefs of Latin@ children, especially those of Mexican origin. Delgado-Gaitan and Trueba (1991) and Delgado-Gaitan (1990, 2004) looked at the forms of socialization that take place in the home. They discovered that families have the expectation for children to become successful. They also observed that parent–child interactions are linked to parents' home values. Likewise, Machado-Casas (2009) research illustrates ILI families and socialization practices:

> Using their past experiences from their country of origin, and their experiences as immigrants in the US, these indigenous parents are able to transmit to their children—in a natural and organic way—the need to be able to navigate multiple spaces and languages, and the ways in which they can survive as undocumented peoples in the US. These parents are aware that as children of transnational indigenous immigrants, they will face oppressive treatment not only from majority groups but also from their Latino counterparts—as they will never be able to escape from the fact that they live under constant surveillance as undocumented immigrants and as members of indigenous groups that continue to suffer from xenophobic treatments even after migrating to the US.
>
> (p. 12)

For ILI families in the US, socialization is intricate, complicated, done in multiple languages, and sophisticated.

Vasquez, Pease-Alvarez, and Shannon (1994) affirmed that schools do not take into consideration that there are many differences within ethnic groups: language, family organization, size, language spoken at home, and different forms of language socialization. Vasquez et al. (1994) were able to look at the traditional oral practices often performed in Latin@ households and saw them as beneficial to children's learning. They discovered that children attain problem-solving skills and use several language sources to create meaning. The authors argued that language socialization is very much tied to multicultural transactions that provide life skills for maintenance and survival.

Vasquez et al. (1994) also showed that schools fail in that they devalue home culture and children's multicultural language identity—turning them into cultural and language deficit problems instead of seeing them as complex intercultural transactions that draw meaning from the second language.

Further, Delgado-Gaitan and Trueba (1991) spoke of the transcendence of families that despite financial, social, and linguistic barriers, manage to elaborate their current values, and gain a new set of social values. In following children from school to home and back to school, it became evident to them that schools disregarded the children's assets. The deficit model of education restricted which home values or practices counted as part of the equation for student success. Delgado-Gaitan and Trueba (1991) argued that participant families and children were not deficient. Instead, they were not provided with the opportunities to use their cultural beliefs in participating in mainstream culture. In looking at ways in which parents and children communicate and interact with each other, Delgado-Gaitan (1990) found that oral forms of communication, such as cultural narratives or *consejos* are often used by parents to give guidance and socialize children.

This is particularly the case for ILI families who are transnational brokers—who provide multiple services back and forth from one's culture or languages to several others. Transnational brokers is based on Trueba's (2004) definition of Transnationality: "A unique capacity to handle different cultures and lifestyles, different social status, different roles and relationships and to function effectively in different social, political, and economic systems" (p. 39). To that end, multilingualism then becomes part of their everyday learning and social practices that teachers and schools should see as assets, not deficits.

Methodology

This chapter incorporates data from a larger research study (Machado-Casas, 2006), which addressed the migration, mobility, and survival of US Latin@s and ILIs. Narrative research methods (Merriam, 1998) that included multiple interactive methods (Creswell, 1998) were used to collect data in multiple settings. Narrative research is especially appropriate when working with indigenous communities with long histories of oral communication. Clandinin and Connelly (2000) state that "understanding ourselves and our worlds narratively, our attention is turned to how we engage in living, telling, retelling, and reliving our lives within particular social and cultural plotlines" (p. 20). Open-ended interviews were used to understand the experiences of the participants.

Data Collection and Analysis

Thirty ILI parents from Mexico, El Salvador, and Guatemala agreed to be interviewed and to share their life stories. For the purposes of this chapter, we focus on three of the ILI participants because they had children in elementary and secondary schools. They were interviewed in Spanish at local libraries, restaurants, schools, or in their homes. Interviews lasted approximately two to three hours and were recorded, transcribed, and analyzed. During the interviews, the participants were asked to expand on their life stories (Gándara, 1995), to include life experiences, schooling histories in their countries of origin, migration, their experience with the children's educational system, and finally, how residing in the US has affected their cultural, linguistic, and social identity.

Some participants had native multilingual translators that provided translation when they were having difficulties expressing themselves in Spanish. These interpreters and translators supplied the necessary transnational language negotiation; in other words, they provided scenarios, settings, examples for words or situations that do not exist in a particular language register—in this case, Spanish.

Given the current research on the history of exploitation and marginalization of indigenous communities throughout the Americas, the three case studies presented here were the ones who described in detail the survival knowledge of raising ILI children in the US. For example, Otomi, Quiché, and Nahuatl are not only written and oral languages, but also mark ethnic indigenous identity. The following are descriptions of the case studies.

Case Studies

Iza

Iza is an Otomi woman from La Sierra Puebla in México. She was married, had two children, and has been in the US for about six years. Iza worked her entire life; working when she was only a child. At the age of seven she was taken to Mexico City to work and only attended school when she was taken back home. She thinks she completed second grade.

Juana

Juana is a Quiché woman from Guatemala who has been in the US about seven years. She was married, one child was born in Guatemala and two children are US born. She attended some school in Guatemala.

Maria

María is a Nahuatl woman from Mexico. She is married, has one child, and has lived in the US for about three years. She had limited schooling.

Findings

Multilingualism as Multiple Ways of Knowing

When expressing the diversity of their realities as indigenous Latino immigrants in the US, three themes emerged: 1) They were forced to live under the discourse of the Spanish language; 2) Indigenous was synonymous with "uneducated" and therefore "not teachable and unreachable;" and 3) Multilingualism as multiple pedagogies of survival for indigenous Latino immigrants became an everyday social practice. We found that because ILI's realities were so diverse and different to survive in the US, they were forced to live and learn different ways of knowing.

Living under the discourse of the Spanish language

In discussing some of the issues, the women were most disturbed with teachers' assumption that they all spoke Spanish. Iza reflected:

A lot of people would speak to us in Spanish and sometimes we would not understand; then they would get upset with us. Many thought that we were mean but we really didn't know how to say many things right away. Now I go to school every Tuesday and Thursday (to learn Spanish) and it's going pretty good.

Like Iza, Juana also had the same experience. Although they both knew Spanish, they were not fluent. Both felt the necessity to learn Spanish—to fit in with others. According to Juana:

I try to go to the school when I can. Many laughed at her because she didn't know how to speak Spanish very well. But I have learned it because it is good to know it well.

For these families having to learn Spanish became another form of colonization—a language imposed upon them out of necessity. In Meso-America, Spanish has always been used as a form of colonization and though not fluent Spanish speakers, they were considered part of the communities. In the US, they had to learn it enough to be able to survive as Latin@ immigrants in a Spanish-English context. Hence, not speaking Spanish meant not belonging as US Latin@ immigrants, which resulted in isolation, fear, and vulnerability.

Indigenous Synonymous with Uneducated, Therefore not Teachable and Unreachable

These three ILI women described the unresponsive manner in which they were treated by teachers and school officials. They felt that this indifference occurred because they were indigenous and that teachers automatically assumed that they were "uneducated." Although they were not formally educated—all had life and home experiences. Nonetheless, they were treated as if they were not teachable and therefore, not reachable. For example, María's interaction with her daughter's teacher:

When we took our daughter to school, the teacher knew that my daughter was Nahuatl. My daughter told her, and she didn't know what that was. I looked it up in the dictionary and found the word and gave it to her. Then she started to ask what we ate, wore, what we did, and everything. She thought that we were like in books "*con una pluma en la cabeza*" (with a feather in our heads). I don't know but I think she did learn that year. With my bad English I had to search for things so she would know us. This is how the year went by. I didn't like when she told the class that we were Indians. I hadn't been called that in a long time and I was surprised that it happened here! My daughters did not want to go back to school until I sent a letter to the teacher in Spanish. She told me that she didn't know it wasn't very nice to call someone an Indian and that the girls were wrong … If it's this bad. Then why don't they bring somebody that speaks Spanish? I don't understand and I have to learn it through others, about the homework and meetings. I'm always the last one. This teacher that called us Indians stopped sending us letters, because we were not going to understand. I was so angry; I told my daughter that I was going to take care of it.

This teacher's insensitivity and ignorance is evident in that she considers them "*indios*," which can be a derogatory humiliating term. This teacher's deficit perspectives are prototypical of many teachers who have worked with non-English speaking families. Some teachers form a deficit impression and do not feel obligated to communicate with ILIs in their language.

Multilingualism as Multiple Pedagogies of Survival for ILI

We began the chapter with a vignette whereby the teacher had advised Iza and Juana to stop speaking to their children in their indigenous languages. However, these astute "uneducated" mothers reasoned that it was very poor advice. The mothers, instead, surmised that multilingualism is indeed a necessary survival toolkit for their children in their new home country. It would enable them to communicate within the family and community across multiple contexts and situations. They also recognized the importance of acquiring English in order to survive in the US, as María indicates:

> I was still taking English classes once a month. Now it is just much more important because my daughters started school already and they don't know English. They speak Nahuatl and Spanish, but it was hard for them.

These women further realized that they and their children had to move in and out of different social and linguistic spaces, which meant the use of multiple languages as part of their everyday utility and ability to live in the US. Participants also recognized that to be treated in a more equitable manner in schools, they had to learn to use multiple languages.

Conclusion

The narratives of the three ILI women illustrate the continued disconnection between US society, schools, and the realities of ILI families and children. They also bring to light the power and astuteness of families who day-to-day struggle as undocumented immigrants in the US. These narratives show how these ILI families use multilingualism as everyday social practice to assure that their children will have the necessary transnational strategies to survive as indigenous immigrants in the US. The ability to use these everyday social practices to pass on multilingual, multisituational, multipurposeful strategies within a transnational social network is what transforms ILIs into teachers and models of the art of becoming global citizens.

By telling these stories, we are building a bridge for teachers to *trabajar* (work) with the families and their children. We are providing a counter story to the pervasive deficit ideology regarding the linguistic and cultural diversity of our Latin@ and ILI communities in the US.

Transforming Teacher Preparation

Candidates need to become more knowledgeable about ILI children's family's cultural ways of knowing, languages, and class backgrounds and view these as cultural capital. Given the narrative testimonies of Iza, Juana, and María, we need to respect them as knowing human beings. We must resist making false assumptions or operate from a deficit perspective regarding indigenous communities. We must understand that Spanish is not their mother tongue and just because they do not speak it well, they are not uneducated. As teachers, we have the moral responsibility and obligation to educate all children regardless of class, culture, language, or gender. We can reach out to parents and families using intercultural interpreters, learning about their cultures and languages, creating different ways of getting to know each other, and working together to build success. This relationship is reciprocal; that is, we also need to share with them about our multiple cultural ways, language, and history as well.

We need to provide candidates experiences in which they not only document the challenges, but also the multiple ways that school-parent-community relationships are solved. What are the issues? How are these issues addressed? How do schools develop rapport with multilingual parents? What resources are needed and used? How do all those involved authentically communicate and learn about each other's cultural ways?

We need to use the aforementioned knowledge about ILI families to change or broaden our attitudes. To do this, we must have the courage to name and interrogate these deficit beliefs and ideologies that interfere with our students' educational success and our pedagogy (see Chapter 4 and 6). For example, when ILI parents are told to speak only Spanish because they are affecting their children's academic potential is no different from telling Spanish-speaking parents to speak only English to their children. These statements represent the myopic and stereotypic deficit ideology that is pervasive in this country, i.e., that bilingualism and/or multilingualism is a detriment to learning and academic achievement.

This type of deficit thinking is irrational. Research shows that the more languages one knows the more intelligent s/he is. By reading, discussing, interrogating, and critically examining the consequences and origins of such negative beliefs, we can begin to transform and replace these beliefs in order to support children and their families. Teacher candidates' negative attitudes and ideology about race, language, culture, and class can change, and positively impact their practice, curriculum, and pedagogy (Flores et al., 1991; Nieto, 2004; see Chapter 4 and 6). We can begin to shift the tide of low expectations, blaming the victim, and misunderstandings, to a more cooperative, collaborative, and meaningful intercultural communications with the parents, families, and the community at large.

In the case of ILIs, the bilingual education teacher can be the multilingual sociocultural mediator between the school's cultural expectations, values, and traditions as s/he mediates this knowledge to the parents (Díaz & Flores, 2001). Reciprocally, as s/he comes to know the cultural ways of the ILI parents, s/he can mediate cultural ways of knowing, communicating, and expectations with school officials and colleagues. Establishing a trusting relationship through respectful ways is the beginning of authentic communication. Developing these skills should occur within the teacher preparation program.

Conducting community ethnographies (Moll, Amanti, Neff, & González, 1992) would be one way to learn about how community members interact within the community (see Chapter 17). Funds of knowledge research has shown that once teachers learn about the parents and the community, they become more adept at communicating, teaching the children with culturally responsive curriculum, and ways of teaching that are more innovative and relevant (González, Moll & Amanti, 2005). In the case of ILI and other Latin@s, it is important for candidates to document the use of the different languages within the different contexts.

Research Directions

Based on the salient findings, we also strongly suggest the following areas for in-depth research that would enhance bilingual education teacher candidates' sociocultural knowledge about ILI children, their families, and communities. We need to:

• document multilingualism as an everyday social practice in the home and in the school;
• explore teacher candidates' notions and knowledge about ILIs;
• examine teachers' ideological shifts in terms of ILIs;
• collect teacher's personal narratives of transformations of practice; and
• conduct longitudinal studies of ILI families and their children in US schools.

Continued narrative research on ILIs will provide powerful stories for teachers' understanding and transformations. Telling our stories about our intercultural ways of communicating, our ways of solving problems, and our ways of cooperating will mark the pathways toward working together for the well-being of all children's education.

References

Anderson, W. (1997, October). *Familias purépechas en el sur de Illinois: La (re)construcción de la identidad étnica* [Purepecha families in southern Illinois: The (re)construction of ethnic identity]. Paper presented at the XIX Coloquio de Antropología e Historia Regionales, organized by El Colegio de Michoacán, Ciudad de Zamora.

Clandinin, D. J., & Connelly, R. M. (2000). *Narrative inquiry: Experience and story in qualitative research*. San Francisco: Jossey-Bass.

Creswell, J. (1998). *Qualitative inquiry and research design: Choosing among five traditions*. Thousand Oaks, CA: Sage.

Delgado-Gaitan, C. (1990). *Literacy for empowerment: The role of parents in children's education*. Bristol, CN: Falmer.

Delgado-Gaitan, C. (2004). *Involving Latino families in schools: Raising student achievement through home-school partnerships*. Thousand Oaks, CA: Corwin Press.

Delgado-Gaitan, C., & Trueba, H. (1991). *Crossing cultural borders: Education for immigrant families in America*. London: Falmer.

Díaz, E., & Flores, B. (2001). Teaching to the potential: Teacher as sociocultural and sociohistorical mediator. In M. de la Luz Reyes & J. Halcón (Eds.), *The best for our children* (pp. 29–47). New York: Teachers College Press.

Flores, B., Cousin, P. T., & Díaz, E. (1991). Critiquing and transforming the deficit myths about learning, language and culture. *Language Arts, 68,* 369–379.

Flores, N., Hernández León, R., & Massey, D. S. (2004). Social capital and emigration from rural and urban communities. In J. Durand & D. S. Massey (Eds.), *Crossing the border: Research from the Mexican migration project* (pp.184–200). New York: Sage.

Fox, J., & Rivera-Salgado, G. (Eds.). (2004). *Indigenous Mexican migrants in the United States.* La Jolla, CA: University of California, San Diego, Center for Comparative Immigration Studies, and Center for US–Mexican Studies.

Gándara, P. (1995). *Over the ivy walls: The educational mobility of low-income Chicanos.* Albany, NY: SUNY.

González, N., Moll, L. C., & Amanti, C. (Eds.). (2005). *Funds of knowledge: Theorizing practice in households, communities, and classrooms.* Mahwah, NJ: Erlbaum.

Grande, S. M. A. (2000). American Indian geographies of identity and power: At the crossroads of Indigena and Mestizaje. *Harvard Educational Review, 70*(4), 467–498.

Machado-Casas, M. (2006). *Narrating education of new Indigenous/Latino transnational communities in the South.* Ph.D. dissertation. University of North Carolina, Chapel Hill.

Machado-Casas, M. (2009). The politics of organic phylogeny: The art of parenting and surviving as transnational multilingual Latino indigenous immigrants in the US. *The High School Journal, 92*(4), 82–99.

Merriam, S. B. (1998). *Qualitative research and case study: Applications in education.* San Francisco, Jossey-Bass.

Moll, L. C., Amanti, C., Neff, D., & González, N. (1992). Funds of knowledge for teaching: Using a qualitative approach to connect homes and classrooms. *Theory into Practice, 31*(2), 132–141.

Moll, L. C., & Greenberg, J. (1990). Creating zones of possibilities: Combining social contexts for instruction. In L. C. Moll (Ed.), *Vygotsky and education* (pp. 319–348). Cambridge, MA: Cambridge University Press.

Murillo, E. (2002). How does it feel to be a problem? In S. Wortham, E. Murillo, & E. T Hamann (Eds.), *Education in the new Latino diaspora: Policy and the politics of identity* (pp. 215–240). New York: Ablex.

Nieto, S. (2004). *Affirming diversity: The sociopolitical context of multicultural education* (4th ed.). New York: Pearson.

Passel, J. S., & Suro, R. (2005). *Rise, peak and decline: Trends in US immigration 1992–2004.* Washington DC: Pew Hispanic Center Report.

Riojas-Cortez, M., & Flores, B. B. (2009). *Sin olvidar a los padres:* Families collaborating within school and university partnerships. *Journal of Latinos in Education, 8*(3), 231–239.

Rivera-Salgado, G. (1999). *Migration and political activism: Mexican transnational indigenous communities in a comparative perspective.* PhD dissertation. University of California, Santa Cruz.

Stephen, L. (2007). *Transborder lives: Indigenous Oaxacans in Mexico, California, and Oregon.* Durham, NC: Duke University Press.

Suárez-Orozco, M. (1988). Psychosocial aspects of achievement motivation among recent Hispanic immigrants. In H. Trueba, G. Spindler, & L. Sprindler (Eds.), *What do anthropologists have to say about dropouts?* (pp. 99–116). New York: Falmer.

Trueba, E. (2004). *The new Americans: Immigrants and transnationals at work.* New York: Rowman & Littlefield.

Valenzuela, A. (1999). *Subtractive schooling: US-Mexican youth and the politics of caring.* New York: SUNY.

Valdés, G. (1996). *Con respeto. Bridging the distance between culturally diverse families and schools.* New York: Teachers College Press.

Vasquez, O. A., Pease-Alvarez, P., & Shannon, S. M. (1994). *Pushing boundaries: Language and culture in a Mexicano community.* New York: Cambridge University Press.

Zabin, C., Kearney, M., García, A., Runsten, D., & Nagengast, C. (1993). *Mixtec migrants in California agriculture: A new cycle of poverty.* Davis, CA: California Institute for Rural Studies.

17 Growing Quality Teachers

Community-Oriented Preparation

Carmen I. Mercado and
Carol Brochin-Ceballos

Jimenez and Gertsen (1999) argue that the greatest challenge facing teacher education is teacher learning, or how to help candidates and teachers shift from traditional teaching approaches to culturally relevant pedagogies. What we have learned from three decades of bilingual education teacher preparation may provide a strong base for the preparation of all teachers. As programs focus on recruiting, developing, and retaining teachers for high-need urban and rural areas, they must address the nature of field service.

In this chapter, we present two cases, which engage candidates and teachers in guided fieldwork in local communities, through supervised placement in schools and informal field-based projects. Both build on the concept "funds of knowledge," coined by Velez-Ibañez (1995) to organize field experiences. Funds of knowledge refer to skills, experiences, knowledge of habitat, and the social knowledge households develop for survival. These community resources have pedagogical value. The two cases in this chapter include candidates and experienced Latin@ teachers from different institutions and geographic contexts.

The first case is in a Hispanic serving institution (HSI) in the southwest with strong ties to local Latin@ communities attracting candidates from the immediate area. The teachers in the second case come from a teaching, research, and service institution in the northeast with long traditions of preparing women teachers. These cases share a common concern—knowing students, local communities, and understanding how homes and communities shape what children know about the world, especially those who live transnational lives.

Case One

Learning Sitios

Latin@ communities as *sitios* for learning build on funds of knowledge, which emphasize the wealth of knowledge and resources present in bilingual, Latin@ communities. In this case study, Brochin-Ceballos (second author) documented how a bilingual teacher education preparation program at a large HSI in the southwest prepares candidates to think broadly about ways to incorporate funds of knowledge. Community ethnographies examined literacy activities as cultural resources.

This case is part of a larger qualitative study examining how candidates cultivated a *maestra* (teacher) identity. Using case study and literacy research methods, data was collected from candidates enrolled in the Spring 2008 bilingual block which included four courses. All candidates were bilingual Mexican American (Spanish/English). The community ethnographies and reflection papers required candidates to critically examine ways to build on the funds of knowledge found within the community. To determine what the candidates learned about the communities from these activities, I analyzed written texts and oral discussions, and identified ways that participating in this activity helped cultivate their *maestra* identity.

Maestra Identity Components

How *maestra* was used by professors in the bilingual block was observed. It was common to hear phrases such as, *Buenos días maestras* (Good morning, teachers). Observational field notes also recorded multiple uses of this term. Although teacher is the literal translation for the word *maestra,* I became interested in how this term might have different connotations by applying Valenzuela's (1999) analysis of the cultural difference between the terms education and *educación.* I documented how *maestra* might be conceptualized differently from teacher. Valenzuela explains that while *educación* is the literal translation for education, in the Latin@ culture to be *bien educado* describes someone with or without schooling who is respectful and thoughtful across multiple settings and situations (see Chapter 1). In English, to be educated only refers to academic schooling.

The following themes emerged from the data. Becoming a *maestra* was not a homogenous, linear construct, but rather a process of becoming grounded in a socially mediated space within the bilingual block. A *maestra* identity included the following tenets: (1) critical self-reflection and cultural recovery; (2) affirmative practices building on cultural and linguistic resources of Bilingual Learners (BLs), their families, and communities; and (3) an awareness and advocacy for BLs within the broader sociocultural, historical, and political context of education.

Participation in the community ethnography assignments required candidates to study schools and their surroundings from an asset-based perspective and to reflect on their experiences as a way to develop a *maestra* identity. They critically examined their own ideologies, including previously held uncovered deficit views toward Mexican American communities (see Chapter 4).

Community Ethnographies and Cultural Resources

As a course requirement, candidates conducted two community ethnographies and one reflection paper. Written papers were submitted in Spanish. They discussed how a site near their school field-based placement could be integrated into classroom activities in three broad areas: mathematics, social studies, and science. Candidates took photographs, conducted informal interviews, and observed the community's funds of knowledge. They wrote a brief ethnography and included three ways to incorporate the location's cultural resources into classroom lessons.

This experience connected them to the broader program vision. One goal identified by the university program director was to develop relationships with the community, particularly with cultural arts organizations and other community resources so that when they are teachers they know how to bring the community into their teaching and how to link it to the types of language and cultural resources that can enrich the teaching in a bicultural bilingual program.

The program philosophy shaped the content and experiences in the courses and advanced the concept that Latin@ communities are rich *sitios* for learning. Candidates were prepared to learn from the students' communities through meaningful course assignments. Professor Gutierrez described why she developed the community ethnography assignment during her first-semester teaching in the bilingual block:

> I was surprised that when we were working in the Westside in one of the schools where we prepared the teachers, I heard some comments during the break that it was kind of scary to come to this neighborhood and park and that they always came the same route because they didn't want to get jacked in their car. And I just went, "wait, wait. You are Latinas. Some of you have lived in neighborhoods like this. ..." I got really worried that maybe I wasn't doing a good job ... that this community aspect was not sinking in.

She developed the community ethnography assignment because although candidates spent a significant amount of time in the schools, they did not explore the communities surrounding the school and often displayed stereotypical views toward working class, Mexican American communities. Although candidates shared the same ethnic make-up as the families in the school communities, they did not live in the communities where they were placed for field experiences. Some stated, "being in the *barrio* is scary." Therefore, professors developed activities to help candidates see the linguistic and cultural richness and resources available in the students' communities.

Candidates wrote essays about various *sitios* such as recreation places, restaurants, bakeries, grocery stores, parks, service stations, tire shops, and beauty salons. In this chapter, I do not focus on the types of activities they developed around each *sitio*, but rather what they learned about visiting the community and how they planned to incorporate this knowledge into classroom lessons. Using textual analysis, I analyzed reflection papers and found examples of how this activity impacted their views of the community and how it cultivated their *maestra* identity. The findings were organized around three shifts: views toward bilingual Mexican American communities, understandings toward incorporating funds of knowledge, and developing ideologies as future *maestras*.

Shifts in Views Toward Bilingual, Mexican American Communities

Although many candidates grew up in working-class families, they now live in middle-class neighborhoods or in apartments near the campus. In their essays, many described how their views of what these communities offered shifted due to participation in these activities. Rosana reflected:

Cuando comencé a observar en esta escuela, no sabía qué esperar. No conocía ese lado de la ciudad. He oído algunas gentes diciendo cosas muy negativas sobre ese lado de la ciudad en donde está la escuela y yo ya había tenido esa mala impresión de la comunidad ...Cuando hice mi primera etnografía, fui con confianza a conocer la comunidad. Despejé todas las cosas negativas que tenía en mi cabeza y empecé con una mente abierta. La comunidad es muy amistosa. Cuando les pedí a los negocios si podía tomar fotos de afuera, todos me dejaron y unos empleados me dijeron que estaban orgullosos de mí porque estaba enriqueciendo el conocimiento de los estudiantes de la comunidad ... [When I started to observe at this school, I didn't know what to expect. I didn't know this part of town. I had heard some people say very negative things about this part of town where the school is located and had a bad impression of the community ... When I did my first ethnography; I went with confidence to get to know the community. I let go of all the negative things I had in my head and I started with an open mind. The community is very friendly. When I asked the businesses if I could take pictures outside, they all let me and some of the employees told me that they were proud of me because I was enriching the knowledge of students from the community].

Roxana, born in Nuevo Laredo, Mexico, moved to San Antonio, Texas when she was two years old. She grew up in a working-class, Spanish-speaking household; however, she admits that she did not know the part of town where she was placed to do her fieldwork. She felt encouraged to incorporate community businesses in her lessons. She admitted hearing negative comments about the area surrounding the school, but after completing the community ethnography, her perspectives towards this community shifted; she developed a more positive perspective. Roxana felt encouraged to incorporate community businesses in her lessons.

Jennifer was placed for field observations at the same elementary school she attended as a child:

Vivo en la comunidad, pero nunca tuve la oportunidad de explorarla con tanta atención. Aunque yo vivo muy cerca de la escuela, la mayoría de el tiempo estaba en casa de mi abuela ... Para poder entender los estudiantes y sus familias las maestras tienen que ser como detectives. Tienen que entrar a los restaurantes y a las tiendas para poder conocer los lugares que visitan los estudiantes. Pude ver con más detalle las activ[idades] que ofrece la comunidad para los estudiantes. Fue algo positivo que cambió mi perspectiva de la comunidad. La tarea es buena si la maestra toma el tiempo para conocer toda la comunidad. No solamente es de pasar por varias calles, tiene que darse la oportunidad de investigar las tiendas, los restaurantes, los lotes de carros, los salones de belleza y los parques [I live in the community, but I never had the opportunity to explore it with so much attention. Although I live really close to the school, the majority of the time I was at my grandmother's house. In order to understand students and their families, teachers need to be like detectives. They have to enter restaurants and stores to get to know the place where students visit. I could see in more detail the activities that the community offers students. It was something positive that changed my perspective of the community. This activity is good if the teacher takes the time to get to know the community. It is not just about driving down several streets; they have to give themselves the opportunity to investigate the stores, restaurants, car lots, beauty salons and the parks].

This example shows the importance of these activities for all candidates, including those who grew up in the same neighborhood.

Shifts in Understanding How to Incorporate Funds of Knowledge

Prior to the bilingual block, candidates were introduced to the theoretical concept, funds of knowledge. The community ethnographies integrated this concept with practice. To illustrate, Cristina acknowledged the importance of incorporating the community into the classroom, but did not know how to do it. This project helped her apply theory to practice:

> *Antes de hacer este proyecto, creía que era muy importante a incorporar la comunidad en la clase pero no sabía cómo hacerlo. Ahora, comprendo cómo crear y organizar lecciones en una manera significativa para los estudiantes ... Si conoces a tus estudiantes, puedes ayudarles a aprender en la clase utilizando conexiones con la comunidad...Finalmente, creo que escuelas deben de incorporar la comunidad en la clase más para qué estudiantes comprendan que su comunidad es muy importante en su aprendizaje* [Before working on this project, I believed that it was very important to incorporate the community in the classroom but I didn't know how to do it. Now I understand how to create and organize lesson plans in more significant ways for students. If you know your students, you can help them learn by making community connections. Finally, I believe that schools should incorporate the community in the classroom so that students can understand that their community is very important in their learning].

Rosemary, born and raised in San Antonio, Texas, also grew up in a neighborhood near the school where she was placed for her fieldwork. To select her *sitio*, she asked fourth grade students where they shopped. They mentioned Chicho Boys Fruit Market. She also realized that building on the funds of knowledge in the community helps students connect what they are learning to real-world situations. Rosemary theorized the impact of this experience on students:

> *Utilizando lugares que los estudiantes conocen y que frecuentan les ayudaría a estar más motivados. Los estudiantes también estarán más atentos para aprender y explorar los diferentes temas. Los fondos del conocimiento que están disponibles en las comunidades de estudiantes deben ser utilizados para hacer la enseñanza más efectiva e interesante* [Utilizing places that the students know and visit would help them be more motivated. The students would also pay more attention in learning and exploring different themes. The funds of knowledge that are available in the community should be used to make learning more effective and interesting].

Ximena realized that workers at a tire shop have vast knowledge to share with children. She saw this as an opportunity to invite parents to the classroom to teach students about auto-mechanics. She felt that teachers can link the funds of knowledge of community businesses to scientific concepts:

> *Los conceptos que se podrían enfocar en un negocio como el de la vulcanizadora Hernández son innumerables. Pero lo más importante es el que podamos mostrarles a estos trabajadores que ellos también tienen mucho que contribuir en la educación de nuestros niños. Creo que también habría la oportunidad de invitar a los papás al salón para dar pequeños talleres sobre mecánica a los niños y niñas* [The concepts that can be taught from a business like the Hernández tire shop are vast. Most importantly, we can show the tire shop workers that they too have a lot to contribute to the education of our children. I also believe there could be an opportunity to invite the parents to the class to give mini-lesson about auto mechanics to boys and girls].

Shifts in Ideologies as Future Maestras.

For candidates, conducting community ethnographies and incorporating them into lesson plans has strong implications for teacher preparation. Many wrote about how these activities helped them shift their ideologies (see Chapter 6). Ximena realized that not all candidates are aware of the funds of knowledge in the community. She also felt that this activity influenced her ideology as *maestra*: "*Definitivamente, es parte crucial de la enseñanza, que desafortunadamente es omitida por la mayoría de los maestros, será una parte esencial de mi ideología como maestra*" [Definitely, this is crucial to our learning, that unfortunately is omitted by most teachers, and will be an essential part of my teacher ideology].

Erika had a similar response and plans to study the community at the beginning of the school year: "*Para mí, conocer la comunidad de mis estudiantes va a ser de gran importancia antes de comenzar el año escolar*" [For me, getting to know the community of my students will be of huge importance before the school year starts].

Yadira saw the community ethnography as a way to break student-teacher borders: "*Como futura maestra podré romper las barreras y crear lecciones más autenticas las cuales los estudiantes de mi salón podrán incorporar la comunidad para aprender más culturalmente*" [As a future teacher, I can break barriers and create more authentic lessons in which my students incorporate the community].

Incorporating Funds of Knowledge in Future Classrooms

Generally, the resources that bilingual teacher candidates bring to the teaching profession are understated and undocumented. However, these case studies show that candidates benefit by conducting community ethnographies, especially those with internalized deficit views towards bilingual, working-class communities. It is important that they be given multiple opportunities to explore and examine Latin@ communities for the rich resources that can support the teaching-learning process. Participation in community ethnographies serve as an important element in the preparation of curricula because of their potential to transform the candidate-view of Latin@ communities as *sitios* for learning. Through ethnographies, candidates learn to link the student-community resources to the classroom activities. This experience allows them to view students' languages, cultures, and community resources as assets, as well as help them challenge deficit views toward Mexican American communities. Community ethnographies support: shifts in how candidates view community resources; application of theory to practice; spaces to reflect on ideological shifts, and cultivation of a *maestra* identity.

Case Two

Funds of Knowledge: Ways to Learn, Teach, and Build Community

Mercado (first author) discovered funds of knowledge as a powerful way for candidates, teachers, and teacher educators to learn about children and families. In Case Two, learning about children and families involved a traditional graduate bilingual research course. This collaborative research activity encourages practitioner research in Latin@ homes. As Zeichner (2006) has pointed out, teachers' insider perspectives are still relatively absent from the scholarship on teaching, a serious omission shaping the quality of the knowledge base on teaching Latin@ children. Studying funds of knowledge generated practical and theoretical knowledge towards transformation of classroom pedagogy.

Documenting my practice through the scholarship of teaching is part of a moral commitment to address inequalities, and documenting the study of funds of knowledge is scholarship of teaching as activism. Through self-study, I seek to gain insights and find answers to questions that traditional research forms may not explicitly address and this guides what I do as a teacher educator.

Adapting Funds of Knowledge to Learning Settings

As a former elementary school teacher, I approached the study of funds of knowledge from a pedagogical stance (Van Manen, 1993) as did the teacher-researchers in the course. This orientation defined what we sought, how we related to others, and ways we collected and interpreted data. This collaborative research was part of a graduate course that met 150 minutes weekly for 15 sessions. It involved mostly bilingual teachers in two to three guided home visits in local Latin@ communities. The teacher-researchers frequently met to prepare for or debrief their experience, usually at a local restaurant, homes of colleagues, or my office.

As course instructor, I guided and assisted in the research process by discussing key ideas in academic readings, specifically funds of knowledge; explaining social networks and literacy as a social practice; and, coaching ways to scaffold home observations and discussions. I also organized the teacher-researchers into teams and helped them reflect on the challenges of learning from this unusual approach to a familiar activity. Presentations at major professional gatherings after the semester ended made it possible for a few teacher-researchers to appreciate their work from the perspective of a broader community of scholars. We managed to create an authentic community of practice that modeled how researchers work.

Two broad questions shaped my role in this process:

- How does studying funds of knowledge change the way teachers conceptualize and make use of students' funds of knowledge?
- How do I learn to assist teachers through participant-observation when studying students' funds of knowledge?

These questions reflect conceptualizing teaching-learning from sociocultural learning theory perspective, which informed the original funds of knowledge studies by González, Moll, and Amanti (2005). A goal was to prepare teachers to teach outside the whitestream by including principles such as:

- experience is incomplete without reflection;
- learning through participation means you need to try to change it; and
- learning is change, which is why we study phenomena in the process of changing it, over time.

Through side-by-side participation, I learned to assist teacher-researchers throughout an intense and challenging semester by lessening apprehensions and misgivings about their capacity to do research which many felt was beyond their reach. Clearly, adapting the study of community funds of knowledge to a graduate research course stretched us in different ways and expanded the boundaries of our learning community. It connected four distinct communities: schools, families, schools of education, and the broader scholarly community. While Zeichner (2006) considers connections among schools, families, and colleges of education as essential to strengthen teacher education, I added the broader educational research community where the voices of ethnic minority teacher educators are typically missing in the empirical knowledge base for teaching about teaching.

Lessons Learned

I have previously studied teachers' experiences of home visits and the funds of knowledge uncovered in the local Latin@ communities where they work (Mercado, 2005; Mercado & Moll, 1997). In this section, I focus on personal and professional learning that informs my work as a teacher educator.

Guided home visits to learn about funds of knowledge in local communities is premised on the belief that candidates and teachers need to know the socio-historic-political realities beyond the school, that constrain much of what happens in classrooms. Fieldwork methods, central to the study of funds of knowledge, brought me out of my institutional setting to learn about and understand local communities where teachers labor and students live. Even though I supervise early field experiences in these same communities, workload and other responsibilities leave little time to examine how changing demographics impact on the curriculum and the learning-teaching process. Therefore, focused, intensive ethnographic fieldwork in local communities is a form of professional development. In the next section, I explore four themes that emerged from the data: a) bilingual communication as resource, b) multiple ways of learning, c) strengthening relationships with teachers, and d) connecting funds of knowledge to community needs.

Bilingual Communication as Resource

Of the 80 households in our study on funds of knowledge, 54% were Latin@, a mix of recent immigrants and long-term Puerto Ricans. The 59 teacher-researchers licensed in Spanish/English bilingual education, were 30–40 years old, and had four years (median) classroom experiences in schools located in low-income communities. Many identified themselves as first and second generation Puerto Ricans and some had lived in the communities we studied.

I began as a classroom teacher in a dual language school and have devoted more than 20 years of my life to college teaching and supervision. Even so, I did not necessarily feel advantaged during home visits. We did feel confident in our ability to communicate in Spanish. Ability to communicate bilingually, and the metalinguistic awareness associated with bilingualism, as Vygotsky (1978) explains, heightened attentiveness to language and its influence in shaping understandings and relationships (Chapter 5). For example, as we reviewed and adapted questions from three questionnaires, we engaged in lively and sometimes heated discussions over the meaning, appropriateness and implications of terms like work, job, and income producing activities, or questions such as, "Are there books in the home?" This eye-opening experience has implications for the preparation of candidates and professional development of teachers even if they are not bilingual.

Focused conversations with children's caregivers were shaped by teachers' bilingual competence and sociocultural knowledge, needed to establish *confianza* (trust), build solidarity, and elicit information, or even making spot decisions of what not to ask. Some teacher-researchers engaged in playful or colloquial use of Spanish to lessen the social distance when esteem and respect for teacher authority interfered with understanding day-to-day activities from a funds of knowledge perspective, such as childrearing practices.

During home interviews, we paid close attention to activities in spaces where interviews took place. We observed how family members interacted, especially with children who were almost always present, and often participants in conversations, much to our delight and surprise. In the majority of homes we visited, it is no longer the case that *"los niños hablan cuando las gallinas mean"* (children speak when hens pee, which is never!). Witnessing these exchanges were always more illuminating than elicited responses. One teacher captured the essence: "we were looking for funds of knowledge, and it was right there," as we observed interactions between children and caregivers and noticed communicative competence seldom visible in the classroom.

One memorable moment occurred when I was greeted by a third grader who opened the entrance gate with a question she delighted in asking "*¿Cómo se porta, Mic i … en la clase?* (How does Ms… behave in class?). After about 4 hours of conversation, this student's bilingual teacher was stunned to learn about maturity and playfulness with the Spanish language that she had not witnessed in the classroom. On this day, in this home, a caring bilingual teacher who thought she knew her students was taken by surprise in confronting what she did not know.

Teachers struggled with the choice of words to represent families in field notes, usually written in English, especially when describing seemingly ambiguous relationships involving the head-of-the-household. Males were often referred to as boyfriends, seldom husbands, and never partners. While we found that teachers need appropriate language to use for home-school communication, this is rarely given attention in preparation programs and professional development experiences. This form of communication is distinct from the way teachers communicate with children in the classroom or with colleagues. Learning through bilingual and culturally appropriate conversations was key to accessing useful information.

Multiple Ways of Learning

Being in students' homes, we learned from the physical environment. This tangible evidence added depth to our conversations. Usually photographs, other artifacts, and visual memories of significant experiences were on public display. Photos of a child's communion, a birthday celebration, or holiday gathering were prominently displayed. The physical space spoke its own sensory language: confining and cluttered with artifacts of lived lives; sparsely furnished; distinct colors, sounds, smells; well lit or dark; and, even cold or overly warm. The space in the homes we visited shaped our interactions with families and impacted us in far more powerful ways than words. This experience was not unlike experiencing a dramatic performance in which the stage setting is deliberately crafted to evoke emotions, consistent with the playwright's message, only in our case it was not crafted; it was real.

Telling or explaining "where you live" affects how you experience life and the quality of the educational experiences and services you receive. Experiencing what these words mean to real people, how it affects their lives, as we discovered in the homes of the modest-income families we visited, is both emotional and intellectual. For Ita's family living in a dilapidated tenement in East Harlem, not knowing if or when their apartment would burn was a real fear for her and for her children, and unimaginable to those who experience life in more affluent parts of the city.

> For seven years, Ita has lived with her second husband Luís, and her five children (sons, age 21 and 17, and daughters. aged 20, 13, and 9) on the fourth floor of a tenement near the overpass to the commuter train to the wealthy suburbs. The railroad apartment is small, everything appearing to be scaled down in size. "Ita's world is like Macondo," writes the teacher, to describe impoverished living conditions she did not expect "in America," Macondo, being the setting for *One Hundred Years of Solitude*. This novel is symbolic of poverty. "Why bother to fix this apartment," Ita explains in Spanish. "If there's a fire, everything is lost."

Notes from a Mexican immigrant family residing in Queens capture another dimension of reality:

En cuatro pequeñas habitaciones conviven tres parejas, un soltero, y cuatro niños. Al entrar por la puerta principal se empieza a sentir las limitaciones de movimiento que la falta de espacio nos impone. Tan estrecho es la entrada que la escalera que nos conduce al segundo piso donde vive La Familia Rojas (pseudónimo) toma la mayor parte de este estrecho pasillo, apenas 3 pies de ancho, según mis cálculos. Se abre la puerta y nos encontramos de repente en la cocina y tan pequeña que nos obliga a sentarnos en la mesa de comer. Luego Wilda (del equipo) admite que este modo de vivir no le sorprende, pero se asusta al sentir el calor de la estufa en su espalda [Three couples, four young children and a single male relative live in four small rooms. Entering through the door you begin to feel how space constrains our movements. The entrance is so narrow that the stairwell leading to the apartment where the Rojas family lives takes up most of a narrow hallway that I estimate to be about three feet wide. The door opens and we find ourselves in a small kitchen, where we are forced to sit around the dining room table for lack of space. Afterwards, Wilda (a member of our team) admitted that she worried when she felt the warmth of the stove on her back even though this way of living came as no surprise to her].

Strengthening Teacher Relationships

Fieldwork methods, central to the study of funds of knowledge, brought me into the social worlds of teachers and children. This experience increased an already high-regard and admiration for hardworking bilingual teachers with high levels of commitment to children and communities. Many bilingual teachers I have worked with do not ask for merit pay, or compensation for the long hours they put in generally unrecognized by supervisors and peers in other settings. Understandings and emotions derived from this collaborative learning experience created a bond with teachers not unlike those who go through hardships or struggle together. Changes in my relationships to the teacher-researchers who were technically my students was the parallel to what teachers experienced in their relationships with students and families. This outcome of the funds of knowledge approach is not surprising, given that it is grounded in respect for the intellect of the teacher-researchers and equally respectful of the knowledge and wisdom in local households.

Connecting Funds of Knowledge to Community Needs

In this study, the median family income was below $20,000, in a city where the median income for a family of four is $50,000. Consequently, we came face-to-face with the poverty that is at the root cause of many social and educational problems we witnessed during our home visits. It is this economic reality that is at the core of health, social, and schooling problems that has been documented that require attention through social policy. Preparing candidates to engage in culturally relevant pedagogies, while important, is insufficient. Methods courses generally pay little attention to the out-of-school factors that influence schooling, which teachers need to understand to be effective. Even so, it is important to clarify that in the modest income homes we visited, poverty did *not* hinder children's capacity to learn. However, poverty causes a scarcity of material resources that affects how children live and limits their access to needed material resources.

The funds of knowledge we identified in the Latin@ households, including, but were not limited to, entrepreneurship, medicine, music, and home repair. One caregiver we interviewed volunteered to assist her son's teacher in the classroom. Then school administrators sought her out to do clerical work because of her ability to read and write in Spanish and English. This parent was an unpaid volunteer; however, she possessed teacher-aide skills. Clearly, teachers can build on community funds of knowledge to connect the knowledge, skills and competencies found in local households. Although bilinguals are in high demand in careers tied to service and communication industries, BLs seldom receive encouragement to develop their bilingualism other than in bilingual programs. Teachers do not have to be bilingual to promote and encourage children's bilingualism and biliteracy through career awareness, but they need to know why this is important.

Summary and Conclusions

In this chapter, both cases illustrate the power of guided field experiences in establishing and strengthening relationships with students, parents, and communities. It helps connect home and community resources to schools. Although Latin@ candidates and teacher-researchers varied in the developmental continuum, both groups discovered, how little they knew about the Latino@ communities where their schools were located. This is not an indictment of candidates and teachers, but rather on the preparation given and the changes occurring in large urban centers. Alarmist discourses by politically motivated advocates and scholars raise concern that the new diversity is compounding the gap in achievement between mainstream majority and ethnic minority students, or that Spanish poses a threat to English. These ideas are disconcerting to candidates and teachers who may be ill-prepared to deal with the realities in their students' lives.

Transforming Teacher Preparation

Our case studies showed that collaborative, guided field experiences, central to the study of funds of knowledge, may be considered as a first step to understanding ways to teach candidates and teachers cross-cultural competencies to help them communicate effectively with Latin@ families. In addition to communication and collaboration, adaptability and resourcefulness are essential competencies that candidates and teachers need. Through participating in supportive learning communities that engage candidates, teachers, faculty from schools of education, and local communities, it is possible to learn about and build upon the positive resources found in local homes and communities, in mutually beneficial ways. Policy is also needed to support and sustain these types of learning communities or mentoring partnerships between faculty from schools of education and teachers.

Research Implications

We need research that responds to the following questions:

- How are schools of education, located in districts experiencing major demographic shifts, promoting faculty development directed at understanding how these changes affect candidate preparation?
- To what extent do preparation programs encourage and support collaborative field experiences with local schools designed to understand and respond to the changing needs of teachers in local schools and school districts?
- Are preparation programs preparing candidates to communicate effectively with families through a variety of techniques that may or may not require developing basic communication in the primary language of the home?
- How do candidates incorporate in practice what they learn in their bilingual teacher preparation programs?
- How can candidates and teachers use ethnographic field experiences to encourage and challenge candidates to discard previously held deficit views towards students, families, and communities?
- To what extent are teacher education programs preparing all teachers to become *maestras*? How can we extend the principles and theories emphasized in bilingual teacher preparation programs into general education programs and transform how all teacher candidates are prepared to work with BLs?

References

González, N., Moll, L. C., & Amanti, C. (Eds.). (2005). *Theorizing practice: Funds of knowledge in households and classrooms.* Mahwah: NJ: Erlbaum.

Jimenez, R. T., & Gertsen, R. (1999). Lessons and dilemmas derived from the literacy instruction of two Latina/o teachers. *AERA Research Journal, 36*(2), 265–301.

Mercado, C. I. (2005). Seeing what's there: Language and literacy funds of knowledge in New York Puerto Rican homes. In A. C. Zentella (Ed.), *Building on strength: Language and literacy in Latino families and communities* (pp. 134–137). New York: Teachers College Press.

Mercado, C. I., & Moll, L. C. (1997). The study of funds of knowledge: Collaborative research in Latino homes. *CENTRO, the Journal of the Center for Puerto Rican Studies, IX*(9), 26–42.

Valenzuela, A. (1999). *Subtractive schooling: U.S.-Mexican youth and the politics of caring.* Albany, NY: SUNY.

Van Manen, M. V. (1993). *Researching lived experience.* Albany, NY: SUNY.

Velez-Ibañez, C. (1995). The challenge of funds of knowledge in urban arenas: Another way of understanding the learning resources of poor Mexicano households in the U.S. Southwest and their implications for national contexts. *Annals of the New York Academy of Sciences.*

Vygotsky, L. (1978). *Mind in society.* Cambridge, MA: Harvard University Press.

Zeichner, K. (2006). Reflections of a university-based teacher educator on the future of college and university-based teacher education. *Journal of Teacher Education, 57*(3), 326–340.

Zentella, A. C. (Ed.). (2005). *Building on strength: Language and literacy in Latino families and communities.* New York: Teachers College Press.

18 Apprenticeship

Affirming Consciousness within Learning Communities

*Belinda Bustos Flores, Claudia Treviño García,
Lorena Claeys, Aracelia Hernández,
and Rosa Hernández Sheets*

A component of the Academy for Teacher Excellence is the Teacher Academy Induction Learning Community (TAILC), University of Texas at San Antonio, which provides induction for novice teachers working in high-need areas such as mathematics, science, bilingual, and special education with Bilingual Learners (BLs). A specific goal of TAILC is to assign mentors to scaffold teacher candidate-novice learning and development, while also reducing isolation, within a community of practice. In this chapter, we share the induction component, which supports teacher candidates commencing their final year of study and continues during their novice years of teaching. Using Vygotsky's (1978) theory of Zone of Proximal Development (ZPD), where learners/apprentices are guided by experts as knowledgeable others; we maintain that candidate-novices can benefit from these social interactions. In this chapter, we focus on novice-mentor dyads.

Theoretical Framework

The novice-mentor's relationship, when viewed as a learning-teaching process, is by nature, situational and contextual; and, as such requires mentors to mediate instruction within the ZPD. This sociocultural perspective suggests that novices' actions in learning-to-teach is grounded in social interactions and nurtured through membership in a community of practice (Lave & Wenger, 1991).

Many consider induction support critical to teachers' professional development. López, Lash, Shields, and Wagner (2004) explored the effects of induction on retention and student achievement. Research shows that effective induction includes: mentors who model best practices; positive mentor-novice relationships; presence of supportive, collegial work environments; quality, structured mentoring; common planning time with mentor; and participation in learning communities (Feiman-Nemser, Carver, Schwille, & Yusko, 1999; Whisnant, Elliot, & Pynchon, 2005). Participation in learning communities of practice provides opportunity for novices to explore personal, ethnic, and teacher identity; examine assumptions regarding students' ethnic, cultural, linguistic, and economic backgrounds; acknowledge pedagogical epistemologies; and help teachers make connections between theory and practice. This communal reflection and dialogue encourages novices to identify with and advocate for their students (Moll & Arnot-Hopffner, 2005; Flores, 2001; Wood & Bennett, 2000).

Torres-Guzmán (1997) adds that bilingual education mentees and mentors should share a common language and ideology because mentors help novices evaluate the sociocultural schooling context. This analysis encourages novices to view communities as rich sources of knowledge with assets worth documenting and sharing. Other work suggests that induction support for bilingual education teachers must include personal development strands, such as exploration of identity, ethnic consciousness, efficacy, and belief systems (Clark & Flores, in press; see Chapters 3 and 4). The case study in this chapter uses a sociocultural theoretical framework defining induction as a support system where mentors, as knowledgeable others, guide novices through their ZPD within a community of practice.

TAILC Induction Case Study

Data sources for this qualitative study were surveys, interviews, and observations. We surmised that effective induction support assists novices as they transition from a teacher preparation program to a learning community of practice. Participants included novices (69), in their first-year teaching culturally, linguistically diverse students and six mentors. The mentors as a group averaged 20 years of teaching experience. Specifically, two were doctoral students in bilingual education; two had masters in math or science, and two had doctorates in education.

Our finding showed that novices felt challenged and overwhelmed in their first-year. They questioned their competency and doubted the effectiveness of their university preparation. Typical comments were: "No one told me it was going to be like this!" or "The professors painted a perfect picture". We also observed that transition from candidate to teacher and understandings of theory to practice was not only difficult, but, developmental in nature. To guide novices through this frustrating period of questioning, disillusionment, and abandonment of goals, mentors promoted—*confianza*—a sense of mutual trust and caring (see Chapter 17). An immediate focus was to establish cooperative relationships rather than exhibit evaluative attitudes. Mentors provided a variety of services, such as explanation of curricular programs, discussions of pedagogical approaches, suggestions for classroom management techniques, and help with ways to access resources. We found specific induction components, which appeared to support and reaffirm novices' commitment to teaching BLs. These included: communiqués, conferencing, coaching, mentoring, and interactive learning experiences.

Communiqués

Novices and mentors used different ways to connect, such as conference meetings, e-mail, and telephone calls. Novices sought guidance and responses to their concerns. For example, John e-mailed his mentor:

> I need your advice on two situations. First, I have a student that refuses to do her work even when I work problems on the board she will not copy them. All

she does is talk. Do you have a form letter or any advice how to handle this? I want to do it right. Second, in sixth period two boys received verbal warnings for being disruptive. It's like pulling teeth to get them to do anything but talk.

Yet, others felt overwhelmed, frustrated, or were resistant. Olivia described a tenuous relationship: "I do appreciate everything you do. I want to apologize for my attitude and behavior. I need to get over being paranoid and nervous when you're in my classroom while I'm conducting a lesson. I know you are here to help me." However, once trust was established, venting about difficult or uncomfortable situations allowed novices to release stress and generate plausible solutions. A mentor stated: "They seek advice about challenges such as classroom management or ways to involve parents."

Conferencing

Individual conferences prior to and after classroom visits provided opportunity to discuss challenges or accomplishments. Using the *LIBRE* model (Guerra, 2005), allowed novice–mentor dyads to engage in problem-solving activities through active listening and reciprocal conversations. Novices also found unscheduled face-to-face meetings and telephone conferences helpful.

Coaching

This approach promoted development and allowed novices to showcase newly acquired skills. Mentors were able to show novices how to create classroom conditions to improve BLs' learning opportunities and demonstrate specific teaching strategies. Coaching with relevant feedback supported growth in a non-threatening context. A mentor reflected:

> Mr. N. rearranged seats for better classroom management. He's trying to determine which groupings minimize disruptions. This lesson was more engaging than the previous one. I recommended that students draw or cut pictures of organisms to create the food chain rather then just use word lists. He did less lecturing and more hands-on group activities.

Mentoring

Our findings showed that mentor support was needed during the first year. Trusting, non-judgmental relationships between mentee and mentor encouraged novices to question school policies and procedures or request assistance without fear of reprisal. Often fear of being perceived as incompetent or even disrespectful limited open-dialogue with and assistance from school supervisors. Novices preferred to share their concerns with mentors. This support reduced anxiety and enhanced feelings of self-efficacy.

Interactive Learning Experiences

Additionally, novices and mentors participated in multiple interactive learning experiences through workshops, seminars, and institutes delivered by master teachers, Academy for Teacher Excellence (ATE) staff, professors, and consultants. Participants found these sessions meaningful as well as relevant since topics were identified by the mentors and novices.

In sum, our findings confirmed that successful induction addressed the academic, personal, and professional needs of novices. Participation in a learning community of practice promoted development and provided an open network for safe communication. A novice captures the value of induction: "I have nothing but gratitude for this program. It helped me get through my first two months."

Transforming Teacher Preparation

Given the critical shortages of teachers in bilingual, mathematics, science, and special education, preparation models must consider the inclusion of induction programs to insure successful transitions from university classrooms to public school settings. Mentoring supports novices' development and promotes sustainability in the field. We must recognize that novices continue to be learners and mentors can serve as experts within novices' zones of development. While preparation programs may address candidates' zone of proximal development, these experiences only approximate the realities that novices face in their classrooms working with BLs. Induction services must be an essential part of preparation programs. Based on this preliminary analysis, we contend that engaging novices through their zones of development, within a learning community with mentors may be the bridge that connects preparation and practice.

Research Directions

There is a need to examine the nature and the impact of induction as a support for novice teachers working with BLs. We suggest the following topics:

- Induction delivery: Comparison of innovative online interdisciplinary learning communities of practice with traditional face-to-face services.
- Impact of induction: Analyze and document how/if induction support affects teacher effectiveness and student learning outcomes.
- Effects of mentor preparation: Examine the process of specific mentor professional development in areas such as cultural diversity, self-empowerment, identity development, and teacher resistance to change.

Acknowledgment

The Academy for Teacher Excellence is grateful to the Greater Texas Foundation for their financial support to implement and research the Teacher Academy Induction Learning Community.

References

Clark, E. R., & Flores, B. B. (in press). The metamorphosis of teacher identity: An intersection of ethnic consciousness, self conceptualization, and belief systems. In P. Jenlink, *Teacher identity and struggle for recognition*. New York: Routledge.

Feiman-Nemser, S., Carver, C., Schwille, S., & Yusko, B. (1999). Beyond support: Taking new teachers seriously as learners. In M. Scherer (Ed.), *A better beginning: Supporting and mentoring new teachers,* (pp. 3–12). Alexandria, VA: Association for Supervision and Curriculum Development.

Flores, B. B. (2001). Bilingual education teachers' beliefs and their relation to self-reported practices. *Bilingual Research Journal, 25*(3), 275–299.

Guerra, N. S. (2005). LIBRE stick figure tool: A graphic organizer to foster self-regulated social cognitive problem solving. *Intervention School and Clinic, 44*(4), 1–5.

Lave, J., & Wenger, E. (1991). *Situated learning: Legitimate peripheral participation*. Cambridge, UK: Cambridge University Press.

Lopez, A., Lash, A. M., Shields, P., & Wagner, M. (2004, February 11). *Review of research on the impact of beginning teacher induction on teacher quality and retention*. Washington, DC: U.S. Department of Education.

Moll, L. C., & Arnot-Hopffner, E. (2005). Sociocultural competence in teacher education. *Journal of Teacher Education, 56*, 242–247.

Torres-Guzmán, M. E. (1997). *Mentoring bilingual teachers. Directions in education and language series,* Washington, DC: NCBE.

Vygotsky, L. S. (1978). *Mind in society: The development of higher psychological processes*. Cambridge, MA: Harvard University Press.

Whisnant, E., Elliot, K., & Pynchon, S. (2005). *A review of literature on beginning teacher induction*. Center for strengthening the teaching profession. Retrieved from http://www.cstp-wa.org/Navigational/Policies_practices/Teacher_induction/A_Review_of_Literature.pdf

Wood, E., & Bennett, N. (2000). Changing theories, changing practice: Exploring early childhood teachers' professional learning. *Teaching and Teacher Education, 16* (5–6), 635–647.

Part V

Revolución

The solution is not to integrate them into the structure of oppression, but to transform that structure so that they can become beings for themselves.

Paulo Freire, P. (1970). *Pedagogy of the oppressed.*
New York: Continuum International Publishing, p. 74.

19 ¡Ya es Tiempo!

Revolutionary *Transformación*

Ellen Riojas Clark, Rosa Hernández Sheets, and Belinda Bustos Flores

La lucha seguirá ...el que persevera triunfa. El que persevera alcanza ...
... the time has come for all the lessons that we have learned as bilingual teacher educators be used to enrich the field of teacher preparation and to prepare the next generation of teacher educators. According to the Mayans, the upcoming era of *el Sexto Sol* will be one of transformation. With the *Educar* model of transformation, we can now say that a knowledge base for bilingual education teacher preparation for Bilingual Learners (BLs) has been developed, examined, established, and now can be advanced. We can attest that the issues of cultural and linguistic diversity have to be at the core of teacher preparation programs in order to affect student learning, especially the learning of BLs. We have come to know the importance of understanding the social, cultural, historical, and political context of each community and its children in order for teachers and schools to respond in an efficacious manner.

Oddly enough, professor of war Petraeus points out: "as intellectuals we know what men [women] of action do not: ideas precede and determine acts. If you want to change something as big as an army [teacher preparation], how better than to change the way it thinks" (Bowden, 2010, p. 197)? This is what we have to do, we must alter *habitus* of mind—change how teacher preparation is conceptualized, take over how they are prepared, and establish a new prototype. This revolutionary thinking creates a new language—so we at the front line can change preparation to mirror who we are so our children can realize their dreams. *Del derecho nace el hecho.*

We know identity is central to the development of efficacy and epistemological belief systems and to the acquisition of all the components of knowledge for teachers to become culturally efficacious. Our teacher preparation process is articulated through *Educar's* overarching framework of *transformación* and *revolución* within the dimensions of *iluminación*, praxis, and *concientización*. Rather than a destination, we engage in a continual journey of critical reflection, for we know that *poco a poco se anda lejos.*

Educar incorporates the exploration of self, the formulation of a definitive identity, and the effecting of social action as a motive. Freire (1970) described an ideology or the developing of *concientización* as critical consciousness—an essential component for the *Educar* model. Our teacher preparation model dissolves filters and concentrates on broadening *aspirantes'* worldviews, perspectives, and consciousness. As risk takers, they will develop resistance principles and take transformative action to improve their praxis. Through this journey, we expect a change of *habitus* of mind to occur in *aspirantes* in terms of their personal and professional identity, which will propel them towards a bilingual bicultural transformative pedagogy and a commitment to social justice.

Preparation of Culturally Efficacious Teacher Educators

Cultural efficacious teachers have a positive teaching efficacy and a strong teacher identity, and can exhibit socioconstructivists' notions of learning and positive cultural competence, as well as demonstrate passion. To *transformar* our praxis, we, as teacher educators, need to have a deeper understanding of how *aspirantes* learn and how they acquire a knowledge base. Thus, the preparation of new teacher educators must include interdisciplinary approaches where identity is reconstructed, universal themes are explored, and connections among cognition, diversity, language, and technology are mediated. Thus, *iluminación, praxis,* and *concientización, y revolución* will inform their teaching philosophy and actions forming their advocacy for the importance of identity and language in the construction of knowledge, the actualization of a social cultural context in students' learning, and a social justice perspective. Therefore, the curricular content and academic experiences in doctoral programs, as well as development events for faculty must include exploration, discussion, and understandings of a bilingual bicultural transformative pedagogy. This transformative knowledge has potential to change their educational philosophy and influence teacher preparation.

Call to Action

> Cultural action ... is an instrument for superseding the dominant alienated and alienating culture. In this sense, every authentic revolution is a cultural revolution.
>
> Paulo Freire (1970, p. 180)

In this, our legacy of revolutionary thinking creates a new language—so we at the front line can change preparation to provide all students with cultural efficacious teachers that demonstrate cultural competence, critical consciousness, social responsibility, and social activism. We trust that this emerging work supports scholars and practitioners in the field of bilingual education teacher preparation, and perhaps serve as a framework for the creation of a new cadre of *aspirantes bien educadas.*

Ya es tiempo ...

References

Bowden, M. (2010, May) Professor of war. *Vanity Fair, 597,* 197.

Freire, P. (1970). *Pedagogy of the oppressed.* New York: Continuum.

Afterword

Implementing a Critical Bilingual/ Bicultural Pedagogy

Lourdes Díaz-Soto

I was honored to review several of the papers included in this volume, *Teacher Preparation for Bilingual Student Populations: Educar para Transformar*, at an AERA Conference. What struck me at the time was how the overall theme of the papers could be viewed with a Freirian lens of *educar para transformar*. Freire's idea includes the understanding that we must be aware of our conditioning in order to engage in the possibility of transformation as a form of liberation.

I have gained tremendous respect for the bilingual/bicultural educators of Texas. These are educators who are willing to advocate, teach, conduct research, and give their hearts to learners and communities. Even former President Lyndon Baines Johnson worked with bilingual children in Texas (Blanton, 2004) providing a possibility that we can someday pursue this struggle along with like-minded educators interested in making a difference in the lives of bilingual/bicultural children.

In this volume, we learn about *dar luz*, as an avenue to: transform ways of being, value transformative action, acknowledge *Sí se puede* as a hope-filled endeavor, give back to the community, use contemporary indigenous knowledge; and, examine the complexities of identities. Important components in this text are chapter sections calling for future additional research.

This book also helps to reveal that our work as educational leaders includes the sociocultural context of learners, teachers, and families. More specifically, we can address the complacency that our country is experiencing with regard to inequity in our nation. Political phenomena linked to larger societal forces such as xenophobia and racism continue to impact the daily-lived realities of bilingual/bicultural learners. Evidence of the latter is the hysteria over immigration leading to the continued demonization of children and families.

Freire (1970) supports learners' ability to think critically about their own situation so connections can be made to the social context. Understanding our own *concientización* is a needed first step to praxis, the power and knowledge to take action against oppression, within the context of a liberatory educational model. Freire relates how praxis involves a cycle of theory, application, evaluation, reflection, and return to theory. Praxis leads to transformation at the collective level. Antonia Darder (1991) further elaborates:

> Unlike traditional perspectives of education that claim to be neutral and apolitical, critical pedagogy views all education theory as intimately linked

to ideologies shaped by power, politics, history and culture. Given this view, schooling functions as a terrain of ongoing struggle over what will be accepted as legitimate knowledge and culture. In accordance with this notion, a critical pedagogy must seriously address the concept of cultural politics y both legitimizing and challenging cultural experiences that comprise the histories and social realities that in turn comprise the forms and boundaries that give meaning to student lives.

(p. 77)

Our goal as liberatory and emancipatory bilingual/bicultural educators is to reach bilingual learners (BLs) and their families so that a basic premise of our work engages BLs in "reading the word and reading the world" (Freire, 1985). This work becomes critical bilingual/bicultural pedagogy. A critical bilingual/bicultural pedagogy ensures home language maintenance, second-language learning, biliteracy and biculturalism. Critical bilingual/bicultural pedagogy will be academically rigorous by centering on children's daily-lived realities and the cultural wisdom of our *abuelitas* and *abuelitos*. Additional important components of a critical bilingual/bicultural pedagogy include: democratic participation with authentic voice; decolonization and liberation; critical examination of electronic technologies that are affecting our lives; anti-racist, anti-sexist, anti-classist projects; explores spaces of healing for our common good and our love for each other (Soto, 2010).

My former Texas graduate students and I embarked on a project with decolonizing *mestiza* ways of knowing. We explored spaces of healing by raising consciousness, cultivating cultural intuition (Delgado Bernal, 1998), and learning that it is possible to pursue decolonial, emancipatory, and feminist action projects. Bilingual/bicultural Texas educators may be well-positioned to pursue this avenue in their search for education for transformation. The graduate students in this project were careful, respectful, critical pedagogues who found a "sacred space" that we will not forget. The possibilities are endless for pursuing community projects that are participatory as well as liberatory educational projects (Soto, Cervantes-Soon, Villareal, & Campos, 2010).

In the continued pursuit of the complexities of identities as described in this volume, I have also found the piece of my friend and Texas colleague, Luis Urrieta (2003), *Las identidades tambien lloran* to be most valuable. As he retells his grandmother's story as an *indigena* who worked to create crossroads in *San Miguel de Pascuara, Méjico,* we are reminded not only of the complexities of identities but of misunderstandings, miscommunications, and cruelty. I am certain that writing the piece was painful for Luis as he recounts his grandmother's stoning.

The Latin@ families and children I am meeting in Northwest Georgia have not been stoned (that I know of), but they have been incarcerated, terrorized, oppressed, check-pointed (asked for driver licenses at stores and while driving), children separated from their mothers (including a child that was not permitted to continue breast feeding), and faced with open hostility by an under-educated majority. The struggle continues on a daily basis especially with the draconian measures initiated by Arizona.

In the latter community, I have also had the honor of supervising student teachers but with some trepidation. One of the candidates shared, "In this class we have the bottom of the heap—the Hispanic children who will be the janitors and will not amount to much. But I did learn that some of these Hispanics are real friendly!" I responded rather annoyed, "Yes, we are!" I remembered that my own father was indeed a janitor. He and my mother, a factory worker who brought piece-meal work home, labored to ensure that their children would someday have a better future. We stand on the shoulders of our elders whose wisdom has nourished us and helped us to become the professionals that we are.

Charise Pimentel and Octavio Pimentel relay the multiple layers of complexities their young children face relating to bilingual/bicultural abilities. Their children, and Charise herself, face tremendous misunderstandings because they neither look like the stereotypical families nor educate their children in stereotypical contemporary ways. The Pimentel children speak Spanish but look *gueritos* and this has created challenges for the family and the children (see their chapters in Soto and Kharem, 2010).

The bilingual programs themselves can present challenges that we may not have anticipated. In a piece about dual language programs we ask: "¿*Quiénes Ganan*? Who stands to win with dual language programs?"

> It has been more than ten years since Valdés (1997) raised cautionary notes concerning the racial dimensions of dual language programs. Considering the absence of significant research in this area since Valdés' work, the goal of this article is to pick up and continue discussion of the possible subtle, yet marginalizing practices that may emerge in dual language programs for language minority students. There are a number of practices that may create or reproduce deficit and/or assimilationist discourses and pedagogy.
> (Pimentel, Soto, Pimentel, Urrieta, 2008, p. 205)

Our work as bilingual/bicultural educators is most often interlaced with issues of power. As Joe Kincheloe (2008) taught us: "Advocates of critical pedagogy are aware that every minute of every hour that teachers teach, they are faced with complex decisions concerning justice, democracy, and competing ethical claims" (p. 1). This volume speaks to teacher preparation in ways that promotes dialogue leading to transformative teacher educators. The teacher educators hold the key to opening avenues and possibilities for the candidate and ultimately, the teacher in the classroom. I often ask myself, "Will I want this candidate to ultimately teach my very own grandchildren and family?" Will you want to open that classroom door and see this teacher? What are our ethical roles to ensure that we are graduating bilingual education teacher candidates who will understand the importance of liberatory and critical perspectives? One of my favorite pieces is Freire's (2006), *Teachers as Cultural Workers*. I am especially fond of the fourth letter that relates the '*Indispensable Qualities of Progressive Teachers for Their Better Performance*' (p. 39). I like to share these with my students and I will share them with you:

1 Humility allows us to listen and learn as we speak and teach; and embrace a democratic instead of an authoritarian classroom.
2 Lovingness is a form of devotion, even in the face of struggle and injustice.

3   Courage helps us to face and overcome our fears as we become willing to stand against unjust power.
4   Tolerance is a form of respect.
5   Decisiveness permits us to seek justice and be confident when making difficult choices.
6   Tension, between patience and impatience, helps us strike a balance as we begin to understand the power of words and how to use them responsibly.
7   Joy of living provides a balance in our lives and in our teaching.

In concluding, I would like to commend the hard work that is evident in this endeavor. Future teacher educators can enter into dialogue with the contributors as they themselves chart a course toward implementing a critical bilingual/bicultural pedagogy. Most of our candidates come to us with idealism and joy for their chosen profession. It is up to us to harness these elements and ensure that children and families are the beneficiaries of an education that is transformative and liberating.

References

Blanton, C. (2004). *The strange career of bilingual education in Texas, 1836–1981.* College Station, Texas: Texas A&M University Press.

Darder, A. (1991). *Culture and power in the classroom: A critical foundation for bicultural education.* Westport, CT: Bergin & Garvey.

Delgado Bernal, D. (1998). Using a Chicana feminist epistemology in educational research. *Harvard Educational Review, 68*(4), 555–582.

Freire, P. (1970). *Pedagogy of the oppressed.* New York: Herder & Herder.

Freire, P. (1985). *Teachers as cultural workers: Letters to those who dare to teach.* Boulder, CO: Westview.

Freire, P. (2006). *Teachers as cultural workers: Letters to those who dare to teach. Expanded Edition.* Boulder, CO: Westview.

Kincheloe, J. (2008). *Knowledge and critical pedagogy: An introduction.* Dordrecht, London: Springer.

Pimentel, C., Soto, L. D., Pimentel O., & Urrieta, L. (2008). The dual language dualism: ¿Quiénes ganan? *TABE Journal, 10*(1), 201–223.

Soto, L. D. (2010). *Educar para transformar:* Toward a critical bilingual/bicultural pedagogy. In S. Steinberg (Ed.), *19 urban questions: Teaching in the city* (2nd ed.) New York: Peter Lang.

Soto, L. D., Cervantes-Soon, C., Villareal, E., & Campos, E. (2010). The Xicana sacred space: A communal circle of compromise for educational researchers, *Harvard Educational Review, 79*(4), 755–776.

Soto, L. D., & Kharem, H. (Eds). (2010). *Teaching bilingual/bicultural children: Teachers talk about language and learning.* New York: Peter Lang.

Urrieta, L. (2003). Las identidades también lloran, Identities also cry: Exploring the human side of indigenous Latina/o identities. *Educational Studies, 34*(2), 147–168.

Valdés, G. (1997). Dual-language immersion programs. A cautionary note concerning the education of language-minority students. *Harvard Education Review, 67*(3), 391–430.

Contributors

Iliana Alanís, Assistant Professor, University of Texas at San Antonio. Her research interests include early childhood biliteracy, two-way bilingual programs, and oral language development.

Blanca Araujo, Assistant Professor, University of Texas at El Paso. The focus of her research lies in the areas of bilingual/ESL education, immigration, migrant students, and family/community advocacy, all within teacher education.

María Brisk, Professor, Boston College. Her research interests include bilingual education, bilingual language and literacy acquisition, literacy teaching methods, and preparation of mainstream teachers to work with bilingual learners.

Carol Brochin-Ceballos, Assistant Professor, University of Texas at El Paso. She uses critical sociocultural literacy research methods to examine issues related to identity, literacy, and teacher preparation with a focus on Latin@ children.

Gloria Calderon, Doctoral Candidate, Texas Tech University. Her research interests include Latino high school retention rates and native language loss among second- and third-generation Latinos.

Sylvia Celédon-Pattichis, Associate Professor, New Mexico State University. Her research interests include linguistic and cultural influences on the teaching and learning of mathematics with Latin@ bilingual learners.

Claudia Cervantes-Soon, Doctoral Candidate, University of Texas at Austin. Her research focuses on empowering education for disenfranchised women and issues related to linguistically diverse students and teacher development.

Lorena Claeys, Doctoral Candidate, University of Texas at San Antonio. Her research interests include teacher preparation, retention, and novice teachers' motives for teaching culturally and linguistically diverse students.

Ellen Riojas Clark, Professor, University of Texas at San Antonio. Her research examines self-concept, teacher identity, ethnic identity, gifted language minority students, and efficacy.

Courtney Clayton, Assistant Professor, University of Mary Washington. Her areas of research include language and literacy development for bilingual learners, bilingual education, and teacher preparation.

Lourdes Díaz-Soto, Professor and Goizueta Endowed Chair, Dalton State University. Her recent publications include two edited volumes: *Teaching Bilingual/Bicultural Children Teachers Talk about Language and Learning* and *Childhoods: A Handbook.*

Lucila D. Ek, Assistant Professor, University of Texas at San Antonio. Her research focus on the intersections of language, literacy, and identity in Chican@/Latin@ immigrant communities.

Mariella Espinoza-Herold, Assistant Professor, Northern Arizona University. Her expertise and publications examine multicultural/bilingual education and teacher preparation for Latin@ students.

Barbara Flores, Professor, California State University, San Bernadino. She engages in collaborative action research with teachers and administrators in their implementation and transformation of whole language with diverse children.

Belinda Bustos Flores, Professor, The University of Texas at San Antonio. Her research focuses on teacher development including self-concept, ethnic identity, efficacy, beliefs, teacher recruitment/retention, high stakes testing, and family cultural literacy.

Claudia Treviño García, Doctoral candidate, University of Texas at San Antonio. Her research interests include bilingual education, diversity pedagogy, induction, and teacher preparation for culturally and linguistically diverse populations.

Eugene E. García, Professor and Vice President for Educational Partnerships, Arizona State University. His research areas include effective schooling for linguistically and diverse populations.

Kimberley Gomez, Associate Professor, University of Pittsburgh. She studies relationships between reading and science achievement in urban high schools and students' development of media literacies.

Virginia González, Professor, University of Cincinnati. Her expertise and research focus on the application of assessment and instruction of diverse students, and pedagogy for bilingual Latin@ children.

Michael D. Guerrero, Associate Professor, University of Texas at Pan American. His research centers on the development and assessment of teachers' academic Spanish language proficiency, and language socialization and policy.

Aracelia Hernández, Lecturer at University of Texas at Austin. Recently she completed her doctorate from University of Southern California. She was an induction field specialist for the Academy for Teacher Excellence.

Mary Esther Huerta, Assistant Professor, Texas State University. Her research and publications center on issues of biliteracy, bilingual education, and equity in urban schools.

Linda Guardia Jackson, Lecturer, University of Texas at San Antonio. Her research examines autobiographical storytelling and the dialogic process shaping ethnic and professional identities of bilingual educators.

Indiatsi John, Doctoral Candidate, Texas Tech University. His research focuses on teacher consciousness, professional development, school transformation, teacher socialization, and identity.

Margarita Machado-Casas, Assistant Professor, Wright State. Her research interests include migrant, indigenous and transnational communities and their agency in the fields of education and family involvement.

Carmen I. Mercado, Professor, Hunters College School of Education, CUNY. Her scholarship examines literacy, bilingual education, and urban education with a focus on linguistically diverse populations.

Bertha Pérez, Professor Emeritus, University of Texas at San Antonio. Her research focuses on biliteracy, language and literacy development in bilingual settings, sociocultural context of literacy, and bilingual teacher education.

Linda Prieto, Assistant Professor, Midwestern State University, Texas. Her areas of work include cultural studies in education, bilingual education, teacher preparation, and educational assessment for linguistically diverse students.

Mari Riojas-Cortez, Professor, University of Texas at San Antonio. Her research and publications focus on Latino family involvement, Mexican American children's play, and early childhood teacher preparation.

Francisco Rios, Professor, University of Wyoming. His research interests include ethnic minority teachers in rural communities, Latinos in education, teacher education with a multicultural focus and ESL preparation.

Patricia Sánchez, Associate Professor, University of Texas at San Antonio. She uses a sociocultural lens to examine globalization, transnationalism, teacher preparation, immigrant students and families, and teacher identity formation.

Rosa Hernández Sheets, Associate Professor, Texas Tech University. Her work examines learning–teaching connections between culture and cognition, and the preparation and development of teachers and teacher educators.

Guillermo Solano-Flores, Associate Professor, University of Colorado, Boulder. His research interests include educational measurement, intersection of psychometrics and sociolinguistics, and language and culture in international test comparisons.

Lucinda Soltero-González, Assistant Professor, University of Colorado, Boulder. Her research interests include biliteracy, and development of bilingualism and early biliteracy in young Spanish speaking children.

María Torres-Guzmán, Professor, Teachers College, Columbia University. Her publications explore alternative perspectives on relationships among languages, cultures, and learning, including personal historical narratives.

Thao Tran, Doctoral Student at Teachers College, Columbia University. Her research includes bilingual education, Asian American and diasporic communities, immigrant youth identity development/transformation, and sociocultural curriculum.

Marcela van Olphen, Assistant Professor, University of South Florida. Her research focuses on world language teacher education, integration of technology, ESOL, and heritage languages teaching and learning.

Concepción M. Valadez, Associate Professor, UCLA. Her specialization and scholarship within bilingual education include: language acquisition, mathematics education, teacher development, and program evaluation nationally and internationally.

Angela Valenzuela, Professor, University of Texas at Austin. Her research interests include the sociology of education, minority youth in schools, educational policy, and urban education reform.

Index